DEATH OF A DIVISION

DEATH OF
A DIVISION

**Eight Days in March 1918 and the Untold Story
of the 66th** (2/1st East Lancashire) **Division**

David E. Martin

*"We must look forward to maintaining the struggle for at
least eight days"* –

General Sir Hubert Gough, March 1918

Frontline Books

DEATH OF A DIVISION
Eight Days in March 1918 and the Untold Story of the 66th
(2/1st East Lancashire) Division

This edition published in 2018 by Frontline Books,
an imprint of Pen & Sword Books Ltd,
47 Church Street, Barnsley, S. Yorkshire, S70 2AS

ISBN: 978-1-47384-472-8

CIP data records for this title are available from the British Library

For more information on our books, please visit
www.frontline-books.com
email info@frontline-books.com
or write to us at the above address.

Printed and bound by TJ International
Typeset in 10.5/12.5 point Palatino

Contents

Dedicated to

Rufus, a loyal dog

Acknowledgements

I would like to extend my thanks to John Grehan and Martin Mace at Frontline Books for commissioning this book and their involvement. I would also like to thank Philip Mather at the Fusilier Museum in Bury, Greater Manchester, for his assistance. Also the staff at the Imperial War Museum archive and photo archives, and the National Archives. I would like to extend my thanks to the staff at the Midland Hotel, Manchester, and especially Barbara Frost for her architectural and historical information, without which I would have not been able to set the scene at the hotel. I would also like to extend my sincere thanks to Lady Avon and the staff of the Cadbury archive at Birmingham University, who hold the papers of Anthony Eden. I would also like to thank the staff at the Tank Museum, Bovington, for their assistance.

The publication of the 1911 census online has been a tremendous aid in getting to know the soldiers themselves and paints a more realistic and personal picture of the men and who they were before the war. I would like to thank the men and women of various online sites who publish the 1911 census information as they are anonymous. Also of great help were the family of Major General Charles Blomfield, who was the first commander of the East Lancashire Division, and I extend my thanks to the late Jan Blomfield for information and her hospitality.

Jane Davies and the staff at the Lancashire Infantry Museum in Preston have been most accommodating, and it was a pleasure to meet Lynn Turp, a relative of Gilbert Wilkinson, and to see around the parts of Preston where he lived and worked.

Thanks are also due to my friends and family who have all helped, including Sue Maxen and family, and especially Jess McKinnon for

ACKNOWLEDGEMENTS

reading the first copy, my editor Paul Middleton, and John Crackett for the Foreword. Also to the families of Peter Hall, John Gore, Tom Hardman, Withinshaw, Norman Dunkerley, R.C.A. Frost, Roland Bate, Tin Westmacott and William Little, all for copyright permissions vis the Imperial War Museum.

Foreword

My local church, St Chad's Shrewsbury, is holding a short service every week to remember the Shropshire dead of the First World War. The service is a simple one; some prayers, the names of those who died in the same week a hundred years ago are read out, a wreath laid, a two-minute silence and a dedication. In a cool and airy military chapel, light streams in to pool on the oak woodwork and pick out the fading regimental colours, while the notes of the *Last Post* resonate around the congregation. This is where I met the bugler: David Martin. Curiously, he picked up the bugle again just so that he could take part in this weekly remembrance service.

You would be right to suspect that Martin is an unusual man. Born in Shrewsbury, his interests span a wide range from historic buildings to warfare. With a twenty-year background in the heritage industry, he is a landscape historian and archaeologist, and works in various museums. Significantly, he has spent five years as a tour guide on the Somme and Ypres battlefields; here is someone who has laid on the ground to see how much the commanding officer could really see from his trench, and someone who has personally walked back the long and difficult roads of a retreat. His first book, *Londoners on the Western Front*,[1] tells the story of one territorial division in which an ancestor served; in this book we have another.

So why – when there is so much First World War literature – read a history about a seemingly obscure Lancashire Territorial Division? After all, 66th Division was, unlike its sister 42nd Division, a second line outfit. It spent the early part of the war in the UK forwarding reinforcements to the front, and only arrived in France in February 1917. Having fought for just over a year it – shattered and depleted – was reduced to a cadre, before being re-formed and seeing action in the last month of the war.

The reason lies in two of the iconic First World War campaigns: the 3rd battle of Ypres and the March 1918 Retreat. The East Lancashire Division took part in both, and both form part of commonly accepted narrative about the Great War. The famous Lancashire-born historian A.J.P. Taylor called the battle of Passchendaele, as it became known, 'the blindest slaughter of a blind war'.[2] There were more than 230,000 casualties on each side; men apparently dying senselessly in the mud due to the politicians' desire for another 'push' and the generals' incompetence. Much less is generally known about the March Retreat, except perhaps that it was one of the worst defeats in British Army history, where bungling lost the hard-won gains of earlier years and the Germans almost won the war. But these deeply ingrained perspectives are flawed. Though costly, Plumer's tactics of the creeping barrage and 'bite and hold' were ultimately successful in enabling the Canadians to reach Passchendaele village. The Retreat, far from being a disaster, proved to be a defensive victory. Even Churchill conceded that 'contrary to the generally accepted verdict, I hold that the Germans, judged by the hard test of gains and losses, were decisively defeated'.[3]

It is only by understanding all of the reality of these battles – political, strategic and tactical – that we can arrive at a balanced judgement. And this is where Martin does great service in following the story of a single division. Here we see the impact of the decisions of the great men: Lloyd George, Foch, Haig, and Gough, on individual units and soldiers. Drawing on his understanding of the ground, and detailed research of primary sources, Martin's narrative is clear and logical. It seems to go into slow motion as the hours and minutes of critical engagements tick by. Interwoven throughout are the stories of soldiers and officers; their backgrounds, what they did, what they felt. I am struck by the tale of Lieutenant Colonel Little, who, relaxing on leave in the Lake District, read about the March offensive in the newspaper. Leaving his motorbike with the stationmaster, he set off by train for the front, determined not to let his boys down. There are the grumblers such as James Jessiman, who tried constantly to get discharged, and heroes such as machine gunner Herbert Columbine VC, who remained firing in his gun position to let his men get away. There are eccentrics such as the Corsham vicar who gave up his calling, commanded a regiment and ended up in the War Graves commission. But most are ordinary, decent men, doing a surprisingly good job in very difficult circumstances.

I don't think it odd that I should recognise these men. I have been an Army Reservist – a Territorial soldier – for nearly forty years. My civilian career has been designing, building and running power stations; managing electricity companies and ultimately sitting on the board of one of the UK's largest energy companies. As a reservist I have been fortunate to command a Lancashire unit, lecture at the staff college, and work with government ministers on the future of the Reserve. I am currently a member of the Executive Committee of the Army Board, where I am responsible for the policy and strategy for reserves: why we have them, how they are trained and organised. Our understanding of the history of volunteer soldiering illuminates the present, and helps judge where we can go in the future.

Wind the clock forward 100 years from the events described in this book, and we find reserve soldiers serving their country in the early years of the 21st century as their forebears did in the early years of the 20th century. Not in as great numbers maybe, but since 2003 we have mobilised around 27,000 reservists – most of them from the army, and most to serve in Afghanistan and Iraq. Thirty-two have given their lives for their country and a good handful have won gallantry medals. While the uniform, weapons and vehicles would be unrecognisable to their antecedents in 66th Division, their motivations, feelings, spirit and experience of volunteer soldiering would not. Let us hope that such people will always be ready when we need them.

Major General J. Crackett CB, TD, DL, VR
Director Reserves,
British Army

[1] *Londoners on the Western Front, The 58th Division in the Great War,* Naval and Military Press.
[2] Taylor, *First World War.* p.194.
[3] Churchill, *World Crisis, 1911–18,* Vol II. pp.1923–31.

Prelude – Legend

Passchendaele Village, 6 November 1917

The Canadian soldiers crept forward in the mud and drizzle, attempting to stay on the remains of the road and buildings and yet keep under cover. To wander away from the rubble and dust that had once been a village, back into the battlefield over which they had just come, meant the possibility of drowning in the water-filled shell holes that were death traps. Of the village nothing remained, just bricks and rubble pummelled into dust. It was 6 November 1917 and the final few days of the Third Battle of Ypres, not that the soldiers knew that; did the generals back at Headquarters even know it yet? As they advanced over the mound that had been the village church, there was no cover, so they began to dig in, a shallow trench to the south-east of the church. If they were lucky they would find a cellar that had survived the pounding bombardments of the last month. There they stayed, dug in against German counter-attacks, until relieved again by 66th Division.

This spot, this village, and the surrounding ridge had been pounded by the massed guns of Fifth Army. It was the most heavily shelled place on the planet, stone had been shattered and then turned over again by heavy shells. Not until the advent of the atom bomb would anywhere receive such a heavy weight of explosive fire. By that evening the men had scraped an effective length of trench on the south-eastern side of the village, the next morning a German biplane flew over to take photographs of the Canadian positions here. In this photograph the trench is visible in the shell-ravaged terrain and in the trench are pinpricks of light. These are the helmets of the Canadian soldiers. If, as is likely, the Germans had retreated a sensible distance from this highpoint then there are two lines of British trenches here. Once the situation had settled down slightly then a few of these Canadian soldiers crept over the ground to find anything of use and any surviving cellars or walls that might give cover for a command post. Legend has

xiii

it that in doing so they uncovered the remains of a number of Lancashire Fusiliers and Manchester Regiment bodies, identifiable by their metal shoulder titles and their divisional arm badges, as being from 66th Division. They had been in an attack here on 9 October, a month before, and had advanced further than any other. If time allowed they buried them in a shallow grave where they remained until after the war, when they were most likely moved to Tyne Cot Cemetery to be buried with many of the other 8,901 British home forces and 2,500 Commonwealth men buried here. Their names will be on the Tyne Cot Memorial, among the 35,000 names inscribed there, those of the missing from August 1917 until the end of the war in the Ypres Salient. Thus was born an enduring legend of the East Lancashire Division.

To acknowledge the sacrifice of East Lancashire at Passchendaele a memorial was incorporated into the new design of the church using old rubble. The chapel of St Cornelius is a stained glass window installed in 1928 showing the arms of the small towns in and around what is today called Greater Manchester; Ardwick, Ashton, Burnley, Bury, Oldham, Rochdale, Salford, and Wigan. This alludes to the fighting for the small village that was the end point of the Third Battle of Ypres. In particular, it represents the soldiers of those Lancashire Fusiliers whose bodies were found here after the battle. These were men of the 3/5th Lancashire Fusiliers and 2/9th Manchester Regiment. The first were from Bury, the second from Ashton-under-Lyne. Casualties were, of course, high; this was the worst of the battles on the Western Front, in terms of artillery, rain and ground conditions, and the sheer seemingly pointless advances for little gain. The apex in disastrous attacks was the month from 9 October to 10 November 1917, when nothing seemed to be gained and everything lost.

Introduction

It was to Passchendaele village and the Ypres battlefield I came for three years from 2002, as a tour guide. The world had changed since I had been on the Somme. The attacks of 11 September 2001 in New York and Washington drew me back to the battlefields and into an awful battle of mud and casualties. Passchendaele village was always on the itinerary for my tours. As a spot it is synonymous with the abject horror of the Western Front and is one of those places that should be visited. Most coach groups venture as far as Tyne Cot cemetery, if they pass through the village they don't stop. They maybe claim there is nothing to see. That is not the case, there is everything to see, or to sense, here. I often went to Passchendaele village, usually for a coffee break, a brief talk and then on to Tyne Cot cemetery via the Canadian memorial and down the narrow lane along the valley of the Stroombeek. The importance of the battle of Passchendaele to the East Lancashire Division can be found in a speech in 1929. At the annual officers' reunion it was stated that 'in short, Passchendaele saw the Division enter its first great battle and at Le Cateau was fought its last big fight'. These two battles were the bookends of the division's service in France and Flanders, but not the main event, which occurred in March 1918.

At Le Cateau there is another memorial to 66th Division in the form of a horse trough. British soldiers had great affection for their horses and it is no surprise to me that I am writing another book on a division that has an equine memorial, [as did my first book, *Londoners on the Western Front*]. By the time of the attacks at Le Cateau in 1918 66th Division had undergone great changes and there were few East Lancashire soldiers left in the division. Instead, one brigade was the South African Brigade, and most of the other two brigades were Irish troops. So between these two dates a massive calamity had changed the division out of all recognition.

Passchendaele and Le Cateau are the most remembered battles of the 66th, but not the greatest test, which were the battles fought between 21 March and 28 March 1918. It is this battle that is the primary history covered here, as it was the most interesting and incredible battle to research. It was a battle that, like Passchendaele, encountered extreme conditions in the weather, but it was a battle of movement as well, of river crossings and chance events that open it up to general interest. A sub-heading of this part of the book could be the retirement of XIX Corps, as after initial defence 66th Division was withdrawn and subordinated to other divisions that took up the fight; 24th, 50th, and 8th Divisions all played a part in the withdrawal.

In 2013 I visited the Villers-Bretonneux area on foot. I walked from the station west to the site of the first tank-versus-tank action in history at Cachy, which occurred in April 1918. Continuing south, I reached Domart, where I managed to have a drink and a snack at a little estaminet. It was November and very cold and icy. After a diversion towards Hangard Wood, much regretted as the locals were shooting near there, I was delayed. I was late for the train that runs only every two hours, so I upped my pace to a run to get back to Villers-Bretonneux, but somewhere on the plain south of the railway and motorway I slipped on black ice. More shaken than physically hurt, I did get the train, just, running over the footbridge as it entered the station. My camera took the brunt of the damage as it was in a trouser pocket. It was at Hangard that the East Lancashire division ended its retreat and the Australians and 58th Division, among others, took over the fight. The battles of Villers-Bretonneux were crucial to ending the German advance on Amiens. I wish to walk the retreat from Roisel to Péronne and Hangard, although I think a bicycle would be a better and quicker form of transport. There is plenty in this day and age that can be done online with maps and satellite photographs in understanding the terrain without necessarily visiting the area.

The reader may be wondering why I follow the action at the divisional level. Most history is written at the battalion or regimental level, or indeed of individuals in the whole army. I have increased the number of battalions I look at by nine (1918). The answer is that once the battalion is looked at the brigade is of the next step and after that the division, being formed of three brigades. The division is the highest level at which the experience of the soldier remains the same and there is (often) a regional coherence. A whole division, of around 15,000 men, may be moved around between different corps and still remain an integral unit. I was also much struck by the divisional memorials while I was guiding on the battlefields; they seemed to have a wider range of sentiments attached to them than regimental memorials, which are more prosaic.

The Lancashire Fusiliers is one of the most famous British regiments and the Great War only served further to elevate its prowess. The story of the six Victoria Crosses won 'before breakfast' at the landing at Cape Helles on the Dardanelles in 1915 is possibly the most famous for the 1st Battalion, Lancashire Fusiliers. This was just one battalion of the twelve that were part of 29th Division at Beaumont Hamel on the Somme, where that divisional memorial is to be found. It was here at Beaumont Hamel that my interest in divisional history started, with 29th Division. As far as divisional memorials go it is not very exciting; a large mound of earth with grass and the red triangle of the division on a metal plate. At the far end of the site is the rousing memorial to 51st (Highland) Division, who took the village that 29th Division had failed to take in July 1916. This is a statue of Colour Sergeant Rowan in a Highlanders uniform. The massacre on 1 July 1916 involved the 1st Battalion, Lancashire Fusiliers, who attacked from the sunken road, a position captured by Geoffrey Malins, as an official war correspondent, in the first ever war documentary film *The Battle of the Somme*. It is one of the most poignant places on the July battlefield, an attack that should have succeeded, owing to the powerful force of the mine placed under the Hawthorn ridge redoubt. However, it failed as the men were mown down by German machine gun fire.

The Lancashire Fusiliers raised thirty battalions during the war, but it is the actions of the 1st Battalion which are often the most remembered, and with them the actions of 29th Division. It is largely these actions and the regimental history that is remembered in the seminal history *Hells Foundations; a Town, its Myths and Gallipoli* by Geoffrey Moorhouse. This book looks at the effects of the Dardanelles campaign on the town of Bury and the last veterans, who were still alive then. In this volume I am attempting to return to the military history of the battalions seen through the eyes of one of the Lancashire Divisions, the (2nd East Lancashire) 66th Division.

There were several all-Lancashire divisions. In the Territorial Force these were 42nd Division and 66th Division of East Lancashire and 55th and 57th of the West Lancashire area. In Kitchener's New Army 30th Division was an all Lancashire Division, 31st and 34th Divisions contained some Lancashire interest, and other battalions were placed where they were needed. By mid-1918 the effects of the German offensive were such that the divisional and regimental system was only used in name as forces were amalgamated to bring them up to numbers in any way possible that would offer a fighting force that was able to face the German onslaught. It is to be expected that the majority of men would serve from the industrial centres as that is where the majority of the population lived, although, of course, the countryside was more populated than it is today with most farm work being manual and only some limited use of machinery. This book concentrates on 66th Division, but never without seeing the fuller picture as well through the eyes of the divisions on either flank.

List of Maps

Chapter 1

That Damned Fool

1914

The reorganisation of the military in nineteenth century Lancashire led to the establishment of three major barracks at Bury, Preston and Ashton-under-Lyne. In the wake of various Chartist disturbances in northern textile towns the government ordered a report by Major General Sir Charles Napier, who in turn ordered a rationalisation of military units into defensible barracks such as those at Fulwood near Preston, Wellington Barracks at Ashton and Bury. Fulwood Barracks is today the headquarters of 42 North Western Brigade, a descendant of 42nd Division, the elder brother of 66th Division. These barracks were surrounded by walls and bastions to offer defence against mobs but not artillery, in accordance with the relatively lightly armed rebels expected. Each barracks had accommodation for an infantry battalion, a half battery and a cavalry squadron. The barracks were sited to make full use of the emerging railway network of the region, all being near enough by rail to Liverpool and Manchester to face any regional disturbances and offering three infantry battalions, artillery and cavalry as a control on Chartism. The establishment of these barracks in small towns led to an interdependency with the community, and the foundation of garrison towns where service in the army was seen as an escape from the textile mills. This set the scene for the establishment of the East Lancashire Regiment in 1880, recruiting from its garrison towns.

The traditions of the Lancashire Fusiliers were more than adhered to during the Boer War, and no more so than the attack on Spion Kop in which Colonel Charles Blomfield took part. Born into an ecclesiastical family, he attended Haileybury School and Sandhurst, with a first class pass, gaining his commission in the Lancashire Fusiliers on 11 February

1

1875. He was Adjutant of the Lancashire Fusiliers from 1880, rising to Captain in 1881, married the daughter of a fellow officer, was Adjutant of Auxiliary Forces from 1884, and achieved the rank of major in 1890. He was acting Military Secretary to the Commander of the Bombay Army and further promotion awaited with him becoming Lieutenant Colonel in 1898. He served in the Khartoum expedition that year and was mentioned in despatches and awarded the Distinguished Service Order. He commanded the 2nd Battalion Lancashire Fusiliers in 1900 at Ladysmith and held joint command during the famous assault on Spion Kop.

> Spion Kop was to be attacked that night. The troops which were to be selected for the task were eight companies of the 2nd Lancashire Fusiliers, six of the 2nd Royal Lancasters, two of the 1st South Lancashire, 180 of Thorneycroft's, and half a company of Sappers. It was to be a North of England job. Under the friendly cover of a starless night the men, in Indian file, like a party of Iroquois braves upon the war trail, stole up the winding and ill-defined path which led to the summit. Woodgate, the Lancashire brigadier, and Blomfield of the Fusiliers led the way. Then the leading files found that they were walking on the level. The crest had been gained. With slow steps and bated breath the open line of skirmishers stole across it. Was it possible that it had been entirely abandoned? Suddenly a raucous shout of 'Wie da?' came out of the darkness, then a shot then a splutter of musketry and a yell, as the Fusiliers sprang onwards with their bayonets. The Boer post of Vyrheid burgers clattered and scrambled away in the darkness, and a cheer that roused both the sleeping armies told that surprise had been complete and the position won.[1]

The action was not over but the result was 1,500 killed, wounded or missing; Blomfield was severely wounded and taken prisoner. However, he survived and went on to continue his military career, being promoted to major general in 1909 in charge of the Wessex Division, later the Mhow Division in India in 1911–12 and the Peshawar Division in 1913–15. In 1915 he returned to Britain to command the East Lancashire Division on home service at Colchester until his retirement in 1917. He had a great deal of experience and was a product of the Victorian Army. He was obviously the right material for the command of a division on home service and was typical of the officer class at the start of the Great War. He was the right figurehead to imbue the men with the fighting heritage of Lancashire.

After the dubious success of the British Army in the Boer War the government set in motion a series of reforms that reached their apex in the 1908 Haldane reforms. After this there were two parts to the British Army, Regular and Territorial Force. This structure was formed of professional full-time soldiers and part-time 'weekend' volunteers who were paid and had to attend an annual camp.

Written after the war and so imbued with patriotism and eloquent poetry, Sergeant Alfred Francis described the drill hall of the Field Ambulance at Old Trafford in August 1914.

> Before many hours had passed the drill hall had lost its pre-war appearance. There was bustle and importance on every square foot of ground, mysterious comings and goings, and commands were barked out every moment. Voices broke around us like claps of thunder which interrupt the warbling birds amongst the leaves. Men entering the hall with newspapers were besieged by inquisitive crowds eager to hear the latest battle news.[2]

Alfred Earnest Francis had been born in the village of Stokesay in Shropshire and come to Manchester with his mother to find employment. He worked as a caterer's clerk, with his mother under his roof and a boarder, Alice Whittle, who was a paper bag maker. His ability as an organiser was such that when he joined the East Lancashire Field Ambulance he was promoted to sergeant. This was as high as a working class clerk at that time could hope to advance and he would have been happy with his lot. Albert Francis would become the historian of his ambulance unit, the 2/3 East Lancashire Field Ambulance. He lived in south-eastern Manchester at Longsight. Here the sheds and marshalling yards of the London and North western Railway were cheek by jowl with industry and housing. Terraced housing was built near the railway for the working classes, who flocked to Manchester for employment in the boom times of the textile and railway industries.

Not all parts of the army were destined for glamour abroad. The 3rd (Reserve) Battalion was at Bury at the outbreak of war. Historian George Ashurst was one of the reserve battalion and remembered 8 August 1914 in Bury:

> Crowds of people were outside the barracks. The public houses were doing a roaring trade to both men and women. There was a lot of hand shaking, kissing, and good wishes; women were crying and laughing and quite a number of men were drunk … By about three

3

o'clock in the afternoon the battalion was ready for moving off, with the exception of a few absentees, who were determined to get down as much beer as possible in case the next drink was a long time coming. We formed up in the barrack square and rather sloppily marched out through the gates. Outside the barracks was a big crowd of men, women and children. Some were cheering, some were silent, and others crying. They broke into the ranks, kissing soldiers, shaking hands and wishing us the best of luck. On we marched to the station.[3]

It was a moment of history rarely recorded as a battalion moved off to its mobilisation station. They expected to be shipped off to some foreign destination, but they ended up on coastal defence in Hull. The 4th (Extra Reserve) Battalion went to Barrow-in-Furness to protect the shipyards and then to Barry in South Wales as part of the Severn garrison.

There were three paths into the army in 1914, Regular, Territorial and Kitchener's Army. The regular army was always on duty so could be instantly mobilised. The Territorial Force was represented here by first-line territorials of 42nd Division. This had existed since the Haldane Act in 1908 and that fact meant it could be called upon for immediate service on the outbreak of war. This was almost entirely a Manchester and district division and was mobilised at 5.30 pm on 4 August 1914 with all troops billeted within reach of their headquarters. On 10 August all units were invited to volunteer for foreign service, and on 20 August, after having accepted this the Division moved to training camps. By 5 September the Division was warned that it was to be sent to Egypt to replace regular forces returning to Europe and it began entraining on 9 September to move to Southampton, with the first shipment setting sail on 10 September.

The first line division, the 42nd, was thus the first Territorial Division to go overseas, a rapid movement to overseas station and the units of the division were split up between Cyprus, Egypt, Khartoum in the Sudan, and the canal zone. The 42nd Division was on station in Egypt before the declaration of war against Turkey on 5 November. The first action was the defence of the Suez Canal against Turkish forces in February 1915, before it was concentrated at Alexandria for the operations at Gallipoli, also called the Dardanelles. The men of 42nd Division landed in May 1915 and took part in the second and third Battles of Krithia and the Battle of Krithia Vineyard.

The outbreak of war was received with a great sense of duty and willingness to volunteer in Lancashire. So much so that the complement of 42nd Division was full up very quickly.

In the minds of those who know the history of the Territorial Force during the Great War there is one fact that will always rebound to the honour of East Lancashire. The immediate response within the Territorial units of that area was so great when the call for foreign service came, and the gaps so quickly filled from outside, that 42nd Division was the first Territorial division to proceed overseas. The nucleus of its second line Division left in this country was small in number and required for more recruits than many other second line Divisions. And in addition the training was more difficult, seeing that the requisite number of commissioned and non-commissioned officers had themselves to be trained.[4]

The reality of war was quick to overtake the patriotic fervour of 1914. The description by Private Norman Dunkerley (D Company, 1/10th Manchester Regiment) of the Dardanelles campaign and the horrors of trench warfare was typical. Norman was the second of four sons of a tin plate worker in Oldham; Norman and his brother Thomas were both clerks. The family had moved the very short distance from Friezland to Oldham in about 1897. Norman had progressed to the position of clerk in the Education Board by 1914, joined the colours and in 1915 wrote a letter to the *Oldham Chronicle,* which published it: 'The following letter has been received from an Oldham Territorial who is now in hospital at Malta, having been wounded in the Gallipoli fighting:

I suppose the story of the part the Oldham boys took in Fridays (14 June) grand affair in Gallipoli is now well known at home, so I will give you a short description of our experiences all along since leaving Suez. First we went to Port Said and then by the Cunarder Ansonia to the Dardanelles. The second or third night our company went into the second line or support trenches. Four days I think they were in, and then we went into dugouts at headquarters. Here shells were bursting over us worse than in the trenches, and we had several casualties. Then we went into the firing line. One night there was to be a levelling up of the lines of trenches, and we had to advance 20 yards or so and, as we were in advance of the general line, the regiments on our right and left had to advance about 100 yards.

We had to dig ourselves in, and where no lives should have been lost it turned out to be a little tragedy. I was one of the covering party some yards in front of the trench diggers. We went down this gap dragging ourselves up at the other side by a dead mans' foot. We crawled out all right and the digging commenced whilst we kept watch. If we saw any signs of attack we were to get back to the trench they were digging. The lads had got some three feet down when somebody got alarmed and the word went down the trench that we were surrounded and to get back for their lives, and we being left in the open, retired too. I had not seen the trench diggers, who by then had fair cover, retire, and I fell headlong into the deserted trench choking my rifle from barrel to breach. Somewhat dazed I got into the firing line and we were all lucky, as the supports were all lined in the firing line with fixed bayonets, and some were firing. We were lucky not to have been shot or bayoneted. In a few minutes we were out again, and the lads were now tired and dispirited and when dawn came had not enough cover and it came on to rain. As soon as daylight broke the snipers got to work. We were then knee deep in slush, and there we had to stay all day in a stooping position, and there being no communication trenches, some had to stay there till midnight. We lost several killed and wounded and we went down to the headquarters tired and slushed [sic] from head to foot.[5]

Most of the complement of 42nd Division was filled by long-term Territorial soldiers. These men usually had a professional career of some sort, from labourers to clerks, with the officers being provided by the higher echelons of society and industry. This differed from the regular army, who would take recruits from the unemployed as full-time soldiers, men who had nothing to lose by joining the army. On the outbreak of war the gaps in the division were filled with volunteers and the officers, especially the higher ranks, filled by the army with regular soldiers. So in the end a Territorial division was still a mix of volunteers and regulars, although mostly long-term 'weekend warriors'. All that existed at this stage of the 2nd East Lancashire Division was about twelve officers and sixty men kicking their heels in Manchester, 'all rather disappointed' that they had missed out on sailing with 42nd Division.

There were twelve infantry battalions in a British division in 1914, often as in this case from a particular region, such as East Lancashire. Formed under Major General C.E. Becket in November 1914, the 2nd East Lancashire Division provided drafts to its front line equivalent, 42nd Division, at Gallipoli, and went on to active service in March 1917. Serving in Flanders, it fought at Nieupoort and Third Ypres, going on to fight a rearguard action in March 1918, and it is this action that will take the majority of this history. In this book the regiments are essentially the Territorials of the Lancashire Fusiliers and East Lancashire Regiment with its metropolitan counterpart, the Manchester Regiment. The infantry were organised in three brigades, each with three (originally four) battalions of infantry, which is nine battalions, around 9,000 infantry. The battalions are generally 800 men by 1918 in four companies of 120 men plus headquarters and signals troops, medics, etc.

Reports of far off events would have informed and inspired the second line Territorials back home in what became 66th Division. It was a long way off being formed when 42nd Division left England. For the moment it existed only on paper and as a reserve and draft forming unit for the first line unit in Egypt and the Dardanelles. So for now any recruits would have been sent to the Middle East.

As we have seen there were three Lancashire regiments that provided the infantry for the East Lancashire Division: East Lancashire, Lancashire Fusiliers and Manchester Regiment, which took these titles from 1881. It is not the place of this history to delve further back in time than that as the period this history will cover is largely from 1914 to 1918. Before 10 August 1915 the men were essentially the second line of 42nd Division, and it was on that date that 66th Division was embodied and became a unit in its own right, while a third line was formed to feed drafts into both East Lancashire divisions.

The Territorial Force units of the Lancashire Fusiliers were comprised of the 1/5th, 1/6th, 1/7th, 1/8th battalions, which all went to 42nd Division; the second line 2/5th, 2/6th, 2/7th, 2/8th and the third line 3/5th, which all went to 66th Division. Also formed were the 2/9th, and the home-based depot units 3/6th, 3/7th, 3/8th, 3/9th and 4/5th Battalions of the third and fourth line. The 3/5th was attached to 66th Division in May 1915, which was an event in itself as it was quite rare to see third-line units actually involved in the fighting.

The Manchester Regiment was made up of battalions from the metropolis of Manchester and including the industrial towns of the modern greater Manchester area as far north as Burnley, south to Wigan, Bury, Oldham, Rochdale, Salford and Ashton and the city and suburbs of Manchester itself.

The structure of the regiment was much the same as the Lancashire Fusiliers. The 3rd and 4th Battalions of the Manchester Regiment were reserve and depot garrisons and were moved from Ashton-under-Lyne to the Humber garrison. The Territorial Force battalions were 1/5th, 1/6th, 1/7th, 1/8th, 1/9th, 1/10th of the first line and these ended up with 42nd Division. The second line were 2/5th, 2/6th, 2/7th, 2/8th, 2/9th, 2/10th, while a third line composed of 3/5th, 3/6th, 3/7th, 3/8th, 3/9th, 3/10th, were home service battalions. Those battalions that concern us here were the 2/5th–2/10th in 66th Division.

The East Lancashire Regiment was formed of soldiers from Blackburn, Burnley and Preston, which at the outbreak of war found the Regular battalions in Colchester and South Africa with the Reserve battalion in Preston. The 1st Battalion, East Lancashire moved to Harrow as part of 4th Division and then moved to France on 22 August 1914. The 2nd Battalion, East Lancashire sailed from Wijnberg, South Africa, to join 8th Division in Hursley Park, before moving to France in November 1914. The Reserve 3rd Battalion moved to Plymouth and then became part of the Tees garrison.

The territorial units of the East Lancashire were the 1/4th and 1/5th Battalions, which were in Blackburn and Burnley. On mobilisation they moved to Chesham Fold Camp in Bury and sailed from Southampton with the rest of 42nd Division to Egypt. Of the second line T.F. units the 2/4th Battalion was formed at Blackburn in September 1914 as a home service battalion. In November 1914 it moved to Southport where the elements of the future 66th Division were forming. Later in May 1915 it moved to Burgess Hill, then Pease Pottage and then Crowborough and Colchester in March 1916. It sailed with the rest of the division and served with it in France. The 2/5th battalion was formed in Burnley and had an identical service record with the East Lancashire Division. The 3/4th and 3/5th units were also formed at Blackburn and Burnley in March 1915 as depot units to provide drafts for the front line units. They both moved to Witley in Surrey in early 1916 and on 8 April 1916 they were formed into Reserve battalions. Then, in September that year, they were absorbed into the 3/4th Battalion, moving to Southport, Ripon, Whitby and Scarborough.

To conclude the structure of the brigades, the infantry battalions of 66th Division were the following battalions; the 3/5th Lancashire Fusiliers from Bury, the 2/6th Lancashire Fusiliers from Rochdale, and the 2/7th and 2/8 Lancashire Fusiliers from Salford, which formed 197 Brigade. The 2/4th East Lancashire, 2/5th East Lancashire from Burnley, 2/6th Lancashire Fusiliers, the 2/9th Manchester Regiment from Ashton-under-Lyne and 2/10th Manchester Regiment from Oldham formed 198 Brigade. The 2/5th Manchester 'Colliers' Battalion, from Wigan (with detachments at Leigh, Patricroft and Atherton), and the 2/6th based in Hulme and 2/7th Manchester Regiment based in Burlington Street, Manchester, formed 199 Brigade. The division was based in Southport from September 1914 to August 1915.

The news in the early part of 1915 was somewhat heartening; the bravery of the Regulars of the Lancashire Fusiliers on their landing at Cape Helles, 'six Victoria crosses before breakfast,' was stirring propaganda and is still remembered today. The British got ashore, but with heavy losses, and dug in on the ill-fated peninsula. The game had been given away months before as the Royal Navy nosed its battle fleet around the peninsula and even landed Royal Marines in a raid. The campaign went about as well as the Trojan War 3,000 years before, and cost the British and French 265,000 men killed, missing and wounded and the Turks 300,000 men. The Lancashire Fusiliers and the Manchester Regiment lost heavily here and their names fill the columns of the missing on the Cape Helles Memorial in levels of bravery high above the history of the disastrous campaign.

Until 66th Division was formed as an independent unit it raised drafts for 42nd Division on overseas service in Egypt and the Dardanelles. Men were asked to volunteer as reinforcements, others were drafted as replacements for casualties. Some men joined the Gallipoli campaign in 29th Division, where the 1st Battalion Lancashire Fusiliers were serving in May and June 1915. Two large drafts were sent out in the troop ships *Royal George* and *Royal Edward*, to which we shall return later.

What this three-tier army organisation amounted to was a massive expansion of the army from two battalions of the regular army (plus two reserve) and five territorial for each of the Lancashire Fusiliers and Manchester Regiments. Among this expansion were the twelve battalions that became 197, 198, and 199 brigades of 66th Division. This was accompanied by four heavy artillery batteries, four artillery batteries, an ammunition column, trench mortar batteries, three engineer companies, signal section, machine guns, ambulance, veterinary section, and a divisional train (horse-drawn wagons). By mid-1915 there were approximately forty-four battalions of the Manchester Regiment and thirty-one of the Lancashire Fusiliers in existence with a paper strength of 75,000 men at any one time. That is a total comparative estimate of five divisions from the two regiments in Manchester and the surrounding towns of east Lancashire. Two of these divisions concern us and twenty-four battalions; of these twelve each were in 42nd Division and 66th Division.

The regular army could be stationed anywhere, the Territorial Army traditionally had no overseas obligation, but the men were asked to make the choice and mostly chose imperial service. For those who did not want to serve abroad they were transferred to home service battalions. This was the same for Kitchener battalions. It was some of these men who formed the nucleus of 66th Division.

The men, known officially as 'Other Ranks', were native Lancashire men, and were notably tough and plain speaking. As Territorials they were gainfully employed before the war, and made it their duty to volunteer for the army at the weekends and for the annual camp in order to raise extra wages and to do their duty. These men were from the second line territorial units of the Lancashire Fusiliers and the Manchester Regiment, based around the metropolis of Manchester and its satellite towns, Ardwick, Ashton, Burnley, Bury, Oldham, Rochdale, Salford, and Wigan. These were industrial mill towns that in popular conception hummed with activity in the pre-war period; mines, quarries, steel works, railways and warehouses and docks. The officers were just the minority; the men were the majority, who served and often died in service with the infantry, artillery and horses.

It is amazing, but not surprising, that so many served voluntarily in the Territorials. There were, however, several key figures in Lancashire who pulled in so many of these willing recruits. It was the wealthy and influential that had a say in the war experience of the common man by asking him to sign up. One of these was Lord Derby, nicknamed the King of Lancashire, owing to his wealth and the land that he owned. The fantastic level of recruitment in the autumn of 1914 had petered out in mid-1915 due to the Gallipoli campaign. Lord Derby had personally telephoned Kitchener when it was stipulated that volunteers may have to serve in any regiment as required rather than their first choice. To ask a Lancashire man, one might say, to serve outside his county regiments, was:

> murdering recruitment. We cannot get a man. It really is heartbreaking to find out that some damned fool should send out this order without consulting anybody connected with the Territorial Forces ... recruitment is at a very parlous state at this moment in Lancashire.[6]

'That damned fool' was Lord Kitchener himself, who had his own agenda. He did not want to follow the county system of regiments, but rather use the regular army and his own 'New Army', full of recruits who could be trained up outside the traditional army system. In a week he had gained permission from Parliament for his New Army and had raised 400,000 men who would see action on the Somme before most of the Territorials. Kitchener was a visionary who had speculated and prepared for a war of at least three years, which was close enough to the reality. There was a battle going on at the highest levels between Lord Kitchener, Lord Esher and Sir Ian Hamilton into which Lord Derby plunged himself. They were each in favour of either New Army or Territorial on their own accounts. Kitchener won through and got his New Army of half a million men who were to be trained, clothed and used in battle (the 1916 Somme battle) before the second line Territorials got their equipment. Lord Derby got a scheme of his own where all eligible men would be registered in the 'Derby scheme' from July 1915 so that when required they could be called upon to conscript. The balance would change as Kitchener was drowned on his way to Russia in 1916. Lord Derby worked his way up to the position in government he really desired and became Secretary of State for War in 1916. The men at the top were true Titans, and were prepared to level with one another when the cause they felt for was challenged.

Lord Derby was a great voice in Lancashire for recruitment. He deserves massive credit for the oration he undertook to recruit men and often did the recruitment himself. So hard did he rail that the Prime Minister, Asquith, made Lord Derby National Director General of Recruitment. A typical statement of Lord Derby was:

> I have only two sons. One is at the front. He has been home for a few days' leave and went back to the front on Thursday. My other boy is in the artillery, and when properly trained will go out to the front. If I had twenty sons I should be ashamed if every one of them did not go to the front when his turn came ... When the war is over I intend, as far as I possibly can, to employ nobody except men who have taken their turn at the front.[7]

Ominous threats from a man who had enormous influence in Lancashire. He put pressure on women to release their menfolk. This in a time when girls and women presented white feathers to men not on service; the pressure was great. Men faced possible loss of employment, loss of status and respect; there was really not a lot of choice but to serve in the forces. Once enlisted there was an option to serve at home only, which many may have taken, far more chose to serve abroad and accept their fate in order to be seen to have done their bit. The men who were the Other Ranks did volunteer in huge numbers. Some were pressured, and eventually conscription was used to force service from 1916. Life in wartime Britain was akin to walking the plank, better to face the sharks and survive than to be branded a coward.

Lord Derby had put his name to the scheme in October 1915 that attested men and women to the national register and they would be called upon when needed. They were not required to serve at once but eventually would be called upon if their occupation was deemed as non-essential. This swept many men into the forces, if they could not convince the appeals process that they were in essential work. This at least kept the family and neighbourhood pressures at bay.

The pressures of war meant that 42nd Division got all the resources in 1914 and 1915, and 66th Division was still a long way off establishment. There were three differing objectives for the army recruiters in the Regular, New Army and Territorial Armies, which meant that a second line territorial deployment was barely considered at this stage. Lord Kitchener was one of the few who saw the scale of the war, that there would indeed be a time when the fledgling second line Territorial Force would be needed abroad. For the moment home defence was imperative in case the Western Front collapsed, and there was always an apparent threat of invasion across the North Sea.

NOTES:

[1] Conan Doyle, *The Great Boer War*, quoted online source, The Museum of the Lancashire Fusiliers.

[2] Francis, A.E., *History of the 2/3 Field Ambulance in the Great War*, pp.1–2.

[3] Ashurst, G., *My Bit*, p.29.

[4] *Clickety-Click*, the East Lancs Division Annual Dinner Club, 1924.

[5] IWM Department of Documents, papers of N. Dunkerley, p.48.

[6] Moorhouse, G., *Hell's Foundations*, 1992, p.167f.

[7] ibid, p.166f.

Chapter 2

Urgent Work

1915–16

Many of the men who joined the 2/4 and 2/5 East Lancashire Regiment were weavers and colliers from Blackburn, Darwen, Clitheroe, Church, Oswaldtwistle, Burnley, Accrington, Padiham, Haslingden, Ramsbottom, Nelson, Colne, and Brierfield. Pre-war boom had turned into bust, and many of the men who enlisted were very poor. 'The men were at this time and for long afterwards in mufti. Many were veritably in rags, trade having been bad for a long time and abject poverty reigning in some homes, and despite the efforts made to obtain underclothing and boots by private subscription their condition remained relatively deplorable until Christmas 1914, when service dress and boots were issued.' Men in these circumstances would have done anything to get a wage, to feed and clothe their families and restore some amount of dignity.[1] It is apparent that some of the cause for the enthusiasm for joining the army was economic and some was to avoid suspicions of cowardice.

As a contrast to the poverty and lack of knowledge of some of the infantry, the skilled medical men of the 2/3rd Field Ambulance were to send a draft to reinforce both 29th and 42nd Division in the East and raised three officers and fifty men to go. They embarked at Avonmouth on two steam ships, His Majesty's Troopships *Royal Edward* and, a day later, *Royal George*. At about 9.00 o'clock on the morning of 13 August 1915 the crew of *Royal Edward* and more than 1,376 officers and men were approaching the entry to the Aegean Sea. Aboard the *Royal Edward* were replacements for the 29th Division, men of the Lancashire Fusiliers, men such as Privates McDonough, Thomas McGuire, John McFeeley, and John McHugh from Cobden Street in Rochdale. Also aboard were men of the Royal Army Medical Corps who had been in the 2/3rd East Lancashire Field Ambulance, including its extremely popular and capable former Commanding Officer Colonel Charles Bertram Marshall from Cheadle Hulme, Stockport. Under his command were George J.R. Black of Cheetham Hill, Manchester, Dan Davies from Higher Openshaw, William Fisher from Ancoats, Manchester, and George Frederick Simms from Putney in London. All were well-trained men of the RAMC who looked forward to doing some good in a dreadful campaign, all be it with some trepidation.

Dan Davies was a newly married man in 1915 and lived with his wife Elizabeth on the City Road at Higher Openshaw, about a mile from where he had grown up in Butterworth Street, Bradford, Manchester. His father, Joseph, was a warehouseman for a drapery, his brother Harry was a labourer in an iron works and his sister Lily a machinist in a skirt factory. Dan worked as a store keeper at an electric works and served as a medic in the 2/3rd East Lancashire Field Ambulance.

Another inner city man was William Fisher, born in Ancoats, the beating heart of Manchester's transport network. Even before the railways had come to Manchester the canals were the main conduit for heavy goods. The Ashton canal was completed by 1796 and the Rochdale canal by 1806. These met in a series of basins in Ancoats. Here by 1844 many mills and warehouses had established themselves to make use of the waterway for the transport of goods. The main road here is called Store Street for this very reason. This attracted a workforce who lived as close to work as speculators would let them. By 1900 the canal was still in use, filthy, polluted and poisonous after a century of run-off from the Store Street ironworks and foundry, the Junction Street lead works was nearby. Many of the mills here were vast, others small and in multiple occupancy. The sun hardly shone here as both industrial and domestic chimneys belched out sooty smoke, blocking out what was left of the sky by the buildings. When the railways came in 1842 the company that became the LNWR built its Manchester terminus here, the modern day Piccadilly Station, another vast building in this inhospitable industrial environment. This seemed to be the very heart of the dark Satanic mills popularised by the famous hymn.

The Ashton canal enters the warehouse district over the Store Street aqueduct, and just beside this was Aqueduct Street. This was the home of bargeman Albert Fisher, his wife Sarah and their sons Sidney, William and daughters Hilda and Doris. They also had a boarder, Martha Lloyd, who was a waitress in a draper's refreshment room. Packed into a small house, this was how the poorest families lived. William had had a happy but poor childhood. By the age of fifteen he was working as an errand boy and going to school part-time. Sometimes he accompanied his father out of the city to the purer air of the countryside where he could enjoy nature, even learn to swim in the better waters of the rivers. Having avoided the worst of any industrial pollution or disease associated with slum life it is no surprise in Piccadilly that William Fisher served as a medic as this part of Manchester was traditionally near the home of the hospitals of the city and it is no doubt that here William found his calling as a medic.

Fisher was also among the medics on their way to the Dardanelles on board the *Royal Edward*. One of a pair of ships built for the Egyptian Royal Mail steamship service between Marseilles and Alexandria, they plied the seas as SS *Cairo* and *Heliopolis* before being renamed by their new owner, the Canadian Northern, and used on the Avonmouth to Montreal and Halifax route across the north Atlantic until they were requisitioned with their captain and crew.

Under Lieutenant Commander Peter Watton R.N.R., they were plying their way from Alexandria to Mudros in order to land reinforcements at Gallipoli. Just off the island of Kandeloussa in the Aegean they passed the Hospital Ship *Soudan* going in the opposite direction. They had been on alert and just stowing their lifebelts below deck after a lifeboat drill. Watching this was the captain of the German U-boat *UB-14*, Oberleutnant zur See Heino von Heimburg, who let the hospital ship pass and fired a torpedo from a mile, hitting the troop ship in the stern. Catastrophically hit, the ship listed quickly and slipped under by the stern. The men below decks coming up met men coming down to recover their life jackets and panic quickly took hold. They had no chance and the ship floundered in just six minutes, leaving a mass of humanity and debris on the surface of the ocean. Few would have had time to react to the torpedo hit and the subsequent sinking was only long enough for the ship's wireless operator to send a quick S.O.S. before it was all over. The hospital ship *Soudan* heard the 'Mayday!' and turned around, as did other ships in the vicinity. Only 600 men were rescued out of a possible total compliment of 1,367 officers and men. It was to remain one of the largest ships sunk in the course of the war and at about 935 men lost one of the highest losses of men at sea.

The disaster was not censored and *The Times* reported the sinking:

> The British Transport Royal Edward was sunk by an enemy submarine in the Aegean Sea on 13 August 1915. According to information at present, the transport had on board 32 officers and

1350 troops, in addition the ship's complement of 220 officers and men. The troops consisted mainly of reinforcements for the 29th Division and the Royal Army Medical Corps.

Amongst those drowned were listed as four officers and 143 men of the RAMC and one officer and twenty-seven men of the Lancashire Fusiliers.[2]

By far the highest loss was to the RAMC. That and the hundreds of lives they might have saved in the hospitals and aid posts on Gallipoli, Lemnos and Mudros. It seems that only five men of the East Lancashire Field Ambulance were lost so the majority of the draft may have been on the *Royal George* or serving in Egypt. Two survivors were Captain W.L. Cockcroft RAMC, who was awarded the Albert Medal for his attention to other survivors of the sinking, and Major R.C. Standring Smith, also RAMC, who was rescued after several hours clinging to an upturned lifeboat. Among the lost was William Fisher, the bargeman's son from Ancoats. He is remembered on the Helles Memorial in Turkey, on the fateful headland of Gallipoli that he never reached.

For the East Lancashire Field Ambulance the loss of five men was a heavy burden on those who wanted to do so much good. In Charles Bertram Marshall they lost a man

> a really good Commanding Officer, a much respected gentleman, a man who would have ornamented any profession, an officer of outstanding worth, and his passing was accepted by every member of the Field Ambulance as a personal and tragic loss. He was one who never turned his back but marched breast forward.[3]

To the men of the division who were now encamped in Sussex this was the worst news of the war so far. The loss of comrades and friends was increasing as the war intensified. The army for its part kept the still-forming units of the division busy by moving them to Maidstone. Here, at Burham, they started digging trenches, a practice much-liked by command to toughen the men and also to keep them busy and tired, distil the effect of bad news and make them into soldiers. Sergeant Francis recalled the impact of these field days:

> The Higher Command had suddenly discovered that Burham possessed extraordinary wartime importance and an opinion was formed that in the remote event of the enemy outwitting our vigilant navy the villages and land of Kent, strategic territory, would be placed in danger ... we were ordered to put our field ambulance

16

training to one side and give assistance in the urgent work of building fortifications.[4]

The sarcasm with which they approached the task is all too evident, but there was serious military purpose in alleviating the threat of invasion and toughening up the soldiers, even the unarmed medics: They were evidently becoming soldiers. After this training they went to Crowborough where the East Lancashire Division was now forming with three brigades, 197, 198, and 199, combining their total of twelve infantry battalions.

Accompanying the infantry were the three artillery brigades each of three field artillery batteries and one heavy battery of the Royal Artillery, formed and trained with their three ammunition columns, three trench mortar batteries, and a divisional ammunition column. There was a divisional artillery headquarters, and (originally) four field artillery brigades: 2/I East Lancashire, 2/II East Lancashire, 2/III East Lancashire and 2/IV East Lancashire (Heavy). These were respectively formed from Blackburn, Manchester, Bolton and Carlisle. These were re-designated in 1916 CCCXXX, CCCXXXI and CCCXXXII (330, 331 and 332) of four batteries each (A, B, C and D 'heavy') of six 18-pounder quick-firing guns and two 4.5in howitzers. Two of the men of 330 Battery Royal Field Artillery were Gunner John Gore, from Boothstown, to the west of Manchester, and 516343 Tom Hardman, who lived in Southsea near Portsmouth (census records are unsure as to whether he was from Lancashire or not). John was one of six children from an agricultural family and Tom may have originated from Lancashire. John Gore may have joined the artillery as he would have been used to working with horses.

The field artillery brigades each composed three light and one heavy battery. The 2/I East Lancashire (Blackburn Artillery) composed 2/4 Lancashire from Blackburn, 2/5 Lancashire from Church, and 2/6 Lancashire batteries from Burnley. The 2/II (Manchester Artillery) was composed of 2/15, 2/16 and 2/17 from Manchester, while 2/III (Bolton Artillery) included 2/18, 2/19 and 2/20 from Bolton and district. These batteries were all re-designated in May 1916 as A, B and C in their respective artillery groups instead of having similar numbers to the infantry battalions.

The heavy artillery was formed of a brigade of guns and gunners from Cumberland and Westmorland, still with the designation East Lancashire (Howitzer) Brigade, although this is outside modern Lancashire. Completing the artillery were the 2/I Cumberland battery from Carlisle and 2/II Cumberland from Workington, whose heavy batteries provided the largest firepower. These were supported by the four East Lancashire Brigade ammunition columns designated 2/I (Carlisle?), 2/II (Workington), 2/III (Maryport?), and 2/IV (Whitehaven). There was also a Divisional Ammunition Column designated the 66th 2/II East Lancashire Divisional Ammunition Column. This was spread between Whitehaven and Maryport with a section in each. Problems were found in providing for the artillery, as at first this second line division lacked guns, modern sights and, more distressingly, had no veterinary officer for the 1,000-plus horses in the division.

The three light trench mortar batteries of eight 3in Stokes mortars were each numbered after the division they served with, hence X 66, Y 66 and Z 66 (LTM) batteries. One medium trench mortar battery, V 66, had six 2in mortars supplied by the divisional ammunition column. The firepower of a division was forty-eight guns, of which thirty-eight were field artillery and twelve howitzers. There were thirty-six trench mortars; twenty-four medium and twelve heavy.

Machine guns were organised under the Machine Gun Corps, with the 66th Battalion MGC divided into three companies, the 202, 203 and 204 companies MGC. In 1918 each division had 400 machine guns; sixty-four Vickers and 336 Lewis guns, its lighter and more mobile companion. The battalion was of 800 to 1,000 men in itself under officers. Four men were assigned to a Vickers and two on a Lewis gun, which is around 928 men and seventy-two officers and a headquarters.

There were three field companies of Royal Engineers, a divisional signal company, three field ambulance units of the Royal Army Medical Corps, a mobile veterinary section, an employment company and a divisional train of the Royal Army Service Corps.

In 1900 Manchester was a hub of progress and offered a great deal of potential recruits for the engineers, and so a corps was formed to make use of their talents. This was termed the 3rd Lancashire Fusiliers Engineers (Volunteers). This became the East Lancashire Royal Engineers with the passing of the Haldane Act in 1908. The three Royal Engineers Companies of the 66th Division were the 430th (2/1st East Lancashire), the 431st (2/2nd East Lancashire) and the 432nd (2/3rd East Lancashire). The Royal Engineers base for 42nd Division was at Bolton and Bury, that of 66th Division at Bolton, Wigan and Old Trafford. When the third line was formed this was at the regional headquarters of the Royal Engineers at Seymour Grove, Old Trafford. Three companies of Royal Engineers went to Alexandria with 42nd Division and those men remaining formed the nucleus of the three

Royal Engineer companies of 66th Division.[5] These eventually combined units from Bolton, Old Trafford and Wigan at Southport.

This completes the composition of the division. When the division was embodied in 1916 it became ready for use in home defence. General Force was a group of armies intended for the defence of Great Britain with its headquarters in London. The army headquarters were at Bedford, Aldershot and Luton. Each army was made up of ten mounted brigades, nine first-line Territorial Force divisions and four cyclist battalions. The general commanding this force was also acting as commander of Eastern Command and Central Force and the headquarters moved from the Hotel Metropole to Horse Guards, Whitehall.

By November 1915, Central Force was almost entirely composed of second line Territorial Force units, but not yet including the East Lancashire Division. In March 1916 it ceased to exist and came directly under Field Marshal Sir John French, Commander Home Forces, whilst the administration was under Eastern Command and the armies were styled Northern and Southern Armies.

At the start of 1916 the East Lancashire Division was embodied and new recruits added to its ranks. Gilbert Wilkinson, a cloth worker from Preston, was one of those who joined. He was born in 1898 in Bow Lane and worked as a book-keeper and cloth bundler at Messrs. Bretherton, Harrop and Company at the Marsh Lane Mill. This was an industrial area of cotton mills and expanding housing between the old centre of Preston and the up-and-coming area of Ashton-on-Ribble. Many men from Preston joined the army to get away from grim conditions in Preston, which had some of the poorest housing in the country with back to backs in which disease was rife up to 1900.[6] Even after the Preston Improvement Act of 1880 problems remained and much of this housing still survives today. In 1915 Gilbert joined the General Service Corps and on 12 May 1916 he was called upon to join the 2/5 Battalion East Lancashire Regiment at Reed Hall camp at Colchester as Private 242147 Gilbert Wilkinson.

When the division was based in Colchester officers were still joining. One of these was Herbert Roland Bate from Leicester. Mere Street, where his family, lived is a meandering and gently sloping road of terraced houses on the east side of the town. The houses are small, but well-proportioned in the Midland style, with glazed bricks and a modest amount of ornamentation. This was the sort of house that men who had progressed to the lower level of management would be able to live in. Number 36, where Bate lived, is opposite the current site of the Roman Catholic Church of the Sacred Heart, part of the Catholic diocese of Nottingham, which was only built in 1922. Bate seems to have been influenced by attending the temporary church set up in the school and followed a calling in the church, going to study with a friend at Leeds university and passing his exams in June 1915. Bate had a found a career in the church that was well thought of, enjoyed a modest income and was better than his father's lot in life. Bate's father, John, was a boot and shoe foreman in a finishing department at a shoe factory, while his sister Lillian was also in the shoe trade:

> When I returned to college in September 1914 some of the older students had already joined up. At the outbreak of war the legal age for military service was 19, though a few who were younger did manage to dodge it by falsifying their age … As I was only 18 I was told by my college head I must complete the academic year now beginning, before thinking of enlisting.

After passing his exams he joined the Artist's Rifles of the London Regiment the following year. This battalion was mostly formed of artists, actors, intellectuals and men of an artistic leaning. In fact so many high-calibre men joined this battalion as private soldiers that they were quickly reassigned as officers to other army battalions. In his case, Bate was assigned to A Company, 2/6th Battalion, the Manchester Regiment:

> In Spring 1916 the Division moved to Essex, with which I had become familiar the year before with the Artists' Rifles. This time however the 2/6 Manchesters were under canvas at Wivenhoe on the river Colne. There we remained all the summer exploring the neighbouring countryside by route marches and field exercises so that places like Fingringhoe and Mersea Island became familiar and well known. There arose a rivalry between Battalions of the division as to which could march furthest in a day. Ten, twelve [or] fifteen miles in full kit with pack and rifle, with ten minutes fall out after every fifty minutes, and of course a midday halt, was pretty good going. In the end some battalions overstretched themselves and a limit was set to a day's march.
>
> As summer faded, once again the division moved into winter quarters at Colchester. This time the battalions were quartered close together, most of them in the barracks. Barracks could not hold us all and our battalion was lucky to be billeted in the town, which was much approved, as giving more freedom and greater convenience than barracks afforded. That winter was exceptionally cold and uneventful, but passed pleasantly enough.[7]

Not all the men in the division were born and bred in Lancashire. As the inevitable casualties made holes in the ranks, men were brought in from elsewhere, and with the way the army recruited, these could be from any part of the country. The division moved to Sussex and Suffolk, meaning that the recruitment went with it as it moved. This meant that men such as Thomas Booty, a grocer's boy from Essex, were recruited into the ranks of the Lancashire men as well as Ralph Frost from Cambridgeshire, who worked on the railways.

Thomas Booty was the second son of seven children from Rochford in Essex. His elder brother had already joined up and was in the Sussex Regiment. At the age of eighteen he joined up and was trained with the division at Colchester, taking the place of men who had been drafted into the front line 42nd Division. As a local recruit he enlisted in Southend on 17 January 1917 in the Manchester Regiment; he was less outgoing than his brother, Bill, and would have felt a bit like an outsider but would have mucked in with the rest, and he at least had his mates from Southend in his platoon, seen in a relaxed section photograph (see plate section page 4) at camp near Colchester. He had been recruited in one of the division's recruitment drives at the end of its stay in Colchester and had little time for basic training, moving as it did to a war footing in late February.

Ralph Frost was the son of a railway guard from March, Cambridgeshire, where he lived at 74 Dartford Road. He had been born in 1898 and was fifteen in 1911 when he was working in the engine sheds as an engine cleaner. He was a signed up member of the trade union but soon attested to the military and called up in May 1917 to join the 2/7 Manchester Regiment.

It was not just the men in the division that expressed the identity of the division but also the divisional sign. The story of this is quite distinct from that of some other divisions and in fact had a maritime heritage. Alfred Stuart Little had moved from his home town of Twickenham to Bembridge, Isle of Wight, as a single man of independent means and was serving as the secretary to the town's sailing club by 1911. He lodged at Myrtle Cottage with the Osborne family, whose son, William, was a yacht worker, presumably also at the club. William Osborne was the sole earner in the Osborne household, so Alfred would have given welcome income to the Osborne family. He worked as secretary to the club and at weekends was a volunteer in the Imperial Yeomanry, so he obviously rode as well. As a lieutenant in the Yeomanry on the outbreak of war his experience was desperately needed and he was gazetted as a captain in the 8th Hampshire (Isle of Wight, 'Princess Beatrice's') Battalion on 28 August 1914. He would have paraded at or around

Osborne House, the royal residence on the island, and have been in a certain social set. In 66th Division, Alfred Little became aide de camp to General Lawrence and Camp Commandant.

Little's racing flag was a square with two light blue bands and a central stripe of primrose yellow, all of the same width. He promptly submitted this and for want of a better one it was accepted, so the division went overseas with Little's yacht racing flag as its divisional sign. The correct colours of the divisional flag were thus the most vital part of it. The blue was not a bright light blue, practically a turquoise, and the yellow primrose, not, as was often the case, a kind of orange.

On entering the line in the Givenchy sector the division was in II Corps. It objected to the divisional sign as a square for being too large and as it was not desired to alter it the top two corners were cut off and the resultant triangle became the divisional symbol. At that time the II was added behind the symbol. When the division left II Corps this was washed out and an equilateral triangle was substituted. This was the divisional sign for the rest of the war.[8]

The identity of the division was now complete and the men were trained and ready for use overseas. Initial frustration for the men who did not go overseas was eventually replaced by the task of forming and training the new division. For the men of 66th Division, their time of waiting was over as they moved rapidly to a war footing. Their stay in Colchester was swiftly interrupted as they were warned to be ready for going overseas. Bate remembered the night they left Colchester on 25 February 'at dead of night, marching silently through the streets, to the railway station'. There were no crowds to wish them Godspeed here, this was total war in the beginning of 1917. Along with thousands of others, Bate entrained, some for Folkestone, with other parts of the division travelling to Southampton to embark. They were being swallowed up by the war as it had come to so many of their friends and relatives. All they needed now was a divisional commander to lead them into the maelstrom of the Western Front.

NOTES:
[1] Nicholson C.N., *History of the East Lancashire Regiment*, 1936, p.307f.
[2] *The Times*, 18 August 1915.
[3] Francis A.E., *History of the 2/3rd Field Ambulance*, 1930, p.13f.
[4] ibid, p.15.
[5] Anonymous, *A History of the East Lancashire Royal Engineers*, Manchester, 1920. p.229.
[6] Historical essay by Nigel Morgan, *The Godfrey Edition of Maps, Preston West*, 1909.
[7] IWM Department of Documents, papers of Herbert Roland Bate.
[8] Colonel B.V.M. Balders, quoted in *Clickety-Click*, No.13, 1935, p.21–2.

Chapter 3

Blood Lust

February–July 1917

The first divisional commander of 66th Division in combat was General Sir Herbert Lawrence. As one account noted:

> 'It is no exaggeration to say that Sir Herbert Lawrence made you who you were,' noted one account. 'I do not mean the raising of units, the clothing and equipping of units; I mean a very great deal more than that. I mean that Sir Herbert Lawrence imbued you with his own high ideals of duty and service. He did what was absolutely necessary in the British Army to produce the very best of results; he produced a spirit by which every officer and man in the Division knew that they had at their head not only an accomplished and able soldier but a personal friend. Gentlemen that spirit which Sir Herbert Lawrence imbued you and your men with is the spirit which enables the soldier to face death fearlessly and cheerfully in a cause he believes to be just.'[1]

Sir Herbert Lawrence was the son of a former viceroy of India, who was educated at Harrow and the Royal Military College, Sandhurst. He served as a lieutenant in India with the 17th Lancers, and in England as an adjutant and as a staff officer in the intelligence division. In the Boer War he served as intelligence officer in Sir John French's cavalry and brevet colonel with the 16th Lancers. He resigned after Douglas Haig was promoted ahead of him and became a successful banker with Glyn Mills and Company in London. He commanded the volunteer King Edward's Horse from 1904–09 and on the outbreak of war was recalled to the colours, where he served as commander of the 127th Manchester Brigade, 42nd Division, then divisional commander of 53rd Welsh Division.

Finally, returning to Egypt he was architect of the victory at Romani in the Sinai. Falling from favour, he was returned to England to command 71st Division and then 66th Division from February 1917 to January 1918.[2]

On arrival at Le Havre the soldiers of the division entrained for 'destination unknown', being concentrated at Thiennes after a phenomenally quick train journey of nine and a half hours to cover 50 odd miles to the area of Givenchy and Cuinchy. Headquarters were established at St Venant and the battalions were diverted to the part of the front where they were to relieve the 5th Division in the trenches, with 197 Brigade at Vielle Chapelle, 198 at Calonne and 199 at St Venant. The general officer commanding, Sir Herbert Lawrence, and his General Staff officer, A.R. Burrowes, went by sea via Folkestone and Boulogne. On 7 March General Lawrence inspected 197 Brigade on its way through St Venant, where it was noted that 'the column was very ragged, emphasising necessity for very slow pace at any rate till men accustomed to Pavé roads. Due to the stoppage of the Channel service, some delay occurred in the arrival of certain units. It appears that Division will have to go into line without Pioneer battalion, Trench Mortars, machine gun companies. Application urgently made for those that have not arrived.'[3] It was not a particularly glorious start to a two-year campaign, but no losses had been suffered at least.

The first units into the trenches were those of 197 and 198 Brigade and gas training, organised sports, drill and reorganisation was all under way for all troops. Snow followed and the privations of life at the front were fully realised. On 12 March army headquarters finally admitted that no pioneer battalion would be attached to the East Lancashire Division, which was seen as a serious drawback for the men, who would have to maintain 7,000 yards of front. On the next day it was arranged that 200 men from each brigade would be assigned to the Royal Engineers for this very purpose. Later on 13 March the late arrival of the 202 and 203 Companies M.G.C. was noted, so at least the division would have some firepower.

The condition of the trenches now became worse as those soldiers who had been there to gain experience had visited a wintry scene during a heavy frost. These same trenches were now in the midst of a thaw, and conditions were bad with running rivulets or deep, gluey mud. The sector was a quiet one, according to the East Lancashire Regiment:

> An arrangement of reliefs was made whereby, during the Brigade's occupation of the sector of each battalion, on relieving the front line, took over the same section of trench, thus acquiring a knowledge of

its particular front which became increasingly valuable as the trench strength gradually decreased owing to casualties, sickness, the detachment of men and officers on courses and special duties and the gradual wastage which goes on almost imperceptibly in such conditions. Familiarity with a particular bit of front line enabled it to be held in the circumstances much more thinly than would have been necessary had the knowledge of the holding unit been less intimate.[4]

The conditions of weather and ground conditions were bad enough but the ruination caused by the war had an impact on the soldiers, unused to seeing such man-made destruction:

> We are in a ruined village which was once a flourishing little hamlet with a railway station, school, post office, a couple of churches, two small breweries, and the usual enormous number of estaminets. There isn't a sound house in the village now; every one is a ruin. Some are completely razed, but have some part of the walls standing, others are complete outside but a mere shell inside, while others again are damaged in parts only. There is no civilian population, and the churches are marked by mere piles of stone of stone and brick, which used to be places of worship, and little graveyards, thick with crosses which have been erected over the graves of our soldiers. All sorts of odd corners are used for burying places, but if it at all possible a cross is always erected to mark the spot, and a large number of the graves receive little attentions in the way of wild flowers and so on. Occasionally you'll see, just off a trench, a place where some soldier has fallen and been buried on the spot – but there's always a little wooden cross.[5]

Casualties mounted, not necessarily by enemy action, but by the mere fact of being in such conditions, what was known as 'natural wastage', a horrible term relating to the siege nature of the warfare. Mine warfare was a part of life in this front and a mine was exploded in the front of the 2/4 East Lancashire Regiment at Surrey and Red Dragon craters, but caused no casualties, save to make no man's land more impassable.

There were three field ambulances, the 2/1st, 2/2nd, and 2/3rd East Lancashire, each under a doctor. This comprised thirty officers and 665 men. Each ambulance thus included ten officers and 221 men. The work of the ambulances was followed in a history of the 2/3rd Field Ambulance written by Sergeant Alfred Francis in 1930. The RAMC had been formed in 1898, just pre-dating the Boer War, but due to alleged inefficiencies it too was reorganised. The field ambulances had been the most prodigious output of the reorganisation by Sir Alfred Keogh.

The system of evacuation was dependent on a chain of aid posts. In no man's land the soldier would either crawl back or be stretchered out at night as possible. A first aid bandage would be applied. At the regimental aid post (RAP), a regimental medical officer would assess the casualty, redress the wound, and apply basic splints as necessary. The casualty would then be carried back the 2,000 yards to the advanced dressing station; this might have been done by horse cart, ambulance, push cart or trolley (railway) or motor ambulance. If done by hand there would be a relay of bearer posts where the carriers would hand over to a fresh pair of hands and rest. There was an RAP per battalion in the line, so four for a brigade, and one field ambulance per brigade.

The advanced dressing station was situated above or below ground, often in a bunker as necessary due to shelling, where the casualty would be reassessed, the wound inspected and a hot drink given. Then the casualty would continue on to the main dressing station, often by horse-drawn ambulance. Located in a church, chateau or farm up to 2 miles behind the front, at this station the casualty would have his wound properly re-examined and be helped to warm up and be fed. This was run by the divisional medical officer.

From here the man would go on to the casualty clearing station, run by the corps, some 6 to 7 miles behind the front in marquees or a building. The first treatment would be decided upon here and nurses would help. An operating theatre was used to treat the wound properly and make sure it was healthy and free of infection. From here he would go to a ward to recuperate or further back for treatment to an army hospital. An assessment was now made of the prospects of a return to his regiment, further recuperation or a 'Blighty Wound' that would necessitate return to Britain to one of many hospitals run by the Territorials or civilian hospitals in Britain. One of the early patients of the field ambulance was Gilbert Wilkinson.

Encounters with the enemy were reported on 25 March by 198 Brigade:

> Between 5 and 5.30 a.m. while D company 2/4 East Lancashire Regiment under Captain Brothers was standing next to 201308 Private Arkwright who was in front line trench at Number 3 Lewis Gun Position A.15.d.9550 [map reference] with about a dozen others heard shouting, which he did not understand, behind him. He

turned round and saw four Germans standing at the parados, who commenced firing their automatic pistols into the trench. Three of the Germans then made off to the left and two to the right towards their own trenches, the fourth jumped into the trench. Private Arkwright and 202697 Private J. Fielding seized him and held him while C.S.M. Fairbrother and 200744 Sergeant T. Holland came up and disarmed him. Our Lewis Gun opened fire but it is not known whether any were hit.

From information gathered it would appear that a German patrol had been sent out to reconnoitre our line in the vicinity of the canal bank at the map reference given and had penetrated to the rear of our front line which is only held by posts. The hostile patrol returning came up in rear of our No 3 Lewis Gun post, hence their presence on our parados there. We had one casualty (wounded) by the firing into our trench.

The enemy's attention was concentrated elsewhere so the slowness of the division to attain its full complement went unnoticed. The Germans were moving inferior divisions after their withdrawal to the Hindenburg line further south, and so the new troops opposite were the 7th Division of the IV Corps and the 16th Bavarian Reserve Division. Headquarters noticed that the German troops were uncertain and postulated that a withdrawal may also be about to happen on the East Lancashire Division front, however this never occurred. The divisional artillery was firmly established behind the front line and carried out tests of concentrated fire that brought little response from their German foes.

The month of April had seen the first trench holding for the East Lancashire Division. As the war diary states:

General Herbert Lawrence recorded no occurrence of great importance occurred. The weather had been cold and wet with occasional falls of snow. [Some difficulty was experienced in collecting units of the division in its concentration area behind the lines prior to relieving 5th Division in the front line]. Machine gun companies that had joined this division in England were taken away and no pioneer battalion is forthcoming even at this date. These minor difficulties are of small importance to an old Division, but the fact that in several cases battalions carried out difficult moves without first line transport and during the period preparatory to taking over trenches for the first time, without mistakes, shows promise of good work in the future.

As we have seen, 197 Brigade repulsed an enemy raid almost on its first night in the trenches and captured an unwounded prisoner, who gave valuable information. With reference to the map it will be seen that the division held:

> 9,000 yards of trench line, making work and general upkeep difficult and reducing rest to a minimum. The morale of all troops is good and the offensive spirit is being further developed by increased patrolling. Units were a little sticky over patrols at first, but great improvement has been made and valuable information received.
>
> This applied equally to ordinary routine of trench warfare but great change has been apparent recently. Casualties have been few of which several were avoidable and caused by excessive zeal to have a look at the enemy. These were included in the casualty returns for the first month on active duty and were four Officers wounded, thirty two Other Ranks killed, one hundred and forty seven wounded and none missing.

On Easter Sunday the Battle of Arras commenced to the south of the division but despite noting increased shelling to the south this did not have much effect on the division. That is not to say that losses were not mounting. On 12 April the whole brigade mourned the sudden loss of Brigadier General G.E. Matthews and his brigade major, M.W. Gordon Steward, killed by a 5.9in shell that burst in the doorway of the splinter-proof dugout where they were in conference.

> General Mathews on one side, and Major Gordon Steward on the other side of Lieutenant Colonel Richey were both mortally wounded, the Brigade Major surviving only a few minutes, and an orderly standing behind them was hit, but Lieutenant-Colonel Richey was left untouched – not the only narrow escape that that very gallant officer experienced during the War. General Mathews had not commanded the Brigade for very long – he had assumed command at Colchester early in 1917, but had won the affectionate regard of all ranks during that period. Since the Brigade had been in France he had been a source of constant anxiety by his passion for visiting the most exposed places in the line and his complete disregard of his own safety, which had been so pronounced as to call for the unofficial censure of the officers commanding the units occupying the various sectors held by the Brigade.[6]

The replacement brigadier was Colonel G.T.B. Wilson of the 2/6 Manchester Regiment and Captain L.F.B. Groube (Royal Fusiliers) stepped in as General Staff Officer 3rd grade. The funeral of Brigadier Matthews in Bethune cemetery was attended by corps and divisional commanders and representatives and heads of departments of division.

It was rumoured that the Germans might be about to retreat but this never came about, as the Battle of Arras failed to gain momentum.

April 1917 was the start of British offensives for the year that would initially avoid the East Lancashire Division and then finally find it totally committed. However, it was early days and the division continued to hold a relatively quiet sector of the front, the Cambrin, Givenchy and Canal zone with Headquarters at Locon. Again General Lawrence recorded little of importance happening within his sector:

> Normal trench warfare, patrolling and reconnaissance. Preparations made in case operations further south compelled Germans opposite us to retire. Initial objectives and means of gaining them organised. Repair of roads and communication trenches carried out and schemes for carrying these on over no man's land drawn up, also connecting tramways to German systems. Dumps formed close up to front and ready to draw on in emergency.

The division was still without a pioneer battalion and fourth machine gun company. The lack of the former was a great handicap. On a more positive note, divisional schools had been opened and useful instruction given to junior officers and non-commissioned officers, although they lacked experienced instructors. The weather had improved and this in turn enabled the division to make considerable improvements to the trenches in this sector. Casualties in April were four officers killed, thirteen wounded, 128 men killed, 379 wounded and thirteen missing.

May saw the division remaining in its trench-holding role. The month was quiet and it was reported that the Germans gave little trouble, as if they were troublesome children to be kept in check:

> It has been policy to maintain frequent raids to keep troops in front of us, lower enemy morale and secure identification. Many good raids carried out and all new formations coming into line quickly identified. Germans seldom stay to fight and in spite of hemming them in with a box barrage on all occasions, its density was seldom thick enough owing to paucity of available guns to prevent Germans running through it.

Herbert Bate recalled:

> The most objectionable enemies, however, in this our first experience of Active Service were the mud and rats, to which to be added later, the lice.

He later remembered:

> the other enemy was always with us night and day, as well as in the deep dug-outs, dark and dank. It was not unknown to be awakened from one's sleep by a rat crawling over one's face. Acquaintance with lice came later. During a spell in the trenches no one took off his clothes or equipment. Four days in the front line were followed by four in support and four in reserve. Only then were parades possible, or de-lousing if and when necessary. This pattern of routine continued for about three months. Living, or half living in such conditions and in dug outs which had long held all manner of troops, it was surprising that any escaped invasion by these unclean and vexatious vermine [sic].[7]

Progress was made with preparations for advance on case of enemy retirement. 'Such a contingency does not however appear profitable at present, though our patrols nightly get in touch with enemy to get early information.' In the event the Germans did not retire on the front that was occupied by the division, and it was able to continue the work of forming the offensive spirit in the infantry, with the participation of the artillery.

NOTES:
[1] *Clickety Click*, Annual Dinner Club No.6, 1925, p.10f.
[2] Sir Herbert Lawrence from Royal Bank of Scotland website, 2015.
[3] The National Archives (TNA), WO 95/3120.
[4] *History of the East Lancashire Regiment*, p.284ff.
[5] *History of the East Lancashire Regiment*, p.284–5.
[6] *History of the East Lancashire Regiment*, p.285.
[7] IWM Department of Document, papers of Roland Bate.

Chapter 4

Raids

May–June 1917

The art of trench raiding was something that was being learned by the units of the division. One of the earliest trench raids was that by 198 Brigade on 14–15 May. Two raids were made simultaneously, being named left and right raids. [see map 1] It was a means of getting to know the enemy, most of whom they had never seen, in very close combat conditions, should one be met. It was a question of very close conditions where instantaneous decisions had to be made over whom to kill, or be killed. This was an area of divisional operations that the commanders from Lawrence downwards and the brigadiers were keen to develop to improve the fighting ability of all ranks of the division.

Prisoners and information was the key to these raids as well as causing enemy casualties. Some of this information would have been heartening for the British captors, as shown by a letter written on 11 May:

> We have been in this very dangerous place for two days, where we are continually trench mortared and it is not so easy to get safely through … At 12 o'clock on the ninth, a tremendous mortar fire broke loose and the whole trench was shot to bits. Josef was in a dugout which got a direct hit and he was buried and suffocated. I had to go out on patrol and so got the news later. I could not see him, perhaps I shall find him tonight …
>
> I could not find anything out about Josef, as he was not yet dug out. There were sixteen men with him in the Island and only four came safely through it. The rest were dead and wounded. It happened during a raid by the enemy. 250 bombs and thirty heavy

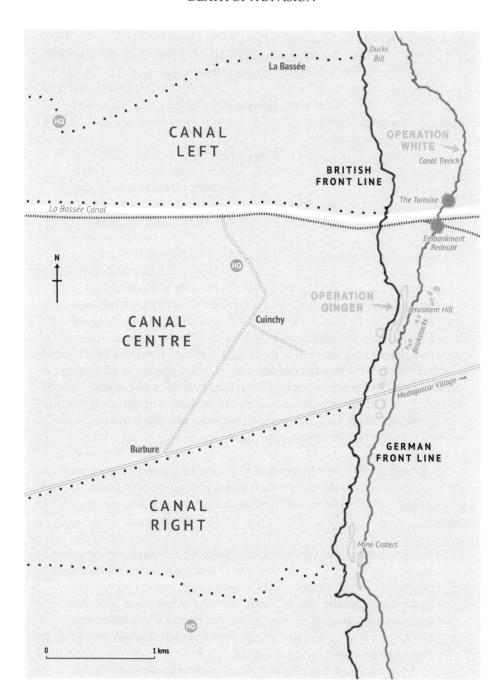

Map 1: Givenchy 1917.

trench mortars were fired on the position. You can't imagine what
the place looked like.

These were men in new units posted to the front from the Bavarian
Regiment. They suffered from being in very poor trenches, especially
around a front line salient where the front was obliterated. There were
no shell-proof dugouts in the front lines, only a few shelters, most of
which were under water. Rations were poor as no hot food was
available and men took five days' bread and tinned meat with them.
Clearly this was not a good sector to be in for the Germans. These
prisoners were so keen to gain favour with their British captors that
they gave away the names of their commanding officers, gun positions,
sites of mine shafts and the names of mining companies working under
the lines.

Enemy artillery started June badly for 199 Brigade, being described
as 'unhealthy' in the forward section and back areas of the brigade. In
the middle of the month, particularly on 14 and 15 June, the section
became much quieter and it was believed that the enemy artillery
responsible had been moved to another part of the front. A successful
raid was carried out on 26–27 June by the 2/6 Manchester Regiment,
which resulted in the capture of a very valuable prisoner that enabled
the British to identify a German unit opposite them, although no enemy
was caught. As reported by the division earlier, it was discovered that
the 185 (Ersatz) Division had replaced the 7th Division.

A larger scale trench raid on 8 June was organised and appears to
have been a great success in tactical terms. This was led by Captain
Walmsley Cotham of the 2/5 Manchester Regiment. This took place at
8.25 pm, so during daylight hours, and was preceded by a five-minute
barrage by artillery, trench mortars and machine guns. At 8.30 the first
wave formed behind the British wire and moved off with a smokescreen
blotting out the flank of objectives known to the British as Dump and
Madagascar Village (a point on the railway near Auchy), all achieved
with only a few casualties. A minute later the artillery lifted off the
German first line and the first wave rushed in. Moppers up accounted
for seven Germans found in the open and two killed by the first wave.

The barrage crept on to the Green line and German machine gun crew
who appear to have surrendered out of Madagascar village on the right
were fired upon and three killed, while two were wounded but escaped.
Another party of Germans jumped up from a shell hole and ran off into
the protecting barrage; two were hit and the rest escaped. At 8.38 the
barrage lifted on to the Green line, where it paused for four minutes.
Another party of five Germans and an officer emerged without

equipment, of which the officer and three men were killed and two men escaped down a tunnel. The moppers up blocked all tunnel entrances and sappers laid mobile charges to destroy the tunnels. The barrage crept on to the Red line, closely followed by the first wave, which arrived at its final objective exactly at 8.48. Following waves dealt with other Germans and took fourteen prisoners. They 'dealt with' nine of these fourteen prisoners, who tried to fight while being taken back and were bayoneted.

Five prisoners were brought in, of which one tried to throw a grenade into a British sap and was killed. The German trenches were thoroughly investigated and tunnels explored and blown up. During the withdrawal thirteen Germans emerged from a tunnel and, showing fight, were killed or wounded, three or four escaping down the tunnel. Several dugouts in the final line were blown up and it was thought that up to eighty Germans were trapped underground by the raid. Other Germans were found dead around their guns and the success of the enterprise was its surprise and destruction. This is a grim reminder of the nature of trench warfare, of kill or be killed. By 9.43 it was all over and the British had returned to their trenches with a few prisoners.[1] The British cost in casualties was one officer wounded and five other ranks killed, forty-five (mostly slightly) wounded and one missing, probably wounded.

The raid was complimented by Lieutenant-General Haking, the corps commander, who wrote to General Lawrence:

> I should be glad if you convey to the General Officer Commanding 199 Brigade to convey to Lieutenant Colonel Hewlett, commanding 2/5 Manchester Regiment, my appreciation of the very excellent raid carried out by men of his battalion under the command of Captain Walmsley Cotham.
>
> The careful preparation beforehand, the able support afforded by the artillery and the gallant manner in which the enemy was attacked by our infantry and his garrison annihilated, reflect the highest credit of all concerned, and will be a fine example to other battalions in the Corps. It was a great pleasure to me to be able to bring these troops for the inspection of the Chief of the Imperial general Staff yesterday.
>
> Signed R. Haking, Lieutenant-General Commanding XI Corps

On 7 June 1917 the British attacked in Belgium at the Battle of Messines Ridge with powerful mines and a successful but limited attack. The only part for the East Lancashire was a successful raid on 8 June, by the 2/5

Manchester Regiment. This took three lines of trenches, many dugouts were bombed and about 100 Germans killed. Again, on 10 June a raid was carried out by 170 men of the 2/4 East Lancashire Regiment and captured one officer and eighteen ranks, killing at least 200 Germans. They destroyed nine underground galleries, having first surveyed them and destroyed any listening apparatus found. This continued on the front all that week, with the Germans retaliating in the Portuguese sector to the north. The trench raids on 8, 10 and 13 June were reported to have inspired 'a genuine lust for blood and generally maintaining the high morale throughout the division'.

A larger operation for the East Lancashire Division on 10 June was meticulously planned, known as Operation Ginger, the soldiers of 2/4 East Lancashire Regiment were trained over similar ground with shallow trenches near Le Quesnoy for ten days prior to the operation under their commander, Captain H. Keay, and Second Lieutenants Cayley, Seddon and Hall, and a total of 185 other ranks.

Operation Ginger was designed to take the enemy trenches in order for special parties of the 170 and 251 Tunnelling companies to inspect, survey and destroy enemy mine systems in this heavily mined area of the front. They would destroy workings and enemy miners who were hard to replace, being specialist engineers. Enemy dugouts were also to be destroyed with phosphorus bombs and any occupants therefore disposed of. The attack was screened by smoke from men of No. 4 Special Company R.E. in the area of the Brickstacks, in addition to which a British mine was blown to add to the effect of the raid:

> The medium trench mortars cut the wire, which was almost entirely invisible from our lines with good effect and neutralised the Brickstacks during the operation. The assaulting troops appear to have acted with dash and coolness.
>
> Their quick entry into the enemy lines over very difficult ground seems to have been largely responsible for their success, and the enemy, probably warned by our wire cutting, seem to have been in much greater strength than usual in this part of the line. Severe hand to hand fighting ensued, particularly on the left, and the blocks were established at the previously arranged points and the trenches and dug outs were thoroughly destroyed. Our troops withdrew quite unmolested. The only counter-attack the enemy made was on the left. This was driven off, causing loss to the enemy.[2]

It was estimated that up to 160 German casualties were caused. One officer and seventeen other ranks of the 161 Infantry Regiment were captured, nine of which were wounded. British casualties were one officer wounded and three other ranks killed, twenty-six wounded (some very slightly remained at duty) and two missing. All in all this was a very successful raid and quite an improvement on previous efforts.

The right raid by men of 2/5 East Lancashire and 2/9 Manchester Regiments:

> was carried out according to programme, except that the Bangalore torpedo was fired at zero plus 22 instead of zero plus 15. This was due to the torpedo coming to pieces, when being carried over the very rough ground.
>
> The raiding and blocking parties entered the German trenches at the West end of Embankment redoubt, but found them vacant. The breastwork on the South Canal bank was also found unoccupied.
>
> The Germans put up some Very lights from these trenches, when the parties originally left our trenches, and presumably slipped away on the Bangalore exploding; our men having a very steep and slippery bank to climb between the wire and the trenches. Casualties to this party were one officer and three Other Ranks wounded with failure to get an identification put down to bad luck.
>
> The left raid carried out their duties as far as the assembly point, owing to parties number two and seven losing direction [and] the Bangalore torpedo was fired about sixty yards to the left of where it was proposed to enter the German Trenches.
>
> The Officer in charge of these parties was wounded, and the sergeant who took over command gave the order to withdraw.
>
> In the meantime party number three had proceeded to the point where the Bangalore torpedo ought to have been fired, and finding that this had not been done, sent for the reserve torpedo.
>
> Whilst this was being done the order to withdraw was heard, and the whole party returned to our lines at about 12.15 a.m. Casualties to this raid were one officer and four Other Ranks wounded and one Other Ranks killed.
>
> Artillery fire was very accurate and gave great confidence to all ranks of both raids.
>
> The Sappers attached from 431 Field Company Royal Engineers did their work with coolness and efficiency.
>
> In spite of the failure to secure and identification, the raids reported on above have been of value.
>
> The officers and men concerned have learnt how a raid should be managed, and also certain things that should not be done.

They will take on their next operation with great confidence in themselves, and in our artillery.

I am convinced that the Embankment redoubt, and the Tortoise, are held, and that in the former case they slipped away by means of a tunnel, the entrance of which was searched for, and could not be found.

Signed
Brig General Commanding 198 Brigade [A.J. Hunter]

Gilbert Wilkinson was involved as a Lewis gunner in an operation on 15–16 June. Operation White was designed to destroy as much as possible of the enemy knife rest wire in front of Canal Trench by blowing it up with mobile charges and setting it on fire with paraffin and petrol. The knife rests for the wire were mostly made of wood and with the grass being long, it was expected that when the charge went off, the paraffin would be so well spread that at least 100 yards would catch fire. The point to be concentrated on was map reference A.16.a.7/2. The stores to be carried were three five-minute mobile charges; three ten-minute mobile charges; one salved [sic] mobile charge, which would fire by concussion of the other charges when placed on top of the other charges; four 2 gallon tins of paraffin; one tin of petrol; and six phosphorus bombs. One can imagine the explosion and the fire that it would produce in addition to the kindling of the grass and wooden knife rests it was designed to destroy.

The party of men detailed to undertake this mission was composed of Lieutenant Baldwin, an N.C.O. and one man to fire the charges, and two carrying parties of one N.C.O and four men each, which totalled seven men to carry the charges. The men were selected by Lieutenant Baldwin from D company 2/6 East Lancashire and it is believed Gilbert Wilkinson was one of these men, although whether he was in the group as a Lewis gunner or not cannot be discerned:

> The covering party will move out first and will consist of Lieutenant Prichard [sic] and two guns. These parties will take up position in the ditch at approx A.16.a.43/12 right party and A.16.a.45/16 left party. The distance between these parties will be approx 30 yards and Lt. Prichard will be responsible for their placement and handling. When they are in position, the carrying parties under Lt. Baldwin will pass through and advance to the enemy's wire, No 2 carrying party in rear. The charges will be inserted at 10 yards interval between each. Ten minute charges will be placed to the right

and five minute charges to the left. The salved charge will be placed at the top of the left hand mobile charge. On the orders of Lt. Baldwin No. 2 carrying party will withdraw to their own lines, passing through the covering party. Similarly No. 1 party will withdraw.

Lt. Baldwin will place over each mobile charge one P bomb and one tin of paraffin over the two most northerly and the two most southerly charges. When all is in position Lt Baldwin and his two specialists will withdraw the firing pins and immediately return to the Lewis gun position. Lt. Prichard will withdraw when all is clear.[3]

The mission appears to have been a total success with a huge conflagration setting fire to the German wire, and no doubt having considerable psychological effect as well.

For the East Lancashire Division life continued much the same but the casualties continued. In May these were three officers killed twelve wounded, sixty-six men killed, 301 wounded and six missing. One of those wounded in June was Gilbert Wilkinson from Preston. After suffering a gunshot wound in the shoulder and face he was evacuated to the 2/1 East Lancashire Field Ambulance, which he reached on 17 June, and 83 General Hospital at Boulogne some days later.

The status quo of raids for the division was relieved only by an imminent move to XV Corps in Belgium. Senior officers started to reconnoitre points around Dunkirk and the coast, and so the division's initiation into trench warfare was coming to an end and soon they would start on the offensive. General Lawrence was allowed leave and in his place Brigadier L. Banon assumed temporary command. The divisional headquarters moved to Goudekerque-Banche, south of Dunkirk, and joined XV Corps. The division was relieved by 2nd Division at Locon. The war diary states, 'units are benefiting from the change of scene and work, and the new Brigade areas along the coast line provide adequate scope and opportunities for rest and training.' They had been in the same sector since early March and were in need of a change, having earned their spurs in raiding and generally settling in to the daily rhythms of trench warfare. It had not been an easy month for the division and the increasing pitch of warfare had cost it 529 casualties. Six officers had been killed, twenty-one wounded and one missing, fifty-seven men killed, 416 wounded and twenty-eight missing. Reinforcements of a 'good quality' had been received across the division.

The joy and enthusiasm that the men of the 432nd Field Company felt for their horses was shared throughout much of the army. On turn

15 June the divisional horse show took place behind the lines at Bethune. Second Lieutenant Derbyshire, in charge of number one section, and the men were thrilled to see their hard work pay off for they won two prizes; first prize for tool-cart turnout and second prize for pontoon-wagon turnout. Major Graves and Captain Berrington shared in the joy that this brought as their company was having a good few days, for just the previous day an NCO and two sappers had been part of a special inspection by General Sir Douglas Haig himself for their work in the trenches at Beuvry. The officers had attended, of course, but the attention had been on the men; it was their day. The first prize awarded for the tool-wagon turnout was enough to advance the team through to the Corps Horse Show, where the company won second prize on 20 June.

They had reason to be happy about their work as they handed over their section of front to 483rd Field Company as they started to move north to the division's next destination. They went into billets at Marles-Les-Mines before going to Loon-Plages and the Petite Synthe near Calais, and on again to Oost Dunkerque, transferring to a canal barge to Furnes and then an attachment to 32nd Division for special duties.

The coast of Belgium at Nieupoort was the extreme northern end of the Western Front, where the barbed wire extended to beyond the low-tide mark. At the English Channel end of the front the fighting continued, beyond the flooded sector of the front held by the Belgians. The front here was on the Yser canal, which ran from Ypres to the sea. The reason that the East Lancashire Division had been rushed in to aid the attack here was caused more by the local terrain and political infighting among the allies. The bridgehead that the allies held was constructed in the sand dunes, and was insufficiently dug in, with only breast works being provided that only protected the soldiers on the German side.

As part of the movement of French forces, General Debeney's Division at Nieupoort was being relieved for service elsewhere. It was to be relieved by the British 1st and 32nd Divisions in the II Corps of General Rawlinson. The French maintained that the British artillery could not cover French troops as they withdrew, but the infantry must be relieved first and then artillery could be changed over. This pause in artillery cover was sensed by the Germans, who saw what was going on and used the opportunity to attack on 10 July 1917.

The engineers of 432 Field Company were caught in the artillery bombardment of the German attack when the billet was struck by a 5.9in shell, causing seven casualties and destroying a lot of equipment. This brief reverse was just the beginning, as they were called in to start clearing roads of rubble and debris and suffered five more casualties on 14 July while they were building screens to camouflage movement on a road. One man not present at this attack was the survivor of Gallipoli. Norman Dunkerley from Oldham, having recovered from wounds received in that campaign, had joined the field company as a replacement but then gone straight out again with impetigo, for which he received his discharge from the army. On 16 July the 432 handed over to 456 Field Company and was given back to 66th Division as it moved up to the Nieupoort sector, where it in turn replaced the 19/ (Pioneer) Battalion Lancashire Fusiliers and settled into billets at Camp Lefevre.

The British infantry were almost annihilated and the bridgehead just about all lost. British casualties were 126 officers and 3,000 other ranks, mostly from the two battalions in the bridgehead, 2nd Kings Royal Rifle Corps and 1st Northamptonshire Regiment. Possible counter-attacks were postponed when common sense ordained that the bridgehead could not be held without better underground defences. This meant that at the end of the month the newly arrived East Lancashire Division would have to undertake this attack itself and retake the lost ground:

> Enemy opened heavy fire along Corps front at 6.30 a.m. Bombardment continued with intensity throughout the day ... At 7.45 p.m. enemy attacked and overran the front system of 1st Division trenches as far as Yser. Front and support line of 32nd Division also taken.[4]

No.197 Brigade was ordered to move to Coxyde-Bains to take command of the three battalions of that brigade in the forward area under orders of the 32nd Division. The Lombartzy sector, which had been taken, was retaken on 11 July by troops under orders of 32nd Division.

On 17 July General Lawrence took over command of the Nieupoort-Bains sector of the front and the 49th Division took over the contested Lombartzy sector across the Yser river. The first task was to improve the trenches on the west side of the Yser, dig tunnels and generally improve the sector. Australian tunnellers were brought in to burrow under the sand dunes, producing attack tunnels and communication trenches that would not be seen by the Germans. Attached to the tunnellers were the field companies of the Royal Engineers from 66th Division. There were four underground tunnels, the first along the promenade of Nieupoort Bains was called Bath Avenue, the second through the cellars of the houses, shops and hotels of the seafront was Bligny Avenue, then further inland was Boche Avenue and a third lay further south. These meant the British could approach and reach the front line overlooking the tidal Yser without hindrance from enemy observation. The beach had also to be defended against an attack from the sea. So defences were built in two general directions, facing north-west and north-east.

The battalions of 199 Brigade spent this period on coastal defence. Unlike the two brigades who were involved facing eastwards, this brigade faced the sea against any possible flanking manoeuvre around the sea end of the trenches. They spent much of their time on working parties but on 25 July moved up to Nieupoort. One of the positive outcomes for the East Lancashire Division was the receiving of a pioneer battalion from 32nd Division in the form of 10/ Duke of Cornwall's Light Infantry, which according to their regimental history was not forgiven by the Cornishmen.

On the relief on 24 July the Germans sensed what was happening and bombarded the relief party, as the earlier source continued:

> Unfortunately during the relief some of the Yser bridges were broken by shell fire, and gas shells were fired into the town. The guides led the 2/6th Manchester regiment through the tunnels where congestion occurred due to the breaking of the bridges, and the air became so thick that some of the men were unable to breathe with their masks on and took them off, a large number of casualties being caused. The relief was considerably delayed and would not be completed that night.

Part of the active operations undertaken by 66th Division during August 1917 were patrols of the enemy bank. Several of these clandestine operations were described in reports:

> A patrol of one NCO and three men left the Lighthouse at 12.05 in the morning and swam across towards the opposite bank. They found the water round the jetty full of barbed wire. The patrol swam to within twenty yards of the opposite bank when they saw an enemy patrol of four men moving in a north-westerly direction along the top of the brick slope. They then returned and landed M.14.b.0.2 at 12.30 a.m.
>
> A patrol of one NCO and three men left the barrel post M.14.a.8/3 at about 12.05 a.m. The patrol leader stayed behind to attend to one man who was seized with cramp. He then swam across and landed on the right of the remains of Richmond bridge and climbed up onto the jetty which runs parallel to and about fifteen yards from the sea wall. A hostile patrol of four then passed along the top of brick slope

in a south-easterly direction and entered a dugout at a point where the barricade turns direction and inland. The patrol leader then swam to brick slope, climbed up and lay on top. The barricade was observed to be knocked about, but is still an obstacle which could only be crossed with difficulty. It consists of sandbags, loose sand, and stones revetted with wicker work. He then returned and reached the barrel post at 1.10 a.m. The remaining two men swam across and passed through a gap in the jetty. They there saw a hostile patrol of four men on brick slope coming towards them from direction of sea. They returned and landed at 12.40 a.m.

If successful the offensive at Ypres was to link up with the coastal attacks and turn the German flank, take the important German naval base at Zeebrugge and thus win the war. Of course, that was the theory. In fact the division faced an uncertain canal crossing under fire, with all bridges having long been destroyed by the Germans. The Royal Engineers had put together rafts and floating bridges for the troops.

One of those awaiting this exposed and dangerous relief was Herbert Bate:

> All this time 'D-Day' had been getting nearer and at dawn on 31 July [this is a mistake by Bate and the actual date of the relief was 24 July] the division attacked on a wide front. To get across the Yser canal was a difficult operation. It was an easy target for the enemy artillery to lay down an accurate and concentrated barrage … Shells were falling and exploding on the banks and in the water. Mingled with the High Explosive were gas shells …
>
> We put on our gas respirators … dashed across the duck-boards and splayed out on the far side and rushed forward. It was not easy to see clearly in a respirator and impossible to shout orders. I was obliged to remove mine several times to shout orders, though this did not account for what happened subsequently. Our respirators were designed for chlorine and phosgene gases only. The Germans were using for the first time mustard gas. Soon my eyes began to water and feel sore and become painful, then my sight began to fail and finally my eyes became fast closed and I was totally blind. I began to stagger and stumble aimlessly and helplessly, falling over the barren and churned up ground, and into shell holes.

For an officer leading his men this, of course, was disastrous, and he and twelve other officers were totally prostrated by the new gas. Somehow somebody saw Bate's distress and led him back over the duckboard bridges, back to the aid station where he was evacuated, unconscious, coming round in a hospital in Cambridge, England. Roland Bate was out of the fighting, and it was to his colleagues that the effort passed. Nieupoort was a sideshow, a locally important attack, for a few hundred yards, made to restore honour to the allies, rather than any particular strategic objective. If they had broken through they might have continued, but it was at Ypres that far more important fighting was taking place.

There were four British divisions involved in the Nieupoort affair, and a casualty list that matched. In July the division suffered four officers killed, thirty wounded, and eighty-seven men killed, 669 wounded and four missing. General Lawrence received a memo on the new German gas known as 'mustard gas', received I am sure as more evidence no doubt of the Huns' ghastliness.

The East Lancashire Division had played its part in the first stages of the Third battle of Ypres by its activities on the coast at Nieupoort in July. Now it was its turn to be actively involved on the ground in the main battle. The men moved from the trenches on the coast on 20 September, just as the next phase of the campaign was under way, the Battle of the Menin Road. This was an important attack that showed the way the battle was starting to move in the allies' favour. Limited though it was in objectives, the initiative and spark of General Sir Herbert Plumer had shown that victory was possible. Although it had been a limited bite and hold attack, they had crept on to the shoulders of Passchendaele ridge itself. It would take them until 10 November to secure the ridge and the village itself and 66th Division would play its part.

NOTES:
[1] TNA, WO 95/3142.
[2] TNA, WO 95/3121.
[3] TNA, WO 95/3131.
[4] TNA, WO 95/3120.

Chapter 5

Night, Storm, War

July–December 1917

General Herbert Lawrence and his headquarters moved from Nieupoort into reserve at Saint-Idesbalde, then to La Panne on 25 September, and Renescure on the 26th. Then they moved by bus to Godvaeerswelte, Wimezeele, on 4 October, and arrived at the casemates near the Menin Gate, their new headquarters, on 6 October. The adjutant and quartermaster branch was located at Brandhoek. However, this was not without its problems as the whole division less the headquarters and Royal Engineers were out in the open. The higher priority was given to the relieved New Zealand and the 3rd Australian divisions, just out of the line. The East Lancashires had missed the intermediate stages of the third Battle of Ypres, the battle of Polygon Wood, and were arriving for the battle of Poelcappelle. They were taking over the sector vacated by the ANZAC divisions, the most distant sector, and therefore troublesome in terms of communications. The sector lay at the foot of the valley of the Ravebeek under the gaze of Passchendaele village, being roughly the road that runs north-west to south-east across the valley and marked the head of the duckboard tracks, the optimistically named 'Jack and Jill' track and K track. Their forward brigade headquarters for 198 and 197 brigades were at Levi Cottage and Springfield, near Hill 40. The immediate task was to improve communications, and they only had a few days to achieve this before the battle began.

General Lawrence soon realised that this was going to be no pushover, with communications in the whole area, not just the forward area, in a terrible state. 'The whole area forward of Ypres being shell holes with one road only fit for wheeled traffic as far as Frezenberg. Beyond that to the front line only pack [mule] and man handled transport available.' A few short days were available to attempt to improve the lines of communication, and the division set to it with gusto.

One of the units in the middle of this work were the engineer companies and the pioneer companies of the 10/ Duke of Cornwall's Light Infantry. Their work was to build a slab road from Wieltje to Spree Farm and on to Kansas Cross and Gravenstafel. Based at Goldfish Château near Poperinghe, they went by lorry each day forward to the work site:

> The work was done in full daylight once the dawn had completely broken, and at first the weather was very good; this was all right in one way, but in others it increased the accuracy of the enemy gunners, whose attention in the salient was quite sufficient even in bad weather. Nevertheless the road advanced very rapidly indeed, the greatest hindrance being the continuous stream of men, animals, rations and water carts across the men at work and the constant repairs to work already done.[1]

Soon though the men were exhausted and were relieved by the Engineers of 49th Division and the New Zealand Engineers. They joined the division near St Omer for a review by the Commander in Chief, Sir Douglas Haig.

> The infantry had been out and cleaned up for over a fortnight. The R.E had been in much longer and had only just got out. No one had much in the way of cleaning materials, and nobody's kit was by any means as good as it had been before going into Ypres. Still the men set to, and with their useful cheerfulness managed to get quite fit and decent in time.

It was not just the men who were suffering, it was the horses and mules. A lack of the necessary toe-clipping equipment and adequate hygiene in the mud led to an outbreak of skin disease among the animals. 'The drivers of the 432 Field Company had a particularly hard time, which however was turned to very useful account by teaching them what to look out for and how to avoid it on future occasions.[2]

A few days later this build-up of the army was noticed by Lieutenant Withinshaw, viewing from the heavy trench mortar positions as the infantry slogged forward into the incessant din of battle. It is:

> wonderful, the way the roads up to Zonnebeke have been made. Although there is a lot of jamming the amount of traffic is enormous,

infantry walking up each side and water carts, motor lorries, caterpillars all coming and going and one a tremendous stream of pack horses with ammo. Country round here absolutely chewed up to ribbons. Not a square patch anywhere without shell holes. Dead horses lie all long the road and on each side of it, derelict carts, motors etcetera.[3]

Another spectator was Gunner John Gore, in the field artillery:

We were next sent to the Ypres Salient. Some were sent up the line, the remainder to Busseboom. I was there attached to the Divisional Ammunition Column and spent a week at an ammunition dump at Oxford Road. This was a rotten job loading mules with 18 pounder shells on panniers. Raining all the time and up to the knees in black treacly mud. No billets. Dug holes. Found a near-new tarpaulin.[4]

They made a shelter with the latter. Having evaded front line duty Gore did not manage to raise any enthusiasm for his military duties in the divisional ammunition column.

The task set for the East Lancashire Division was to push forward in the central sector up on to the Passchendaele ridge, with the 49th Division on the left and the 2nd Australian Division on the right. The main artery of communication, so jam-packed with traffic, was the old Potijze–Frezenberg road leading to Zonnebeke. It was usual that a division would have a line of communication of its own, but in this battle, with the salient narrowing, the whole corps had only a few roads to use for all its divisions, with one-way systems in place as some roads were for movements towards the front, and others for retiring troops, hence the organised muddle that Lieutenant Withinshaw noted. Also, the army had spent months making many routes across the shattered landscape, but with the weather turning the dry weather routes were out of use, and the army crowded on to the wet weather routes. It was a matter of speed now to change tired, spent, infantry for their fresher comrades.

The march was no easy one for men such as Peter Hall, who remembered it taking some four hours to travel from Ypres to Zonnebeke along duckboard tracks, marching in his case via Hell Fire Corner and the Ypres to Roulers railway line. Hall had been an education worker with the Manchester Education Committee. Married to Florence Simcock, he had a young child and lived in Moss Side, Manchester.

The battle of Broodseinde on 4 October had made considerable advances along the whole front, and had taken a part of the

Passchendaele ridge around the hamlet of Broodseinde. This made it feasible to take the whole ridge, but with the weather turning conditions made it more difficult to achieve. The next line to take was the German Flanders II line, which hugged the western slopes of the Passchendaele ridge. The pillboxes facing the allies had been taken on 4 October by the Australian infantry, such as those still existing in Tyne Cot cemetery, an actual part of the battlefield that still exists within the architectural design of the cemetery. The official history states of 66th Division, 'no wire barred its progress, as the Flanders I line had been occupied on 4 October by the 3rd Australian Division.'[5] This gave hope to the British commanders that the next attack would bring justifiable rewards and a significant gain as they thought the Germans were beaten in Flanders.

The ground captured by the Australians had been hard won and it was they who took the positions in the area of Tyne Cot [cemetery] area on 4 October. Advancing from Windmill Hill (Hill 40):

> the barrage was acclaimed as excellent. Strong opposition, met at the outset on Windmill Hill, was at once crushed by the weight of the barrage and by the ruthless determination behind the infantry assault. Bayonets were freely used against the large number of Germans found assembled, 350 dead being counted later in the first five hundred yards of one brigade sector alone [a proposed counter-attack force that was overrun]. As the Australians swept on down the back of Windmill Hill and over the Hanebeek, Germans were seen ahead of them, running into the high explosive barrage, which in the dawn light looked like a 'wall of flame'.[6]

Several Victoria Crosses had been gained by the Australians in this advance. Sergeant Lewis McGee of the 40th Australian Infantry Battalion attacked:

> Armed only with a revolver, he rushed a machine gun emplacement which was causing severe casualties to his platoon, shot some of the detachment and captured the rest. He was foremost in the subsequent advance.

Unfortunately his luck did not hold as he was killed on 13 October and is buried towards the front of Tyne Cot cemetery, overlooking the battlefield where he won a posthumous Victoria Cross.

The bravery and zeal of the Australians had captured a good deal of ground and pushed the Germans back up the hill, clearing the wide open slopes for the next attack by 66th Division. Attacks to the north had not gone so well and the commanding pillboxes at Bellevue were not captured, still holding up the advance of the New Zealanders on 12 October, and threatening 66th Division on 9 October. The slopes here are like the glacis of a fort and easily swept with machine gun fire and enfiladed from the side. Anyone who has stood in Tyne Cot cemetery can see all the way to Ypres, so open is the ground here. The aftermath of the carnage of the Australian advance was plain to see for the East Lancashire Division, such as Lieutenant Withinshaw, at his battery position near Zonnebeke. He noted in his diary:

> … our dead and Boche lie unburied and present a horrible sight and awful smell … Many more dead Boche around Zonnebeke. Of course I was there three days after the advance and no time could be spared to bury these.[7]

In the 2/6th Battalion Manchester Regiment, Peter Hall was part of the infantry marching up to the relief of soldiers in the front line, tramping across the inhospitable moonscape that was the salient. He would have marched out of the Menin Gate, past his headquarters in the ramparts. No mention is made of whether or not the brigadier came out of headquarters to see his men pass, many of whom would never return, or whether he preferred not to. Quite honestly they were too busy as the staff encountered innumerable difficulties in relieving their own tired, wet and cold troops in the front line.

Headquarters noted that:

> owing to the torrential rain the ground had become almost impassable. The men moving from the Frezenberg Ridge to the assembly place had to wade almost waist deep in mud along the assembly tracks. At 3 o'clock in the morning of 9 October it was obvious that all battalions of 197 Brigade would be unable to arrive at the assembly line in time. Two battalions of the 198 Brigade that were holding the line were placed at the disposal of General Officer Commanding 197 Brigade.[8]

It was not an auspicious start for Brigadier Generals Hunter and Borrett, although their training led them to persevere. The East Lancashires were under the command of II ANZAC Corps for this attack, giving some continuity of command that might deliver the same results that the Broodseinde attack had given. The difference was fresh troops, but the weather had broken. As we have seen, the attacking troops were unable to get to the front so tired soldiers were used instead.

The Official History states that the division was new into battle and was largely untried. It had been in trench warfare since February that year and had taken part in the fighting at Nieupoort. It had been put into a dreadful situation in appalling weather, and did no better or worse than any other battalion between 9 October and 10 November 1917. The things that crippled it were the devastation of the artillery on the landscape at Ypres, the breaking of the weather and the subsequent impossibility of using tanks in this ruined battlefield. Lack of communication and the failure of 49th Division at Bellevue meant that the flank was unsecured and the Germans could enfilade the attack.

> The attack commenced along the whole front of Fifth Army. In the north the Fifth army attacked Poelcappelle, the main attack in the south under the command of X Corps, with I and II ANZAC, with 5th, 7th and 21st British Divisions and 2nd Australian Division forming the attacking divisions. Australian 2nd Division was to cover the right of 66th Division with 1st Australian to the south holding their line. The 66th Division attacked on a two-brigade front between the Ypres–Roulers railway and the Ravebeek.

The attacks at Poelcappelle were covered in the previous volume *Londoners on the Western Front*, so there is no need for a long description here. It will suffice to say that tanks were ordered out of the salient on this day, and the attacks were initially quite successful but suffered from German counter-attacks in the Poelcappelle area. These attacks were distant from the 66th Division sector and had little effect on the central sector other than to divert attention away and provide a northern flank to the attack.

The left brigade, 198 Brigade, was, however, hampered by the mud and by a number of water-filled trenches on the lower slopes above the Ravebeek. According to the *Official History*, it was also enfiladed by machine gun fire from the uncaptured pillboxes across the valley, near Bellevue, at a range of 500–800 yards.

Divisional Headquarters noted on 8 October: 'The whole area forward of Ypres being shell holes with one road only fit for wheel traffic as far as Frezenberg. Beyond that to front line only pack and man handled transport available.' Two Brigades, 197 and 198, were to proceed to the Frezenberg area to start work on marking out tracks and the improvement of advanced Brigade Headquarters continued.[9]

There were two ways to the front, over dry and wet weather tracks. In the awful autumn weather wet weather tracks prevailed. Engineers had laid down more than 100 miles of duckboard track across the salient in the autumn of 1917. These tracks were the only way to cross the shell-ravaged terrain, with deep water-filled shell holes for the unwary or unlucky. This system was in theory good for the infantry, in practice it was deadly, barely wide enough to walk on, and lethal to fall off. The German spotters knew exactly where they were and periodically strafed them in the hope of hitting a column of infantry moving to or from the front. For the infantry, trying to get to the start line was difficult enough, in the 2/5th Battalion East Lancashire Regiment Lieutenant Paddy King remembered:

> It was an absolute nightmare. Often we would have to stop and wait for up to half an hour, because all the time the duck-boards were being blown up and the men being blown off the track or simply slipping off – because we were all in full marching order with gas masks and rifles, and some were carrying machine guns and extra ammunition. We were all carrying equipment of some kind, and all had empty sand bags on our backs. We were loaded like Christmas trees, so of course an explosion nearby or just the slightest thing would knock a man off balance and he would go off the track and right down into the muck.[10]

The start line of the two brigades was roughly level with the post-war Cross of Sacrifice but diagonally across the middle of Tyne Cot Cemetery, this being the furthest the Australians had advanced. The right boundary of the division was on the Ypres to Roulers railway line between Dash Crossing and Defy Crossing. The left divisional boundary was on the Ravebeek. This sector was further subdivided in half with a brigade boundary from Hamburg through Augustus Wood and Heine Houses to Beds Wood. The Ravebeek on the left was a marsh extending way beyond its banks and the terrain was generally impossible with water-filled shell holes and slimy mud [see map 2].

It may have seemed clear at headquarters with maps to inform, but for the infantry at the front nothing was clear. Peter Hall and his comrades were still tramping up to the line at this time and he does not recall the battles in any particular form, except to say:

> I find it extremely difficult to have any clear recollection of what happened in these battles – the mind was stunned. The whole world seemed to erupt like a volcano, one had to fix in one's mind the necessity of going forward to reach the objective at all costs. In fact it was impossible to see what was going on beyond about twenty yards from where one was and we had little idea of the battle as a whole.[11]

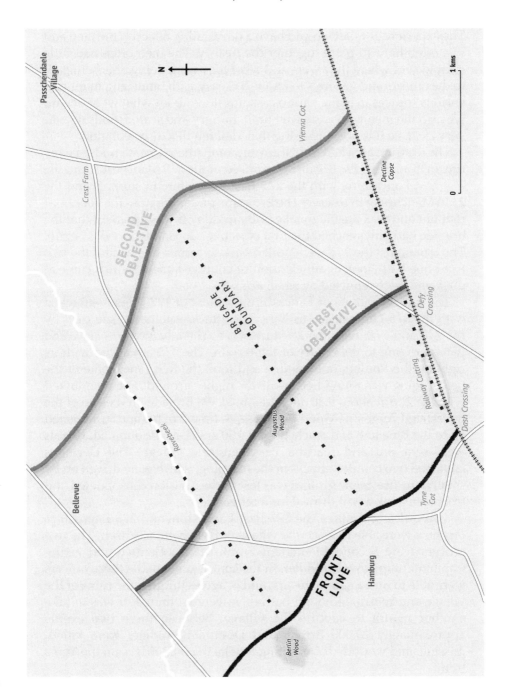

Map 2: Passchendaele 1917.

The experience of battle could have a devastating effect on the men and it is often hard to piece together the history. The men often had little clear idea of where they were and what they were doing, this being left to the officers and generals to know. It is easy with hindsight, maps and various sources to make various assumptions about what went on and why. To the men who were wet, tired, hungry and scared, nothing was very clear, so it is not surprising that Hall felt this disorientation.

The division attacked at 5.20 am and immediately came under heavy fire. In front were 198 Brigade comprised of the 2/9 Manchester and the 2/4 East Lancashire, with the 2/5 East Lancashire in support and the 2/10 Manchester in reserve. The 2/5 came under fire from the Hamburg redoubt and was unable to take it. By midday it was apparent that the brigade had only reached the first objective. Consolidation was begun. The remains of the 2/5 were pulled back to form a line behind the two front line battalions in anticipation of counter-attacks, which came at dusk and were repulsed by small arms fire.

The four battalions of Lancashire Fusiliers of 197 Brigade attacked with the 3/5 Lancashire Fusiliers. The attack was then taken over by the 2/6 and 2/8, with the 2/7 in reserve. The advance was slow and patchy, owing to the nature of the terrain. The 3/5 advanced with its right on the Roulers railway line and took the Red Line, some of the better going was found here as it was higher ground. The men linked with the 2/6 at about 9.30 am and joined 198 Brigade on the site of the devastated Augustus Wood. At the same time the 2/8 and 3/5 pushed on to the Blue line and reached it by 9.30 am and consolidated. Patrols were sent out and reached Passchendaele village. The Germans launched two counter-attacks in the morning, which were driven off by small arms fire. Some ground was lost as the division consolidated and troops mistook a withdrawal for a retreat.[12]

Two officer patrols of the 3/5 East Lancashire and 2/8 Lancashire Fusiliers were able to reach the village of Passchendaele itself. The two officers were Second Lieutenant Frank Mercer Bentley and acting Captain Philip Townley Miller. In the confusion of battle these officers were able to find a gap in the line and progress through the ruins of the village and return, although both men were wounded. It was to take another month to capture the village. Between these two events approximately 29,000 British and Dominion soldiers were killed, missing, and wounded attempting to take the final ridges on the Ypres front.

The legend has been established that when the Canadians took the village of Passchendaele on 6 November 1917 they found some corpses of the two battalions, the 2/8 and 3/5 Lancashire Fusiliers. There is no direct evidence for this. The Canadian troops who took Passchendaele village on 6 November recorded the following:

> As soon as the second intermediate objective had been secured Captain Curran, who was Officer Commanding of the reserve company and at the time O.C. forward report centre, moved his headquarters from the original support line to a dugout adjacent to Passchendaele church …
>
> The final objective was captured at 7.30 a.m. Upon receipt of this information from the flank companies, Major Robinson, O.C. centre company, sent up the pre-arranged signal of three white flares. This was at 7.40 a.m. The spirit and fighting qualities shown by the men was magnificent and the supervision and leadership exercised by the officers was of the highest standard. All ranks made the assault with the greatest dash. The toll of casualties amongst the enemy was extremely heavy for it was not until the later stage of the attack [that] prisoners were taken in any numbers. After the attack no less than 76 dead Germans were counted in a small area in the vicinity of the church. The prisoners were utilised for carrying out the wounded and did their work well. Unfortunately a number of them were killed by their own shells while doing this, for the shelling along the route Passchendaele to the rear was very severe and continuous.[13]

No description of finding British casualties among the dead is given but among such a large number a few may have been missed as being uniforms of East Lancashire soldiers. While the myth can be refuted through lack of evidence, this does not mean to say it might not have happened. The confusion in the myth is that soldiers of both battalions were found, which to me suggests a slightly different scenario. The report quoted above from the colonel of the Winnipeg Rifles reports the use of German prisoners of war as stretcher bearers, which would give a reason for the reported corpses to be of different units used in a similar fashion by the Germans. The only other options are that the men were prisoners who were executed, which I find to be unlikely, or were prisoners who were caught by artillery fire, which is more plausible; if it is recorded as having happened to German prisoners of the British there is no reason why it could not have happened to British prisoners of the Germans. However, at this point I find it to be more myth caused by nightmarish dreams and battle stress. It is possible that among the 250 missing of the East Lancashire Division on 9 October some ended up as prisoners of the Germans. For the relatives of the soldiers and the people of Lancashire this is an important myth and it brings a heavy weight of purpose to the memorial at Passchendaele church to the fallen and their descendants, and the link between Lancashire and the Flemish people of Passchendaele to this day.

However, in December 1917 there were other divisions deployed here, including 8th Division. It had both 2/ East Lancashire and 15/ Lancashire Fusiliers in its ranks. They were used for the failed attack on 2 December, described in *A Moonlight Massacre* by Michael LoCicero. It is possible that casualties from this attack were found later in December, although the divisional flash that it is claimed was found would be different. There are therefore two possibilities; first that it was men of the 66th who were found, and second that it was East Lancashire or Lancashire Fusiliers who were found, but they were of another division. Whatever the truth, the link back to East Lancashire was established and this was enough to promote the legend and lead to the building of the memorial in the 1920s.

The site of Passchendaele church was used thoroughly by the Canadians, who were dug in all around it:

> Communication throughout the action was very difficult and runners were chiefly used. A power buzzer was taken forward to the village but unfortunately was not able to be read [for technical reasons] at the receiving station. A lamp visual station was established at Passchendaele Church and proved useful though the smoke etc. from the continuous shelling interfered seriously with the receiving of messages. No telephone were able to run forward from Battalion headquarters owing to the impossibility of maintaining lines under heavy shell fire which swept the areas through which the lines would have been run.
>
> An evacuation party of one Officer and ninety Other Ranks did splendid work on clearing the battlefield and carrying out stretcher cases. Without the aid of this party it is quite certain that it would not have been possible to evacuate all the wounded, owing to the length of the trail and the terribly heavy going it was impossible to carry out the dead other than the officers. However the dead in advance of the original front line were buried where they fell before the battalion were relieved in the line.

It was only this party and especially the officer in charge who would have been able to establish if there had been any British corpses around the church. They seem to have cleared the battlefield effectively before they were relieved. The battle was so intense and the shelling heavy, especially at the church, that any burials may well have been disinterred by shellfire.

54

That was far ahead, and for the moment the East Lancashire Division settled into its temporary line on Passchendaele ridge. The men of the 2/6 Lancashire Fusiliers sat on the right flank of the division. The route of the Ypres to Roulers railway cut through the ridge line that the British had spent so much energy and blood to reach. The cover afforded by the railway cutting was much appreciated, although this also drew heavy fire from the Germans.

> This record would be incomplete without a description of the railway cutting between Dash and Defy crossings. When speaking of roads and woods and railways it should be borne in mind that we are speaking of features that were once roads, woods and railways before the whole area was reduced to pulp.
>
> The railway cutting, by simple reason of its mass, remained, and the railway line could be traced by the twisted metals and broken sleepers; the cutting formed a concealed approach to our front lines and also a conspicuous target for the German guns. These two reasons caused it to become a shambles. In it the dead lay in heaps, and each time you passed you found increased carnage. The cutting had deep dugouts built in its sides. Most had been blown in but one remained and became an aid post.
>
> The casualties, however, were so numerous that often loaded stretchers had to remain outside and the wounded take the risk of further mutilation or death. Walking wounded at least remain happy in the knowledge that they could make some shift to cover the intervening mile or so of shell holes and make the firmness and comparative safety of the Ypres to Zonnebeke road. The badly wounded lay for some days in shell holes or by a pill box for days with only thirst and pain as their only attendants until the stretcher bearers found them and then after medical attention would have to endure hours of manhandling over the sea of mud until they reached the road.[14]

As the fighting settled down in the winter Lieutenant Withinshaw found himself some more salubrious accommodation, a cellar that had a view towards the German lines and Moorslede. He settled himself in and was able to provide good intelligence to his superiors. He also could see the town square of Moorslede through a telescope, beyond the devastation of the front, a fact that was passed to an officer in the French army who had a wife there. Somehow a letter was got to the resistance in the town and the wife was told to be in the square at a certain time when he would be able to see her, unfortunately she started waving and was arrested by the Germans, who thought she must be signalling, and the whole practice was stopped. The French officer was so enraged that he almost launched a personal offensive to get to Moorslede himself. Later on the hidey hole was given away by a red-tabbed staff officer who tried to find it and almost got shot in the process, Withinshaw had to effect a rapid exit to avoid the mortar bombs that destroyed his hideaway.[15]

The most important lessons of the Passchendaele attack for the division were given in a report at the end of the battle. The report praised the initiative displayed by the battalion commanders, which saved the left hand of the line by providing supports. The failure of the troops to reach the starting line by zero hour was remarked upon, but was unavoidable due to it being impossible to move east of Frezenberg in daylight. The conclusion was that the 'fresh troops' should have been brought up a night earlier as that was better than using those that were exhausted but already in the line, no doubt hoping for relief, as they would have had lower morale. Better communications and knowledge of the front lines would have helped the situation.

After the close of the Ypres campaign the British were starting to go on the defensive. In Russia, the revolution released German divisions to bring to the Western Front. On 22 December 1917, 66th Division received a new commander, General Neill Malcolm. Hubert Gough, the army commander, remembered the changeover:

> It was now that Neill Malcolm was taken from me and sent to command a division. His departure was a serious loss to the Fifth Army at such a moment, when we were taking over a new task of the utmost gravity ... This division, though a comparatively new one, was animated by a great spirit of comradeship, cheerfulness, and esprit de corps which stood it on good stead in the coming battle, and enabled it hold together, heroically carrying on the fight, even after a week of that desperate storm which reduced the divisions to mere skeletons. [March 1918][16]

Major General Neill Malcolm was a man whose face fitted the army command. Malcolm was forty-nine years old in 1918, and a regular soldier, as might be expected of someone of this seniority. He had gained a commission in the Argyll and Sutherland Highlanders in 1889; travelled extensively in India, Tibet and China; fought in various Imperial campaigns in Africa, including with the Tochi field force in Uganda 1897–99; the Boer War in 1899–1900; and was part of the Somaliland Field force in 1903–04. By 1904 he was a staff captain at

Army Headquarters, being promoted to deputy quartermaster general. He moved to be secretary of the Historical Section, and was later appointed to the Committee of Imperial Defence from 1908 to 1910 and by 1912 he was a grade 2 general officer at the Staff College. In 1914 he had a battlefield command with First Army, British Expeditionary Force, then was General Staff officer (1) in 11th (Northern) Division during the Salonika campaign. There he commanded a brigade in Egypt before returning to France as a staff officer in the Reserve Corps. In 1917 and 1918 he commanded 66th Division.

Thanks to Malcolm's illustrious career as a staff officer and general officer he was seen as a rising star in the British army. Also he was someone always on the move, going from command to command. The East Lancashire Division was just one of a list of divisions he commanded during the Great War, which included 39th Division and 30th Division. He was a man whose face fitted the role, in a modernising army it was easy to lose touch and become a casualty of the state of flux. The fact that during his career the army had only fought campaigns in the Sudan meant that after the Boer War modernisation was rapid and accelerated. The Haldane Act of 1908 assured a role for the Territorial Force as a European war became more likely. Malcolm was able to meet the needs of the army and provide a figurehead. The fact that most of these divisions were mauled in the battles of 1918 (not necessarily under his command) does not reflect a failure, but the extreme conditions of warfare they were fighting under. The army had to have the type of commanders who were independent, yet followed their orders, uncompromising yet intelligent. Neill Malcolm was such a commander.

Malcolm's staff were a General Staff Officer (1), Lieutenant Colonel A.R. Burrows; an assistant adjutant and quarter master general, Lieutenant Colonel G.N. MacReady; a brigadier general of Royal Artillery, Brigadier General A. Birtwhistle; and a commander Royal Engineers, normally a major or lieutenant colonel but in this case a captain (acting), C.A. West.

The army commander lost a member of his staff, but the division gained a general with knowledge of the bigger picture and the army command. This was to be crucial in the months ahead.

The Times newspaper carried the following reference on 10 October:

> On the right centre a Third Line [sic] Territorial Division comprising the Manchester, East Lancashire and Lancashire Fusiliers Regiments advanced one mile northwards along the ridge in the direction of Passchendaele, capturing all its objectives under the most trying and difficult circumstances with great determination and gallantry.[17]

The men of the East Lancashire Division held the ground at Passchendaele in the cold winter of 1917-18. The threat of a German spring offensive in France necessitated a move to St Quentin and a date with destiny for the men under Malcolm.

NOTES:

[1] Anonymous, *A History of the East Lancashire Royal Engineers*, 1920, p.234.

[2] ibid, p.236.

[3] IWM Department of Documents, papers of Withinshaw.

[4] IWM Department of Documents, papers of John Gore.

[5] Edmunds, E., *Official History, 1917*, Vol. II, p.302.

[6] ibid, p.308.

[7] IWM Department of Documents, papers of Withinshaw.

[8] TNA, WO 95/3120.

[9] ibid.

[10] Lieutenant P. King, Quoted in McDonald Lyn, *They Called It Passchendaele*.

[11] IWM Department of Documents, Papers of P.R. Hall, p.16.

[12] McCarthy, C., *The Third Ypres, Passchendaele, the Day to Day Account*, 1995, London, p.105.

[13] TNA, WO 95/3183.

[14] Potter and Withinshaw, *History of the 2/6 Battalion*, 1926 LF, p.82–3.

[15] IWM Department of Documents, private papers of Withinshaw.

[16] Gough, H., *The Fifth Army*, 1968, p.223.

[17] *History of the East Lancashire Regiment*, p.294.

Chapter 6

A Very Fine Mess

St Quentin, March 1918

The territory occupied by the division in front of the Hindenburg Line was well chosen by the Germans. This was land made for open combat, few obstacles were apparent. No one describes it better than the Royal Engineers. The country in this sector

> is a land of high rolling chalk downs with long narrow valleys, running east and west from ridges: such a ridge formed the main line of resistance. There are few streams, and the only military obstacles between the Hindenburg Line and the [river] Somme are a number of sunken roads: imagine this open, almost treeless land (except for a few copses) all covered with a thick white mist, its valleys a mass of gas and mist.[1]

The forward zone of the division was more strongly held as it included the important Cologne Ridge, which had been captured during the summer of 1917; three full battalions were allotted for its defence [see map 3]. The trenches here were named Railway trench, Pond trench, Bait trench and Art trench, which formed a slight eastward salient into the German lines. The result was that this forward zone was much more strongly held by the 66th Division than by the divisions on either flank, with a proportionate weakening of the defence of the battle zone [see map 4].

The East Lancashire Division was initially positioned with 198 Brigade on the right with brigade headquarters at Roisel, 197 Brigade to the left with brigade headquarters at Montigny and 199 Brigade in reserve sharing a headquarters with Divisional Command at Nobescourt Farm.

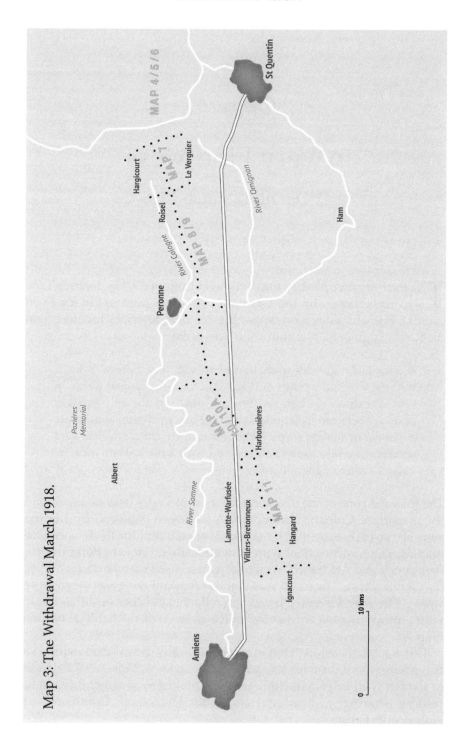

Map 3: The Withdrawal March 1918.

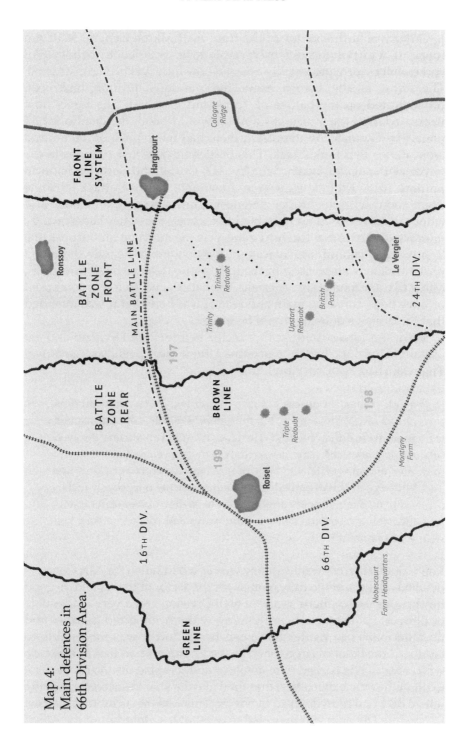

Map 4:
Main defences in
66th Division Area.

On arrival at this sector of the front on 1 March General Malcolm found it was not the defensive system he was led to believe. All commanders were profoundly amazed how little had been constructed. The effort of the British army the previous autumn had been concentrated on the battles of Ypres and Cambrai. The hope, now vaporised, that the attack at Cambrai would break the deadlock had gone. The German counter-attack there had taken most of the ground won in the mass tank attack. This battlefield was just 10 miles to the north of the sector taken over by XIX Corps and 66th Division in January 1918. They now faced an inevitable German attack 'at some point soon' with no proper defences. Time was of the essence and labour was organised and doubled to increase the zones laid down by military doctrine; the forward zone was meant to be an outpost line lightly held, behind which was the battle zone, a heavily defended series of defensive posts in the round, giving defence in all directions, rather like a wagon laager or castle. The battle zone itself was composed of three lines, forward, main and rear. It was here that it was intended that the decisive defence would be made.

Sadly, the forces holding this sector before, 24th Division and 1st Cavalry Division, had not occupied their time well, as the Royal Engineers had been busy building

> a golf course, an officer's club with garden, a very fine battalion officer's mess and theatre, but the defences which every one wanted to see were difficult to find. The latter included an old and decayed outpost line – the same as was first taken up a year before – a poorly sited and made [sic] main line of resistance: a reserve or Corps line with a good belt of barbed wire, but the trenches one foot six inches deep; no deep dugouts or other decent shelter, except at Templeux Quarries; no buried cables; no tramways and roads in a very bad state of repair.[2]

The lack of progress on the defences was a bad omen for XIX Corps. A detailed analysis of the trench maps for the sector in theory shows good defences in the southern sector of 66th Division and a very inadequate or dire state of defences near Ronssoy, with unconnected trenches and no redoubts.[3] The winter had been harsh and it was impossible to construct the defences necessary, so the Engineers had had to make do with constructing barbed wire defences and scraping the top off the bare earth with some expectation that they may be able to succeed in spring where they had been delayed in winter. This was the sector that the East Lancashire Division was expected to defend. It suffered from the Allied doctrine that every yard of French and Belgian soil must be held so there was no thought of pulling back to better ground with better defences. The sector in front of Hargicourt held by the three Lancashire battalions was very near the German line and more advanced than the rest of the British defences to the south.

The British response to the threatened offensive was managed at corps level by Major General Herbert Watts. Lieutenant General Sir Herbert Edward Watts was a pre-war regular soldier who had been commissioned in the East Yorkshire Regiment in 1880. Son of a local vicar in Wisbech, he served with the regiment for thirty years, including the Second Boer War, where he was mentioned in despatches five times and promoted to brevet lieutenant colonel. Watts was married in 1896, to Mary, and he retired with the rank of colonel in 1910. He was described by General Gough as:

> a spare, active man, quiet and very modest in demeanour, but one of our most courageous and experienced commanders. Having retired from the army before the war, he returned on its outbreak and was at once put in command of a brigade of 7th Division intended for the relief of Antwerp. Since then he had been engaged in almost every battle, he had risen to the command of a Corps. His judgement, sane as it was courageous, was an inestimable asset to his corps and me.[4]

Watts held the command of 38th (Welsh) Division in 1916, rising to command XIX Corps in early 1918. It was in XIX Corps that 66th Division would fight in March 1918. The only fault to be found with Watts seems to be that he never attended staff college, so any logistical and tactical planning was left to his clearly capable but quite possibly overstretched staff officers.

It was Watts at XIX Corps that organised the defence of the sector and the divisional defence was to rest on holding the forward zone, while in the red or front zone of the battle zone twelve redoubts were built on a line from Hesbécourt to Vermand. This was a XIX Corps line and ran over sectors of both 66th and 24th Division. From south to north these were Yard, Woodcock, Woody, Worm, Viper, Vixen, Upset, Uplift, Upstart, Trinket, Trinity and Triple redoubts. The redoubts were manned by a company of each brigade plus Royal Engineers and men currently on working parties, with tunnellers at Yard, Upset and Triple redoubts.[5] In addition to this, Kaffir and Zulu Copses were to be manned by machine gunners, as was Bobby Quarry and Bobby Farm, the former having the only deep dugouts on this sector of the front at Bolsover Pit.[6]

The two redoubts, Trinity and Trinket, were in the sector of the East Lancashire Division, the southern four in 24th Division's sector.

The intelligence reaching General Gough showed a completely apposite state of affairs in the German lines opposing his army front. He was sure that the Germans intended to attack on the Fifth Army front, while Sir Douglas Haig thought they would attack against the French Army. This difference of opinion was important for the coming battle as it pitched commanders against each other. Gough had basic evidence:

> Our air service, from reports and photographs, was also showing us the growth in the number of new hospitals and aerodromes on our front, as well as roads, railways and bridges.[7]

Here was incontestable evidence of a military build-up as feared. Even the German commander was the right man for an attack, the victor of Riga, Oskar von Hutier.

While the intelligence was being gathered, units were being disbanded to fill the physical gaps in manning the army after the casualty figures of the previous autumn; the battles of Ypres and Cambrai had had a massive impact on the regiments of the British army. Henceforth every brigade was to be made up of three battalions, rather than the previous four, so each brigade of the division lost a battalion. Three battalions were amalgamated or sent elsewhere. While this strengthened the battalions, there were fewer battalions for reserves.

At the same time as this reorganisation was being undertaken, officers and some men were given much-needed leave. Officers on leave at this time included Colonel William Benjamin Little, of the 5th Border Regiment, who had just moved his battalion to 66th Division as pioneers. This was part of the reorganisation of the army brigades to three battalion units, and they moved from 50th Division to 66th Division and became pioneers. In the meantime, he was enjoying some leave while his men pressed ahead with the expansion and improvement of Bolsover Pit dugouts, which were at Templeux quarries, to provide more underground accommodation.

One man hoping for discharge was an aggrieved James Brown Jessiman, formerly of the Gordon Highlanders. Jessiman was not typical of the men in the East Lancashire Division. Born in 1897 at Rhynie, Banffshire, near Aberdeen, he was a highlander and one of ten children of the local blacksmith. He studied medicine in 1914 and 1915 at Aberdeen university, then joined the 3/4th Gordon Highlanders there. He served at Ripon from June 1917 and then joined 204 Company Machine Gun Corps at Grantham, Lincolnshire. Moving in November

1917, he joined the division at Passchendaele as a reinforcement. He wrote regular letters to his sister, Meg, living at that time at Cornhill, near Banff. His spell with the East Lancashire Division does not appear to have been particularly enjoyable, as he hankered after his chosen career of medicine.

Jessiman was now in 204 Machine Gun Company in the East Lancashire Division. This unit was formed on 11 March as part of the defensive reorganisation of the army. An unhappy soldier, he wrote to Meg:

> I told you in my last note that I had sent in my application for discharge. The Chaplain is off on furlough for a fortnight. I dare say I won't hear until he comes back. I told you my division already, 66th. I mentioned also about 'little Kitchener' in my last note, don't bother, you wanted to know what to send, tins of sardines or salmon, don't send Oxo as we don't care for it, but [do send] a bit of cake or anything edible.

Jessiman wanted to become a doctor and this may have been the reason for his attempts to be discharged. This general theme continued throughout February, although while resting and moving the rations improved:

> We don't need parcels now – We have any amount of canteens around. We have had our pay raised to 1/6- a day so can buy almost anything we want here. Tonight for supper we had plums and apricots à la Crème.
>
> I was to have gone to the 'Lancashire Lads' tonight, only I was picked for guard. They are the Divisional concert party – very good too.

13 February:

> I've had no word of my application yet.

22 February:

> We are still out on rest, billeted in villages which Fritz had shelled about the first days of the war – it is now half deserted so we are in the empty houses, quite cosy billets too, and the weather is better now. I am to see the C.O. tomorrow so will tell you the result before I post this note … I didn't see the C.O. today, I'll write soon as I do.

4 March:

> Just a note to say I'm still alive altho' I'm not just in the pink – I'll be
> alright in a day or two. Just a touch of flue [sic] rotten too. I haven't
> seen the C.O. yet – it isn't for want of trying but such is the army.

18 March:

> Och, that touch of the flue lasted only three or four days but it was
> rotten while I did have it. No, I've had no word yet but the Captain
> has written [to] Brigade headquarters so I expect to hear shortly. I
> wrote last week about sending a letter to him. I dare say it has been
> sent in, the sooner the better as April will soon be here.

The unease in his letters is all too palpable, and it would not just be
April that was coming James Jessiman's way in just a few days' time.

On the XIX Corps front 24th and 66th Divisions were in the line with
1st and 3rd Cavalry in reserve and 50th (Northumbrian) Division in
army reserve 25 miles behind them. Gough complained that the line
to the north of the river Omignon was not in a good state, compared
with the old French line to the south of it. He set to and prepared the
line, with the front south of the Omignon ready in February and that
to the north of it by the middle or end of March 1918. General Gough
was sure he could offer defence here by mid-March, but offered a new
position on the Somme and at Péronne as a defensive line behind the
front as an alternative should the Germans break through. He guessed
that Fifth Army and Amiens would be the main objective. It was VII
and XIX Corps that were placed in the line forward of Péronne, an old
fortified town set at a strategic position on the Somme river. The
importance of this town was not lost on the British or the Germans,
which meant that the venom of the attack would be on the forces
defending this position, termed the Péronne bridgehead. Also of
importance to the Germans was the railway line to Roisel via Péronne
and Chaulnes and the dead straight Roman road from St Quentin to
Amiens.

General Davidson in headquarters at Montreuil replied with an eight-
point plan that included elements of defence but clearly admitted that
a retreat to the line of the Somme river might be considered with a
defence based on Péronne and the bridge at Brie to the south (see
Appendices). The emphasis was still on the battle zone, and the retreat
option only a last resort, as defences on this line and even at Villers-
Bretonneux, back on the Amiens defence line, were scarce at best. The

plan rested upon the construction of two defensive lines of 50 miles in length to secure the Péronne bridgehead.

This was to have consequences for the forthcoming battle. It was to be considered that each division should be covered by a small rearguard of all arms. A statement of the time described how 'by the skilful handling of these, particularly as regards the employment of machine guns in conjunction with wire obstacles, it should be possible to delay considerably the enemy's advance, cause him to expend considerable force and generally dislocate his arrangements'.

This statement made in early February showed that an enormous amount of work was necessary in a short amount of time. Labour had to be brought in and 9,000 men were available for defensive construction. The principles set out above that affected the 66th Division were that the line was thinly held, few reserves were available and Péronne should be held with the Somme river as a defensive line. The commander of Royal Engineers for XIX Corps, Brigadier General A.G. Bremner, bemoaned the labour available:

> On 1 March work commenced on the rear zone defences as rapidly as possible with the labour available. Attention was principally directed to machine gun sites and wiring. Italian labour commenced digging with indifferent results. They [the officers in charge] considered there were too many restrictions imposed on the work, i.e. no work on Sundays, labour may not march more than two miles inclusive to and from work, not to be worked more than seven hours a day etcetera.

As for the stores available for the divisions, the dump at Roisel was too close to the front, and efforts to empty out the stores were too little, too late.

The director of transport for Fifth Army had been busy, providing new narrow gauge lines, building standard gauge lines such as the Tortille valley line and gun spurs at Roisel, as well as road improvements for the bridges across the Somme. The depot had been planned to support an army in supposed offensive operations upon the Hindenburg Line, rather than a British army in potential defence of a line based upon a future withdrawal. On the gun spurs were two 12in railway howitzers manned by the Royal Garrison Artillery. Able to traverse fully and fire a 750lb shell 14,350 yards, these were a considerable asset in the firepower available to XIX Corps.

In researching the Fifth Army artillery it soon became obvious that it was not where I had supposed it to be; it was still up in Belgium in the

Ypres Salient in March 1918. So the question arose as to which artillery was in the Somme battlefield, and an educated guess led to the fact that it was Third Army artillery that was in the southern sector, covering the actual areas of Third and Fifth Armies. While divisional artillery mostly moved with the unit it was commanded by, army artillery might be elsewhere than where one would suppose it to be.

The heavy and siege artillery of XIX Corps was under the command of Brigadier General H.A. Pritchard. This comprised 21, 22, 26, 76 and 68 Artillery Brigades, a total of 284 heavy guns. A last-minute attempt to bring up more guns in the sector brought the guns of Fifth Army to sufficient strength. The gun strength of XIX Corps was brought up to 284 from 236 field guns; twenty-four 60-pounder guns, eight 6in guns and sixty-six 6in howitzers, twelve 8in howitzers, three 9.2in guns, seventeen 9.2in howitzers, and no guns above that calibre. More howitzers were also brought into the area at the army command level, thus there were three command levels for artillery in the corps area: field artillery, corps and army artillery.

In Roisel itself the Royal Garrison Artillery had been building a 'silent battery', fully camouflaged and packing guns of 6 and 8in calibre. The guns of 68th Brigade Royal Garrison Artillery were not registered upon their targets, which might give away their presence. Their barrels were to be cold until the guns were needed in action.

Wilfrid James Woodcock had served with the mounted infantry in the Boer War and with the Lancashire Fusiliers at Gallipoli as a major. Receiving promotion to lieutenant colonel of the 7/ Border Regiment, he then commanded the 2/7 Manchester Regiment in 66th Division and then the 66th Battalion Machine Gun Corps in the same division. Born in Wigan, the son of a wealthy banker and former mayor of Wigan, the family moved to Bolnore House at Cuckfield, Sussex, where his father lived off his means with ten servants and seven children. Born in 1879, Wilfrid had a comfortable existence and went to boarding school in Bournemouth. That was followed by the Royal Military College as a gentleman cadet, and he became a second lieutenant in the Lancashire Fusiliers in 1898. Joining the mounted infantry in Malta, he was rapidly promoted in the Boer War and became captain, twice being mentioned in dispatches. He married Caroline Lawrie in 1907 and retired in 1913 to the special reserve. Called out of retirement in 1914, he was again rapidly promoted and commanded four different battalions in the war. Not indifferent to new technology, he was commanding the machine gun battalion of the division in 1918.[8]

The men of 66th Battalion Machine Gun Corps were alone in having plenty of time to choose their fields of fire, although they too suffered from lack of time to dig in. The commander, Colonel Woodcock, had surveyed the ground and found that: 'The country was undulating and broken by many valleys, giving covered approaches to hostile advances. The left flank, the Cologne valley was entirely dominated by the Ronssoy Ridge, held by the division on our left.' At least they were being aided by what labour there was available. The machine gunners consisted of three companies, not the normal four, with forty-two guns and the 2nd Squadron, Cavalry Machine Gun Corps, with eight guns bringing the total to fifty-three guns. The three battery commanders were Captains G.E. Gilbert with A Company, 197 Brigade, H.E.B. Wilkins with B Company in 198 brigade and R.B. Buchanan with C Company in 199 Brigade.

The disposition of these was thirty-two guns in the outpost line, of which five were within 800 yards of the front line. The forward zone of the battle line had twelve guns and the battle zone eight guns. In addition there was a reserve of eight guns in the battle zone for immediate placement in case of an attack. There was also a general reserve of nine guns that were mostly used for anti-aircraft defence at Hervilly:

> The nature and extent of the front made it impossible for all guns to be actually in pairs, though in all cases control of two or more guns was possible. The necessity of barrage work made it necessary to have batteries in barrage position; [i.e. firing over the curve of the ground to rear areas]. These guns were also allocated battle positions in close proximity. These battle positions were carefully dug and camouflaged. About half the guns in position, thirty-nine, were in trenches or emplacements taken over from the division relieved on 6 March, the others were in fresh positions, newly sited and camouflaged, and practically in the open. The reserve positions were all new.[9]

German intelligence was obviously good, as when later a captured map was inspected, all the old positions in trenches were shown, but not the new positions made within the last two weeks before the attack. All posts were supplied with fourteen boxes of belt ammunition, 10,000 rounds small arms ammunition and reserve water and oil for the Vickers machine guns. This unit was the centre of the defence as it existed and provided a devastating fire when called upon. The essence of the machine gun was to have camouflaged positions unknown to the enemy that could work in pairs and provide enfilade fire.

The cavalry also made good use of their time, planning counter-attacks which they enacted on 6 March with a tactical exercise around the Fervaque Farm position with the commanding officers of the Bedfordshire Yeomanry and the 9/ Machine Gun Squadron. This was to be crucial in a just a few weeks' time. For the soldiers there was a divisional football competition to take their minds off the expected offensive and maintain their morale. On 16 March the 2/5 East Lancashire played the divisional ammunition column and won 4-1.

The front line battalions of 198 Brigade were relieved in the lines on the night of 16–17 March, a normal military process that continued every four to six days depending upon conditions. In 198 Brigade the men of 9/ Manchester Regiment moved from front line back to reserve, 4/ East Lancs from support to front line and 2/5th Manchester Regiment from reserve to support. They carried on a plan of active patrolling of no man's land at night which, was recorded in a detailed report by Second Lieutenant S. Beaumont.

The final disposition of brigades was 199 Brigade on the right flank, 198 in the middle and 197 on the left flank. From right to left the units in the forward zone were 2/5 Manchester Regiment, 4/ East Lancashire, and 2/8 Lancashire Fusiliers. These were split up by company and covered a large front on the southern and northern flanks. In front of Villeret the 4/ East Lancashire Regiment was concentrated in front of Hargicourt. The companies of the 2/8 L.F. were widely spread with three companies in the front line and one in reserve. This was to prove a very weak disposition with just three companies in the front line stretching around 1,500 yards. Each company covered 500 yards but if each company was in several trenches this was around one man every 12 yards. Supporting fire was not possible due to the thick fog and the Germans only spotted once they were at the wire and within grenade and flame-thrower range. The German assault in this area would undoubtedly head for New Quarry, which was undefended, and it would then be able to turn on the lines to the north and south and roll up their flanks.

Behind this forward zone were one company of 2/7 Manchester Regiment in the Grand Priel Woods [all the trees had been cut down the year before], 2/6 Manchester around Fervaque Farm, 9/ Manchester around Hargicourt Quarries, 2/5 East Lancashire to the west of Hargicourt, and in reserve the remains of the 2/7 Manchester around Toine Wood and Orchard Post. The Royal Engineer and attached units were to fill in a gap at the Hargicourt quarries.

Beaumont describes how from noon on 19 March until midday the next day British artillery was active all day and throughout the night. At 3.30 am a barrage was laid down on no man's land for fifteen minutes, the trench mortar batteries were little used and 'quieter than usual'. The medium trench mortars shot off five rounds at 5.45 am, and the Stokes mortars thirty rounds on various points around Buckshot Ravine. British machine guns were not fired. As for enemy operations, little is reported besides some sporadic 5.9in howitzer fire near Pimple Post and six mortar bombs fired at Railway Support trench. No hostile patrols were found or heard.

Seven British patrols were active in the sector held by 2/6th Manchester of 198 Brigade during the night of 20 March. Mostly composed of one officer and two men, their task was to look for gaps in the enemy wire and spy on and report work to repair gaps made by British artillery. These left British lines at intervals between 7.45 in the evening and 3.30 in the morning, and all reported little work or movement in the enemy lines. One patrol was affected by the British artillery bombardment at 3.30 in the morning. However, despite having every excuse to stay in their own lines they returned to a spot 50 yards from the enemy wire, where they remained until just before dawn.

The practicalities of hygiene in trench warfare and the sense of impending action led to some bizarre events as senior officers rallied their men. On the night of 20 March Major William Beaumont of the Royal Engineers was sharing an elephant shelter in a sunken road near Hargicourt with a subaltern having a hot bath in a canvas wash bowl:

> It was beautiful to see him wondering how to salute when Brigadier-General Hunter and his brigade major came in to tell us to man battle stations.

The front that concerns 66th Division was under the XIX Corps under General Herbert Watts, a corps frontage of 12,000 yards. The East Lancashire Division held 4,500 yards of front between Verguier and Ronssoy, which was subdivided into three brigade sectors each of 1,750 yards, roughly lying between the rivers Cologne and Omignon. His divisional generals were Major General Malcolm of 66th Division and General Daly of 24th Division. To the north were the Irish 16th Division under Major General C.P.A. Hull, part of VII Corps under Lieutenant General Sir Walter Congreve. In the East Lancashire Division the forces were arranged with 197 Brigade and 198 Brigade in the front line and 199 Brigade in reserve.

The principal tactical areas of the front of 66th Division were Le Verguier, Fervaque Farm, the Cologne Farm ridge, the Templeux quarries and Ronssoy. The right sector of the division was held by 199 Brigade under Brigadier G.C. Williams. In the forward zone were 2/5 Manchester, including Private Thomas Booty, around Villaret. In the battle zone were 2/6 Manchester with part of 2/7 Manchester with reserve companies marching up.

In the middle of the division 198 Brigade under Brigadier A.J. Hunter held the Hargicourt sector. In the front line here were the 4/ East Lancashire under acting Lieutenant Colonel Arthur Leonard Wrenford and his adjutant, H.A. Mellows. Wrenford was the son of a barrister and a product of Sandhurst and Cambridge who had served in Ireland, South Africa, Ceylon and India. Serving with the North Nigerian regiment in 1914, he came home and served with several units including the Royal Inniskilling Fusiliers before taking command of the 4th East Lancashire in September 1917. With headquarters at Slag Heap Camp at Hargicourt, his battalion formed the central section of the division forward zone defences. They were established in front line trenches at Bait trench, Pond trench and Railway trench with the old narrow gauge railway lines that hugged the contours of this rolling landscape. To their front was Ruby Wood with its gaunt tree trunks and Twisted Tree. To their front was Buckshot Ravine, leading down to Bellicourt village.

The line of 197 Brigade under Brigadier Borrett was formed of the forward zone between Lempire and Hargicourt including Malakoff Farm, with names such as Benjamin Post and Little Benjamin, Sugar Post and Ruby Post. Behind this ran a parallel track, Hussar Track, with Hussar Post, Valley Post and Indian Post. Behind this was the battle zone with Orchard Post, Toine Post, Mill Post, Pimple Post and Consort Post. The final line, based around some phosphate quarries near Templeux le Guerard, Sherwood trench, was a home to many dugouts and the reserve company. Each post was held by a section or platoon of twelve or thirty men accordingly, the reserve companies at the quarries were ten platoons, in total more than 300 men, and two companies of the pioneer battalion, the 2/5th Border Regiment under Lieutenant Colonel William Benjamin Little and his second in command, Major S. Rigg. It was the task of the Border Regiment to open up the phosphate quarries and mine deep dugouts at Orchard and Toine posts while A Company worked on roads and mining and B Company on tramways, starting on 4 March. That gave them a little over two weeks, so we can presume the work was not finished by the time of the attack. Also, Colonel Little left on 13 March for a period of leave, leaving Major Rigg in command. This was to have an effect on the battle, as we will see later. The work at the phosphate quarry was to improve the dugouts, which had suffered several falls and create a new shaft and an air shaft for ventilation. The position created was called Bolsover Pit.

Warnings were received on the afternoon of 20 March that the offensive was likely to begin the next day. This time army headquarters had a number of sources, and captured soldiers, deserters and aerial reconnaissance all pointed to the same inevitable conclusion [see Appendix]. This had happened before, but the intelligence picture was growing rather than diminishing. It was nerve-wracking for the troops to consider the possibility of the attack, which seemed imminent. All working parties were cancelled and troops warned to be ready for an attack, active patrolling was undertaken and vital intelligence gained.

One of those raids was organised for A Company of the 2/7th Manchester Regiment, as recounted by Ralph Frost, a nineteen year old reinforcement from March in Cambridgeshire who joined at Passchendaele after coming through the dreaded Bull Ring camp at Étaples:

> Until 20 March it was working parties and routine drilling. On 20 March A Company should have raided Jerry's lines. After starting out and getting towards his lines, for some unknown reason, we were ordered back to camp arriving at about 2 a.m. At 4.30 a.m. the order was given to stand to, battle order, this was about the time that Jerry opened up with his bombardment. About half an hour later we were ordered to march and get to the front line which was being held by the 2/5 Manchesters. Try to picture us loaded with 120 rounds of ammo, five Mills bombs, wire cutters, two Lewis guns and spare parts, and shells coming over like a hailstorm, and to make matters worse it was foggy.[10]

In 197 Brigade a patrol of the 2/8th Lancashire Fusiliers came back to their colonel, A.E. Stokes-Roberts, with definite intelligence that the trenches opposite the right company in Bone Lane and Sugar Trench were packed with Germans. This was at 3.45 am and without hesitation artillery was called down on this point. It was not going to go all the Germans' way. At 4.20 am Stokes-Roberts considered ceasing this bombardment but he was overruled by Major General Malcolm, who was determined to use every opportunity to attack the enemy.

The division was on full alert and the men were tense, but sentries apart, they slept nonetheless. Though these alerts had happened before, they might need all the rest they could get. Gunner John Gore, in Hervilly, on the Green line, was still not enjoying his surroundings and wrote in his diary on 16 March,

'Getting used to these cramped quarters. We have been re-equipped from Quartermasters stores and plenty of clothes and boots. There is an ominous feeling about, as if something is going to happen,' and on 20 March, 'got the wind up, slept with clothes on'.

Outside the night was chilly and fog crept in:

> The keen crisp air apparent on the night of the 20 was replaced on the morning of the 21 by a chilly penetrating dampness. Wreaths of woolly mist drifted from nowhere, drawn together by some unseen attraction, and by dawn the whole of the Fifth Army was completely blinded by a dense fog extending from far in front of the line miles backwards, even in the higher regions it was impossible to see more than a few yards in front of one, while in the valleys and particularly in the quarries it was so thick that the range of vision did not extend beyond more than six or seven feet on any side.[11]

NOTES:

[1] Anonymous, *A History of the East Lancashire Royal Engineers*, Manchester, 1920, p.239.
[2] ibid, p.238.
[3] Trench maps, National Library of Scotland, 62 c NE and 62 b NW.
[4] Gough, H., *The Fifth Army*, 1968, Bath, p.268.
[5] TNA, WO 95/3121.
[6] IWM Department of Documents, papers of Colonel Little.
[7] Gough, H., *The Fifth Army*, 1968, Bath, p.228.
[8] *The Cairo Gang*, Colonel W.J. Woodcock.
[9] TNA, WO 95/3121.
[10] IWM Department of Documemts, Papers of R.C.A. Frost 09/6/1.
[11] *History of the East Lancashire Regiment*, Liverpool, 1936, p.308.

Chapter 7

The Battle of St Quentin

Thursday, 21 March 1918, 4 o'clock to 10 o'clock

At 4.30 exactly that morning a German artillery barrage started. For the soldiers in the front line this was the beginning of a five-hour bombardment they had to face. Casualties mounted [see map 5].

The 4/ Battalion East Lancashire Fusiliers were one of the battalions in the front line under their commander, Lieutenant Colonel Arthur Wrenford. After the long artillery bombardment, which ceased about 9.30, they were attacked by infantry at about 10.30, who quickly outflanked them in their isolated position and attacked them from the rear.

> A splendid resistance was made but most of the officers and men became casualties or were taken prisoner. The commanding officer was wounded and taken prisoner, to die a few days later. The reserve company fought a magnificent rearguard action under Captain Bolton who was wounded and taken prisoner.[1]

It was over quickly for some front line units. The front line positions on the Cologne Ridge were not easily defended, and should have been abandoned had not military strategy demanded differently. The British front line trenches were part of the German front line system and were in some places still connected to the system with just trench blocks dividing them. It is no surprise that they were overrun. The rest of the men under Captain Cooper withdrew fighting to the Red line, just west of Hargicourt. The survivors of the 4/ East Lancashire numbered three officers and ninety other ranks. At Hargicourt they met Major Paddock with a detail of fifty other ranks to reinforce them.

Lieutenant Colonel Whitehead and his men of the 2/5 East Lancashire Regiment in reserve in Hesbécourt fared little better:

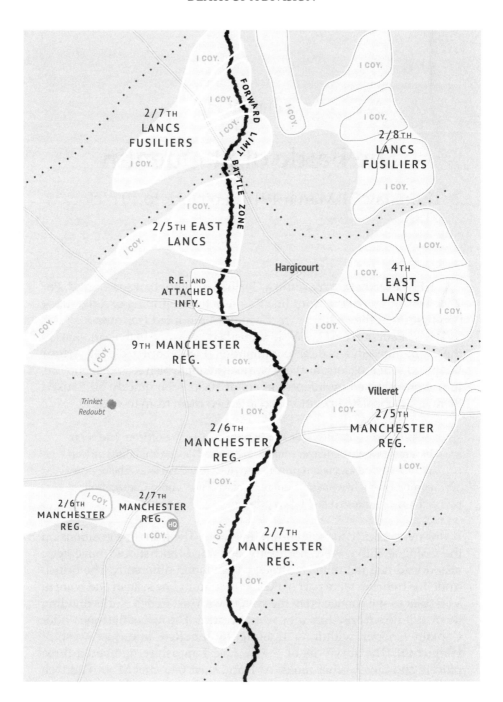

Map 5: Forward units.

On that main street the Boche gunfire descended that morning with devastating accuracy effectively completing the ruin of the semi-destroyed barns in which the men were largely billeted, and causing heavy casualties and considerable confusion before the battalion could even get on parade ... It was obvious that the expected Boche offensive had materialised, and the battalion immediately moved up to its Battle Station where it established itself by around 6 o'clock, having already suffered considerable casualties by that time.[2]

In the front line headquarters of the 2/8 Battalion Lancashire Fusiliers, Lieutenant Colonel Stokes-Sharpe and his men were overrun and captured almost immediately:

Dense masses of Germans advanced and overwhelmed the whole area occupied by the battalion, whose headquarters were captured in a dug out before they had an idea that the attack had even begun. The attack had come in a southerly direction from Lempire towards Hargicourt and had consequently turned the left flank of the brigade. At about 9 o'clock German 'swarms' reached the support position and attacked the 2/7 Battalion [in the second line] in front of the quarries close to Templeux.[3]

The defences were not of a quality to resist determined attack and it appears that here the soldiers were quickly overwhelmed, Colonel Gell was one of the few survivors. Lance-Corporal William Sharpe was in the front lines and gives one of the few testimonies from the men of 2/8 Battalion Lancashire Fusiliers. In his private papers he related how after a chlorine gas bombardment at 5.30 in the morning:

A terrific bombardment had started – a succession of falling shells dropping increasingly near with each successive round. We who had been at Ypres began to compare, saying it was as bad, but it continued to get worse and came to a pitch when it seemed impossible that anything could live in it, and personally I prayed with every reverence.

Soon the shock of the bombardment produced shell shock, especially among the youths in their first combat.

My section included four youths just turned eighteen years, who had only been with our company three weeks and whose first experience of shell fire it was, and WHAT an experience. They cried and one kept calling 'mother!' And who could blame him, such HELL makes weaklings of the strongest and no humans nerves or body were ever built to stand such torture, noise, horror and mental pain.

The barrage was now on top of us and our trench was blown in. I missed these four youths, and I never saw them again, despite searching amongst the debris for some time.[4]

The effect upon the battalion was such that the men wanted to run for it, but were ordered to stay their ground, rum being sent up to steady their shattered nerves. Stragglers from other sections of their company, who had been blown out of their trenches, passed by heading for the rear. But the artillery and the waiting continued until nearly 10 o'clock. Then they heard the sound of the wire being cut out to their front:

We opened with rapid fire, firing some 50 yards into the mist, without seeing anything. We followed this with bombs for some ten minutes and still with no attack. Not knowing exactly what to do, we decided to go for instructions to the command dugout and made our way through what had been trenches to the sunken road although even this could hardly be recognised. The fog was now lifting and the sun breaking through. No sooner had we got into the road when we ran into 'Jerries', who opened fire with revolvers. A few of the lads bolted up [the bank on] the edge of the road and the remainder of us stood still, simply amazed, and were again fired at by a German officer. Directly afterwards a shell burst (one of ours we presumed) just a few yards away and I am sure this saved our lives. We were then told to put up our hands – or actions to that effect – and of course there was no help for it, for the whole road was occupied by Germans. They quickly relieved us of rifles, bombs, equipment etc., and we were simply left.

Thinking there might be some chance of getting away, I helped to attend the German wounded and there were some hundreds and some awful wounds too. They all seemed to be quite decent fellows (as far as we could make ourselves understood) and pressed their cigarettes and food on to me.

One German spoke perfect English and informed Sharpe that they were 'miles behind the lines by now'. Sharpe took his first opportunity to climb the bank of the road and what he saw confirmed the German's analysis:

> As far as the eye could see, on what a day ago were flat green fields scarcely pitted with shell holes, was nothing except the blue grey uniforms of German troops advancing in well-ordered company formation. The British artillery was now in fine form and with spotter planes up had now started to retaliate with a barrage and I was forced to take cover from this, after seeing a German service wagon and horses blown thirty feet into the air.[5]

William Sharpe was one of the few survivors of the 2/8 Lancashire Fusiliers battalion and one of the few eyewitness accounts of the front line fighting. They had been bypassed and surrounded, without orders but forced to abandon their posts they then surrendered.

The attack had quickly overwhelmed many of those in the crowded front line trenches. The 4/ East Lancashire and 2/8 Lancashire Fusiliers were decimated by the overwhelming artillery bombardment and the massed infantry attack. A similar story was told to the north in the 16th Irish Division sector and it was here that the breakthrough had succeeded. Though historians of the Irish attribute the collapse to the East Lancashire Division and vice versa, suffice to say the collapse was on both fronts. The Irish were holding a pronounced salient that was attacked before 9 o'clock. Two companies of the 7/ Royal Irish in the front line suffered terribly with not a man escaping. As the official history states, this made the German task of rolling up the flank of the 16th Irish Division easy, and they advanced on Ronssoy by 9.30 that morning.

The barrage fell on the line where the forward companies of the field companies of the Royal Engineers had their billets, about 1,000 yards behind the front line at Templeux quarries.

> Never even at Ypres had we heard the equal of this – never, not even when the Hindenburg Line was being taken later in the year, was the sound so overwhelming. Being now quite practised in alarm and battle positions, the sappers turned out, only to find a mist so thick they could not see a yard, and that the mist had a large percentage of gas in it, and nearer the front line a quantity of high explosive … respirators had to be worn from 4.30 until after 9 o'clock.[6]

The gas was composed of lacrymator [tear gas] and chlorine gas shells, and though thick in the valleys where it concentrated, it was not so thick elsewhere.

Major William Beaumont recounted:

At four o'clock the [next] morning the biggest bombardment I have heard came down with a crash and in a very short time the Boche were on us. We managed to get our men together somehow – they were living in all sorts of cubbyholes in the phosphate quarry – and got them into a sort of rectangular dry reservoir with good banks around which we were to defend. I went round to try and explode my tool cart but found a shell had done so already.[7]

John Gore was awoken:

The German Somme offensive commenced. About 4 o'clock this morning lying in bed a terrible noise like heavy rain went on. Got up and found the attack had started with thousands of gas shells. Sergeant Manning came to the shack and told me to go round all the huts and bring every man of our batteries that were down the line. Putting on our respirators Clarke and self groped our way through the darkness and warned the boys.[8]

In the trenches opposite the XIX Corps was the German XIV and LI Corps, with the 4th Guards Division, 25th and 208th Infantry Divisions of von der Maritz's Second Army. In reserve were the 13th and 79th Reserve Divisions. To put it plainly, the British XIX and VII Corps of six and a third divisions faced seventeen German divisions of von der Marwitz's Second Army.

Crucially, 66th Division and its northern companion in VII Corps, 16th (Irish) Division, held the trenches opposite the *Souterrain de Riqueval*, the land above the tunnel of the St Quentin Canal at Bellicourt. In anyone's book this was an obvious route for major forces to advance without having to cross the canal on bridges. That this happened to coincide with a British corps and divisional boundary was unfortunate, if not downright disastrous. This was coupled with the packing of troops into the front line as 'this was judged necessary due to the short field of view on the high ground, on which the front line had settled after the battle of Cambrai, and the ease at which the enemy could mass in the defile, through which the Schelde canal ran close at hand, free from ground observation'.[9] The Irish had five battalions in the forward zone, the neighbouring 21st and 9th Divisions four each. The East Lancashire Division had three battalions in the forward and four in the battle zone. The dire situation on the ground coupled with the need to protect the main St Quentin to Amiens road in the 24th Division sector made this area strategically important for Watts' XIX Corps.

This perhaps is why General Gough insisted on the trenches of the outpost line being overmanned. This was disastrous for the Irish, as it was for the East Lancashire Division. The Germans outnumbered the British here in considerable quantity, and unleashed a veritable fire storm on the packed British trenches that made sure they broke through. Once they had broken through, the valley of the Omignon river afforded a valuable route to Péronne and the Somme crossings with the protected flank of the Cologne river. And the key to this was Nobescourt Farm, Major General Malcolm's divisional headquarters. The goal of the German plan was to reach Péronne and turn north and roll up the British line, forcing them back on their lines of communication towards the channel ports.

In the divisional artillery batteries behind the infantry the men awoke to the sound of artillery. Tom Hardman of the 330 Brigade Royal Field Artillery wrote brief entries in his diary: 'terrific bombardment, big battle opened. Germans attacking. It is awful to hear the guns; there must be thousands of them.'[10] The British guns opened in retaliation on their normal SOS lines.

Divisional headquarters at Nobescourt Farm was on a high plateau several kilometres behind the front line. Described as the linchpin of the Green line, or battle zone defences, it was situated on a plateau with flat land all around. Major General Neill Malcolm had his headquarters here and it was defended with a double line of trenches facing north-east. The essential facility of command was communications with the front line positions. But the companies and battalions in the front line were cut off and unable to report: 'All wires seemed to be cut at once, and no message was received at all from one forward post, which consisted of two sections of R.E. from the 431 and 432 Companies and a company of infantry.'[11] Some units would never be heard from again, so sudden and instant was the loss of communication. Without communications and unable to see the front from headquarters, General Malcolm was unable to ascertain the situation. All he could do was to send reinforcements and hope the officers used their initiative and training. At 4.50 am Malcolm sent the order 'take action', at which infantry and machine gun units would move forward to their battle stations.

This set the 9/ and 2/7th Manchesters on their way to the battle positions as well as units of the Machine Gun Corps. The battle positions of the 9/ were at Higson quarries south of Hargicourt under Lieutenant Colonel E. Lloyd, who wrote:

> At 5 o'clock the smell of gas was very apparent but the morning broke with everything enveloped in a thick white fog which added

greatly to the difficulty. C Company, however, got off in good time to take up their positions and were shortly followed by the remainder of the battalion. Two companies at Ruelles Wood H.Q. and one company in L.9.a close to a 2.5 inch Howitzer position. The latter position was reached at 7.15 a.m. and a runner to that effect sent to Brigade headquarters. This man apparently lost his way in the fog or became a casualty as he never reached his destination. The approach to the Battle positions was one of extreme difficulty as owing to the fog which was thickened by the gas cloud, the track was almost indiscernible besides which the enemy having lengthened his range was shelling the approaches fairly heavily and several casualties occurred this way. After having reached battle position headquarters – which at the time was undergoing heavy shelling from a 5.9 inch howitzer (apparently searching for the gun position) gas and High Explosive shelling from all calibres continued until 10.15 a.m. and then ceased.

C company under Captain Butterworth 100 yards to the west of L.10.a as his post in Hargicourt trench had become untenable and obliterated through shellfire. His position was prolonged to the north by A Company under Lieutenant Till. Headquarters were sent forward to the high ground in L.9.a to act as support and the runners, signallers and a few stragglers occupied this trench just above the howitzer battery position; the two Lewis guns attached to this battery were taken over in order to strengthen the defence and sweep the valley towards Templeux Quarries and prevent the enemy from approaching from that direction.[12]

The 2/6 Lancashire Fusiliers moved up to their position in the redoubt line early that morning. A private Harrop recalled that: 'So dense was the fog that each man groped his way to the line maintaining touch with one another by holding on to his bayonet scabbard of the man in front.' They were in position by 6 o'clock and Captain Potter recalled that they were able to enjoy what they could in way of breakfast at 8 o'clock:

Battalion headquarters was established in a quarry rather to the left of the line. The position was chosen because it was possible to see the whole front from the top of it. It was an unfortunate place though as it was away from the road and difficult for messages. The Boche had evidently had instructions to shell it and he carried out his instructions very thoroughly, killing several of the headquarters signallers and blowing the signals officer Ormerod, and myself (they were in a Nissen hut) a considerable distance, all with one direct hit.[13]

The artillery barrage persisted but appeared to die down at 6.40 am. Gas shelling, which had concentrated on the Templeux quarries, ceased. This had pinned down the front line, destroyed communications, killed men in the trenches and confused them as gas mingled with the mist.

At this point the intensity of the German shelling switched from the front lines to rear areas where reinforcements might be grouping, searching out targets that the German air service had mapped before the fog swept in. One of the targets was the depot and railway at Roisel. The first shells had fallen here at 4.30 am, and by 6.20 they were striking the railway with gas, high explosive and shrapnel shells at the rate of six or eight a minute.[14] This effectively cut the railway and caused casualties to those attempting to repair it. The quickest way to empty the depot was now severed, and two railway guns stuck the wrong side of the broken track at Ste Emilie that were abandoned later appeared in a German newsreel with victorious German soldiers posing on the guns.[15]

General Gough at Nesle, in charge of the Fifth Army, heard from his staff:

> All four Corps report heavy bombardment along their front. Third Army report heavy bombardment on about ten miles of the southern part of their front. The French report no bombardment on their front. No signs of any infantry advance as yet. This at once opened my eyes to the magnitude of the attack on Fifth Army ... the whole thin line was involved.[16]

This information was sent to Fifth Army headquarters and sent back to individual divisional commanders as general information was needed at all levels. General Gough rose at 7.30 that morning, issued orders as necessary, and returned to bed as 'the German infantry would not attack for several hours'.[17] The reality of warfare in the Great War was that artillery bombardments lasted for hours and then later the infantry attack started. There are exceptions to this rule, but the idea of surprise attacks was not generally part of the set-up of battle. This also gave the opposing army time to bring reserves up, and this in turn slowed down the battle and any chance of a breakthrough was often lost. The 21

March attack was so overwhelming in its magnitude that this surprise was not going to be an issue. As an army commander there was not much he could do so until the attack began. While General Gough slept the men of the Fifth Army crouched in the trenches, were wounded or killed, and awaited the enemy infantry. In 66th Division the men also crouched in their defences, ready at their battle stations.

The men of the 2/3 East Lancashire Field Ambulance were established at their main dressing station at the sugar beet factory at Bernes, 4 miles south of Roisel. Their orders to 'prepare for battle' was received at 6.10 am, although most of the men were standing to from about 5 o'clock, roused by the magnitude of the bombardment. A walking wounded post was established at Montigny Farm under Captains Bounds and White. Bearer posts were established at sites called after their 'Tommy slang' names: The Egg at Villeret; The Leave Train, also near Villeret; Hussar Post near Ronssoy; Hargicourt Quarry; and Hardy Bank, near Hargicourt. The advanced dressing stations were at Jeancourt and Templeux-le-Grand. The medics sent forward despatch riders on motorcycles to contact the infantry and establish what amount of wounded were to be expected, the mechanical transport drivers (motor ambulances) prepared for duty until word came back with the motorcycle messengers:

> From reports sent down from the Officers in charge of the Advanced Dressing Stations by our motor despatch riders it became plain that the accommodation at the Main Dressing Station would be taxed by the wounded and gas cases to be received, therefore it was considered advisable to evacuate all sick cases to the Corps Rest Station at Doingt and without delay these were all sent forward [back west] to that place by Horse Ambulances.[18]

It did not take long for the first wounded and gas cases to appear and these arrived at about 6.45 am.

The remains of 432 Field Company R.E. were at Hervilly Wood with a small garrison of eight officers and 150 men on the Brown line.

When the infantry attack came at 9 o'clock it was overwhelming. The tactics used by the storm troopers, infiltrating around the British positions, worked most effectively in the fog. The exposed positions on the Cologne ridge were easy targets, being taken in the flanks, and their weak numbers not enough for the onslaught they faced. The 4/ East Lancashire and 2/8th Lancashire Fusiliers were heavily attacked on both flanks. On 66th Division front:

the first waves of the German advance broke through the three trenches of the Forward zone and reached Villeret, the head of a spur behind it, but they were then fired into heavily from the village, now in their rear, and their further progress now checked.[19]

NOTES:

[1] TNA, WO95/3141.

[2] *History of the East Lancashire Regiment*, Liverpool, 1936, p.304.

[3] Latter, J.C., *The Lancashire Fusiliers, 1914–1918*, 1949, pp.288–9.

[4] IWM Department of Documents, Papers of William Sharpe.

[5] Brown, *IWM book of 1918*, pp.46–8.

[6] Anonymous, *A History of the East Lancashire Royal Engineers*, Manchester, 1920, p.239f.

[7] Major W. Beaumont in *Clickety-Click*, Annual Dinner club of 66th Division, 1937, p.30.

[8] IWM Department of Documents, private papers of John Gore.

[9] Edmunds, E., *Official History, 1918*, Vol. I, 1934, p.130.

[10] IWM Department of Documents, private papers of Tom Hardman 84/1/1.

[11] Anonymous, *A History of the East Lancashire Royal Engineers*, Manchester, 1920, p.240.

[12] TNA, WO95/3121.

[13] Potter and Withinshaw, *History of the 2/6 LF*, p.114.

[14] Henniker, A., *Transportation on the Western Front*, p.371.

[15] These I believe are the guns filmed by the Germans 'at Roisel' and available in a Bundesarchive film online.

[16] Gough, *The Fifth Army*, p.260.

[17] ibid, pp.260–1.

[18] Francis, A., *History of the 2/3 East Lancashire Field Ambulance*, Salford (1930) p.93f.

[19] *Official History*, p.179.

Chapter 8

We are Pushing Jerry Back

Thursday, 10 o'clock to Midday

The great majority of the 2/8 Lancashire Fusiliers had been killed or captured but second Lieutenant G.L. Sayer and a few other survivors made their way back and, joining the 6/ Battalion, were of great assistance in defending strongpoints in and near the village of Templeux. Shortly before noon the Germans had captured Sherwood Trench, were working their way past the east of the quarries and were in parts of Templeux itself. While the Germans were now easy targets for the artillery, Major Wike with A and B Companies of 6/ L.F. led a counter-attack. These companies succeeded in clearing the village and establishing a line along its north-eastern face. But the centre was gradually pressed back and fighting took place in the village, the outskirts of which changed hands several times. Finally the Germans managed to turn the left flank of the position and A Company was forced to retire in order to escape being surrounded. It was hoped to make a stand on some high ground at the southern edge of the village, but this was in full view of the enemy, and although the Germans were prevented from coming out of the village in this direction for about twenty minutes, two Lewis gun teams were put out of action and such a concentration of fire brought to bear on the survivors that they were compelled to make a further withdrawal.

The history of the 2/5 East Lancashire Regiment recorded that:

> As the morning wore on the fog began to clear, and the sun finally breaking through about 10 o'clock showed a clear country with casualties streaming back from the font, bringing news of the extent and completeness of the breakthrough. The stories of the wounded were presently confirmed by the appearance of small parties of

Germans on the ridge beyond Templeux-le-Guerrard and these were fought for some time by guns in front of our own front line. The now good visibility rendered the Boche progress apparent, and on its becoming obvious that the enemy had worked round the battalion's right flank, a withdrawal to Templeux-le-Guerrard defences was successfully effected. Lieutenant-Colonel Whitehead departed to report the situation to brigade headquarters at Hervilly, leaving the battalion under the command of Captain J H G Grey, whose cool and courageous bearing on that – and subsequent days – excited the respectful comment not only of the men of his own battalion but those of neighbouring units. He became in his person a rallying point for stragglers, and many were the inquiries for 'that there little Tommy Grey'.[1]

The 2/6 Lancashire Fusiliers on the Brown line moved their headquarters to the roadside. They saw the wounded coming back from the front and recorded:

The fog now began to lift. All this time a steady stream of casualties had been coming down the road from the direction of Templeux. The bombardment appeared to have demolished the front line, and had the front line been thickly held the casualties would have been heavier. From the fact that the bombardment had switched on to ourselves we surmised that the Boche advance had commenced.

By 10.30 a.m. the country was completely clear – it was a beautiful sunny day and as the fog cleared we could see the Boche advance guard on top of the crest of the hill and a German battery coming into action. On our left we could see the enemy advancing in great numbers, almost between ourselves and Epehy; the division on our left had gone too.

We managed to get a battery of 18 pounders onto the gents [sic] on top of Templeux Quarries' ridge and the gunners were able to do great execution, as did a 4.5 Howitzer battery. This battery was at work in front of our line and in full view of the enemy, who continued to come up over the ridge and work away to our left all the morning. Our machine guns had some very good shooting on the left and caused the enemy there to sheer off. This battery was under the command of Major W R Cuncliffe. It fought to the last, keeping the enemy at bay with Lewis guns. Its gun pits were finally rushed by the Prussian Guard, who had been especially brought up for this purpose. Major Cuncliffe was taken prisoner and later awarded the Military Cross for his stand although he deserved a greater honour.[2]

For the Machine Gun Corps there was plenty of work. Lieutenant Colonel Wilfrid Woodcock, in charge of the 66th Battalion MGC, reported later:

> The five extreme forward guns and three others were the only ones that of which I have no definite knowledge of their having been in action, though it is quite probable that they may have been so. Every other gun was in action for a longer or shorter period, some with extremely good targets. Thus the Grand Priel group, four guns, on the right were heard firing for some time after the infantry had been driven back. The Sherwood Group of three, after driving back one attack which reached within 100 yards, were obliterated by hostile artillery and the Bobby Quarry group after firing all their ammunition were withdrawn, the section officer covering their retirement with his revolver, an act of gallantry which cost him his life. In another case, one gun having fired all its ammunition, and all the team, except the gun commander becoming casualties, the N.C.O. destroyed his gun with a mills grenade, escaped and re-joined another gun, coming into action with them.[3]

The machine gunners were often left behind as a rearguard to allow the infantry to withdraw and were often called upon to pay with their lives. At least the foggy conditions allowed men to slip away easily when in good conditions they would have been shot dead.

The 2/5 East Lancashire fought hard all that morning, as recorded by Second Lieutenant V.H. Johnston in this record of C Company under Captain Arthur Emlyn Hopkins written from a PoW camp in Germany to the father of the late Captain Hopkins describing the action:

> The fighting in which your son and myself with my platoon were engaged was very severe and very disastrous to ourselves. As far as I can recollect only three, or at most four, out of thirty came through without being killed or severely wounded. We had a post in the open – a few yards of trench – and were attacked in overwhelming numbers, large numbers of the enemy streaming through on our flanks meanwhile. The Germans had broken through the front line – we were in immediate support – and our post was left behind by the waves of the enemy, like a battered ship, alone, and finally submerged by fresh onslaughts.
>
> We fought for two hours from 10 till noon. Captain Hopkins and I each took charge of a section of trench and carried on with rifle and Lewis-gun fire till there was hardly a man left. About half-way

through the fight, Captain Hopkins came down to me and said he feared he could not go on very much longer as he was wounded in the back and the leg, presumably by machine gun bullets. Nevertheless, with wonderful courage he insisted on carrying on, controlling, directing fire and urging the men like the splendid soldier he showed himself to be. At last when not a single man remained of his party, he himself took a Lewis gun. I was then by his side, getting the other gun into action, and saw what happened.

A bullet struck the gun he was firing and hit him in the lower part of the face. As he sank back he said to me 'Fire the gun Mr Johnston – fire the gun'. The Germans were then swarming upon us from our rear – we were attacked on three sides – and I found myself surrounded. The German Captain was very courteous – professed to be very much concerned to the losses we had suffered, and distinctly promised to do all he could for your son.[4]

Arthur Emlyn Hopkins just was twenty-one years old, the son of a council accountant from Trealaw near Pontypridd in the South Wales valleys. This action earned him his posthumous Military Cross for bravery.

Machine guns were crucial in the defence of the right flank under 24th Division at Le Verguier and this action can be epitomised by the stand of Lance Corporal John Sayer that won him a Victoria Cross with the 8/ Royal West Surrey Regiment. The resistance of a few men at Shepherd's Copse appears to have delayed the Germans considerably and caused large casualties. For this delay meant that the defence of Le Verguier lasted more than a day and night under the direction of Colonel Piers:

For most conspicuous bravery, determination and ability displayed on 21 March, 1918 at Le Verguier, when holding for two hours in the face of incessant attacks the flank of a small isolated post. Owing to mist the enemy approached to within 30 yards before being discovered. Lance Corporal Sayer, however, on his own initiative and without assistance, beat off a succession of flank attacks and inflicted heavy casualties on the enemy. Though attacked by rifle and machine gun fire, bayonet and bombs, he repulsed all attacks, killing many and wounding others. During the whole time he was continuously exposed to rifle and machine gun fire, but he showed the utmost contempt of danger, and his conduct was an inspiration to all. His skilful use of fire of all description enabled the post to hold out until nearly all the garrison had been killed and himself wounded and captured. He subsequently died of wounds at Le Cateau.[5]

The actions of John Sayer would epitomise the stand of 24th Division the first day and night of combat. It appears that his defiance at Shepherd's Copse played a major part in the battle.[6] The direction of the southern thrust on Le Verguier indicates that the Germans had broken through 61st Division to the south of 24th Division and turned north. To the north, though, Sayer and a mixture of units including men of the 11/ Hussars had held them a considerable time. The whole of XIX Corps was caught in a flanking manoeuvre, but it was not to go all the Germans' way though.

The defence of Le Verguier is recorded in the battalion war diary. This was not a front line position, but in the forward zone of the battle zone, in the redoubt line. The original documents were burnt to stop them falling into the hands of the enemy, and written up later when the legend of the defence was already making headlines in *The Times* newspaper. Although we must not doubt the basic facts it appears that some sort of bias may be present. The stand at Shepherd's Copse was isolated from the main defence at Le Verguier and did not come to light until later. Obviously the war diary focuses on events around headquarters and the battle through the eyes of Colonel Piers. It is still strange that the VC is not mentioned in the battalion history.

One of the battalions in corps reserve was 9/ Royal Sussex Regiment of 24th Division, which was at Hancourt. Under Colonel Murray Hill it was ordered into battle positions and was to defend the redoubt line based on the four redoubts: C Company was to defend Trinket redoubt with Captain Saxon, A Company was in Trinity redoubt with Captain Rewell, Upstart redoubt was defended by D Company under Second Lieutenant Bishop, and Triple redoubt was defended by B Company with Lieutenant Surridge. The redoubts had been dug on the night of 19–20 March and only filled with rations and ammunition at midnight before the attack, not only that but some of the trenches were only a foot deep in places. They were supported by the 15th Entrenching Battalion, who dug in front of B Company, Royal Sussex. The march to their battle positions was two hours for the Sussex men, so they were in position just as the attack started on the front line positions. Colonel Hill had been right that there was no hurry for these second line positions. Captain Saxon remembered:

> The Commanding Officer watched us march out. I stopped with him for a minute or two, when he particularly impressed on me the fact that there was no necessity to hurry and that the men should be allowed to take the march up at an easy pace.

As we neared Hervilly we again saw the C.O. who told us that the village was then fairly free from gas. We were then moving sections and passed safely through Hervilly. As we passed along the sunken portion of the road between that village Hesbécourt shells began to fall round us, a few men of the company, on their section commanders order, got up on the top and two or three were wounded before they could be brought down again – not a shell fell in the road. We passed Triple redoubt just as Pullinger's platoon reached it.[7]

The Sussex battalion commanders had reconnoitred the positions the day before and must have advanced with a sinking feeling in their stomachs that the position was untenable and badly prepared. This advance march by the Sussex men was not done without casualties to B and D Battalions as they encountered shell fire. The lack of structure to the redoubts was a serious error by the British, as elsewhere on the front, well-constructed redoubts held on for more than twenty-four hours and held up the Germans considerably, as highlighted by the famous defence of Manchester Hill near St Quentin by Lieutenant Colonel Elstob VC. Most of the men of the Sussex Battalion were engaged in training behind the lines and while they supplied working parties the work was not strenuous and they 'had a glorious 18 days in Hancourt' and spent most of their time on the rifle ranges. The East Lancashire Division had just suffered from having too little time to do too much work. In this sector though, a brave defence was to be made by the Sussex men with elements of 66th Division and XIX Corps.

The reserve battalions had been ordered into their battle positions. At 9.45 am headquarters still awaited information. Runners had been sent out to get information and 199 Brigade reported that the situation was unchanged. Neill Malcolm was totally unaware of the situation in the front line trenches and assumed that as he heard no rifle fire from this direction that no infantry assault had occurred yet, when in fact it was already over and the battle for the outpost line finished. The artillery slackened their fire to conserve shells. This and the break in communications was very damaging, and General Malcolm resorted to sending out his staff officers on horseback or with any means available to gather information, vital to any commander. All he had for the first three hours of the attack was a communications blackout achieved by the German artillery that was instantaneous in its completeness. All he could do was send forward his reserves to the second line and wait to be attacked, and hope the picture would improve.

At Templeux Le Guerard were two companies (A and D) of the 2/6 Lancashire Fusiliers under Major Wilke. The Germans were in the village so a quick counter-attack was organised and the Germans briefly pushed out, but then the British were forced to retire to a sunken road.

At 10.20 am 199 Brigade headquarters was informed by division that an attack had developed in the adjoining Irish Division but not on their own front. The situation was obscure due to the mist. By 10.30 am it was all over in the forward line; all the soldiers were either dead or prisoners of war. Relying on what they heard from the front gave headquarters no idea of what was actually happening; above the tumult of the guns not much could be heard [see map 6].

Gunner John Gore was in the rear areas and although they were told to get all papers and maps ready for burning, there appeared to be no haste. The roads were full of wounded in ambulances and those able to walk, filing back. John and his mortar team made them tea.

> Met a Captain with blackened face, torn tunic, one puttee gone and a trouser leg in ribbons. He said 'It is all right, we are pushing Jerry back.' Later Brigadier Cartwright came down, he had had his jaw tied up and tried to mumble to us as best he could with what appeared to a broken jaw, that Jerry was advancing and that all our battery except four were killed or captured. Corporal Dakin was taken prisoner. The divisional losses were very heavy. After tea Clarke and self burnt all the maps and papers behind the barn … later Jerry started to shell Hervilly. All the huts were shelled and set on fire including officers huts and mess. Later somebody got a GS wagon and we put on it our kits and one blanket per man and marched behind the wagon to Nobescourt where we slept in a large hut by an ammunition dump.

The varied reports of the fighting and the stiff resistance meted out by the front line forces come across in some of the reports.

Life behind the lines was dicey, but for those going forward to meet the German attack it was much worse. Ralph Frost was among the 2/7 Manchester Regiment moving up to the front under Lieutenant Colonel Gell, the charismatic colonel who had served in the Worcestershire Yeomanry in the Boer War as a chaplain trooper and who was the vicar of Corsham in Wiltshire. In 1915 he took off his dog collar and took a commission in the Royal Fusiliers, where he was soon promoted to captain and then major, commanding the 2/7 Lancashire Fusiliers battalion in 1917. Frost remembered:

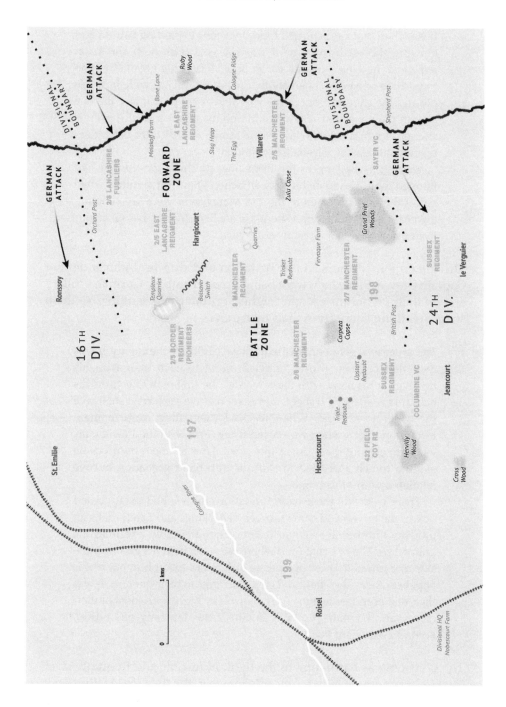

Map 6: The 66th Division front, 21 March 1918.

It was then that I was buried twice by shells exploding behind and blowing the earth over me. I was released with help and I can remember hearing someone say 'poor old Frosty has got one', but no I was all in one piece. I had another lucky escape, we were in single file and the chap in front of me was almost cut in half and the one behind me beheaded. They would only be about a yard from me, strange as it may seem, I did not feel afraid. Shortly after, our officer Lieutenant Beasley was badly wounded.

We still carried on to the front line, by this time the fog had thinned a bit. I should think we marched about three miles, when out of the mist five men of the 2/5 Manchester were seen coming towards us shouting 'don't shoot, we are British, Jerry has taken our front line and we are the only survivors'.

These men joined the Seventh Battalion and dug in under orders of Captain Brown. Since they were being fired on both by German artillery and by their own guns on open sights, a runner was sent to give them some breathing space from their own guns.

The order was given not to fire until we could see the enemy. It was then that Captain Brown crawled along to each man with his revolver in his hand with these words; 'the first man that turns his back on the enemy, I'll shoot, and as soon as we see Jerry, I shall give the order to charge'. When we saw them they were in mass formation, that's when we started firing, and with the Lewis guns we were cutting them down like corn. After a time a patrol came along a trench and tried to shift us with hand grenades, but we retaliated with Mills bombs.

There were still these mass formations but we had them pinned down, then overhead came thirteen aeroplanes and I said that's an unlucky number, we've had it now. They flew low and machine gunned us. The one that fired where we were, held his gun over the side and grinned, three of us were ordered to fire at him but it was hopeless. Away they flew and gave the range to their gunners, it was then that both Lewis guns were blown sky high, with most of their crews, and Captain Brown was killed, this left only one officer, Second Lieutenant Fox.[8]

The division was hardening to the fight, in resolve and in numbers; at least for the moment it had some advantage in the defence. At divisional headquarters Major General Malcolm heard about the stragglers of the 2/5 Manchesters breaking out. It was 199 Brigade that reported the line at Villeret had been penetrated and the Germans were attacking the battalion headquarters of the 2/5 Manchester at The Egg from the rear.

> The extent of the penetration was unknown, but efforts were being made to keep the Battle zone clear of the enemy. Lieutenant-Colonel Maxwell and thirty men had succeeded in cutting their way back through the enemy and fighting was still in progress.

In the forward areas pioneers and sappers all took up arms to defend their posts. At Hargicourt the Engineers under Captain William Beaumont had fought all morning in their banked enclosure with further expertise given by an infantry captain of the Manchester Regiment:

> The enemy got through on the left and used their machine guns on the position from the rear, and our own shells were also dropping on the spot, but when the mist rose and the enemy could be seen driving in the line on the right flank, the infantry Captain decided to defend a trench about three hundred yards behind. Many men had been killed, but they must have done a lot of damage to the Boche. It was the first time that many of the sappers had really had a chance of getting their own back, and they were as happy as sand boys [sic] and full of fun, although at the time it didn't seem likely that they would ever get out of the place. The infantry Captain who was the last to leave the enclosure was killed by a hand grenade.[9]

Also a casualty was William Beaumont, who reckoned the captain felt his time was up:

> The Captain had been queer and listless all morning and I could not get him to come out with the others. By this time we were the last left in, and the Boche had got up on the banks. He and I got hit by a hand grenade, which killed him and wounded me in the arm and head. Before I could get up the Boche were on top of me, and one was just going to shoot me with a revolver when an NCO pulled his arm and said 'Nein, Nein, Offizier, Offizier'. He took me to his Captain, who was a very decent chap, and sent for a Red Cross man to do me up. I took him into my elephant [shelter] and shared the remains of a bottle of whisky with him. Drinking first I said 'After the manner of the middle ages, to show it isn't poisoned.[10]

And so the fighting was over for Captain Beaumont.

This was how it played out: officers were lucky to be taken prisoner, other ranks were likely to be shot out of hand. By now word was trickling back to headquarters that the front line in the region of The Egg was taken, but it took until 11.30 am for 198 Brigade to hear this.

For Colonel Lloyd with the 9/Manchesters in the Hargicourt switch, the fact that the front lines had fallen became quickly apparent:

> A large group of stragglers, composed of all units, were now seen making their way up the valley. These were collected, divided into sections and allotted various sectors of defence – but chiefly to act as a reserve for counter-attack or in case of necessity.
>
> Stragglers from the forward zone arrived from all units. They were utilised to hold localities but not being of any particular unit and under strange officers did not do much good until they realised the necessity of the general situation.
>
> Stragglers were collected and under officers who had come in from the front line were ordered to take up position in Hesbécourt Switch.[11]

Behind the British lines dressing stations became full to capacity, the wounded had come in all morning, starting at 6.45 am and continuing throughout the day. The counter-attack of the Lancashire Fusiliers had bought time for the medics to continue their work. Sergeant Alfred Francis recorded the situation for the medics at the dressing station:

> Although shells were falling all round the station the men seemed to acclimatise themselves to danger, and though they were constantly doubling in and out with stretcher cases, in some miraculous way they escaped without hurt of serious nature. The self-sacrificing work performed by the bearers was beyond praise.

However, the counter-attack brought retaliation from the German batteries:

> Between noon and one o'clock the neighbourhood of Templeux Advanced Dressing Station was so heavily shelled that it became impossible to maintain communication with the Battalion Medical officers in the Forward area, and to enable the wounded to be efficiently treated the medical officers of the 5th Border, 4th East Lancashire and 2/5 East Lancashire were compelled to fall back to this ADS.[12]

Further down the Cologne valley the hutments of the 281st Army Troops Royal Engineers were also bombarded. 'At noon troops shelled out of their camps. Orders from Commander of Engineers to move to Doingt … Bicycle shed destroyed by shell fire, two motorcycle combination sets destroyed along with three push bikes.'[13] It seems they were lucky to get away with only these few material casualties. Some of the cavalry units nearby were not so lucky and the Hussars lost eleven horses in the bombardment.

It was not only the Germans who could retaliate; as soon as the commanders were sure that the Germans were in possession of Hargicourt the village and the valleys around were soaked with almost all the division's remaining gas shells, around 2,000 in all. Now as late morning came and the mist was starting to lift, British aeroplanes were able to get up and spot for the British artillery.

It was time to prepare for the fight for the battle zone, the main line of redoubts established as the Red line. Some troops made it out of the forward positions. As late as 2 o'clock that afternoon one company under Captain Cooper of the 4/ East Lancashire withdrew fighting to the Red line. Major Paddock, the second in command, had a detail of about fifty men; the survivors of the battalion then numbered three officers and ninety other ranks. In the former front line trenches of 4/ East Lancashire and 2/8 Lancashire Fusiliers the battle was over, quiet now restored, many dead lay around; fewer and farther between were the prisoners, who were escorted to the rear. It was like a charnel house.

NOTES:
[1] *History of the East Lancashire Regiment*, Liverpool, 1936, p.305.
[2] Potter and Withinshaw, *History of the 2/6 LF*, p.114.
[3] National Archives, WO95/3121.
[4] *History of the East Lancashire Regiment*, Liverpool, 1936, pp.305–6.
[5] *The London Gazette*, 9 June 1919 (It is worth noting that this VC was gazetted the same day as Colonel Elstob).
[6] Murland J., *Retreat and Rearguard – Somme 1918*, p.81f.
[7] TNA, WO95/2219, Royal Sussex Regiment.
[8] IWM Department of Documents, papers of R.C.A. Frost.
[9] Anonymous, *History of the East Lancashire Royal Engineers*, p.240.
[10] *Clickety-Click*, The 66th. No. 14 (1937), p.31.
[11] TNA, WO95/3121.
[12] Francis, A., *History of the 2/3rd East Lancashire Field Ambulance*, p.94f.
[13] TNA, WO95/547.

Chapter 9

Johnny's Coming!

Thursday midday to midnight

Up to this point the battle had been fought by infantry and artillery. This was about to change as the reserve elements of the British defence were brought into play. Where were the crucial reserves? The reinforcements that were so urgently needed were still far away. Now that the battle had some element of open warfare about it, cavalry was needed. Horse cavalry was attached to the division in the form of 2nd Cavalry Brigade and was being concentrated in Roisel. The remainder of 2nd Cavalry (Pioneer battalion) remained at Hervilly with 198 Brigade.

At 12.30 pm it was reported that the enemy was in possession of Ronssoy on 197 Brigade front and hence that Malcolm's left flank had been turned. The result of this loss of cohesion of the front was to imperil the Red line defences and Neill Malcolm lost no time in calling down the whole of the Red line barrage to cause as much destruction to the Germans there as possible. This may have caused considerable damage to the advancing German forces but what was not known was how far the Germans had penetrated in force. The reserves were deploying and to add to the forces in the line the Pioneer Company, the 2/5th Border Regiment, was alerted to be at disposal of 197 Infantry Brigade, under Brigadier General Oswald Borrett.

Major Rigg and the Border Regiment were becoming embroiled in the fighting; a Captain Feetham wrote to Colonel Little after the war.

> The first idea we had as to the advance was through machine gun fire directed into the quarries from Ronssoy direction, this would be about 10.45 a.m. You will remember there were four posts in that long stretch of Sherwood trench. Well the Boche managed to get into

the trench unseen – a perfectly easy job owing to the fog – and commenced mopping them up. He then moved on round to the posts on the right and did the same. At about 11.30 the fog cleared somewhat and from the top of the Slag Heap we could see what had happened. Graham was still holding the Horseshoe and we were also holding the ground on the right of the Quarries close to the tunnel entrance. The Sherwood Trench and all the other posts had gone, and the Boche was well in possession of Lempire ridge – Hargicourt valley and Bolsolver Switch and was attacking in force towards Fervaque Farm. The barrage had lifted off us and we could move about although sniping and machine gun fire was very heavy and likewise our casualties. The Boche left us in this position and sweeping round attacked Templeux village, this was about noon. A counter-attack followed but he had complete possession by about 2 p.m. I got this information from Roberts (Medical Officer) who stayed with the wounded and saw the whole battle for the village.[1]

The 527 men of the 15th Hussars were split between a working party who were digging trenches in the Brown line and their mounted component who were back at Le Mesnil, south-east of Péronne. At 07.45 the cavalry were brought to readiness, packed and ready to move, but they were held while the men and horses were fed. The horses of the working party were sent up to them at Vendelles, just north of the Roman road from Amiens to Brie, whilst the men would rally at Roisel, only leaving for that place at 12.55 in the afternoon.

The Germans under Von der Marwitz had attacked the Fifth Army with thirteen divisions with reserves of four divisions against five divisions of the XIX and VII Corps with one division in support and the equivalent of a brigade in the form of the 2nd Cavalry Division. The Germans were well resourced and their reserves were close, those of the British XIX Corps were only the 50th (Northumbrian) and 20th (Light) Divisions. These were more than a day away and could not be brought up until 23 March. Until then 66th Division and its neighbours were on their own. The Germans reckoned that the scale of the attack would drive the British back to the line of the Somme and Crozat Canal to the south by the end of the first day, a belief that was to be overturned by the resolve of the British soldiers. But troubling news was filtering through to Gough's headquarters about the northern flank of 66th Division, which was being turned. Gough needed reinforcements, and he had got them, with the agreement of General Haig; they were still incredibly up to three days away. Gough had ordered the reinforcing divisions to move that morning by telephone. For the moment he was not able to counter-attack, that would have to wait. He had to delay the enemy advance as much as possible. All he had at his disposal were his front line infantry divisions, a cavalry division and a tank battalion.

In the lines of the 2/6 Lancashire Fusiliers there was plenty of determination for the fight and a counter-attack was begun:

> No more movement occurred until 12 noon when it was determined that the time for a counter-attack had arrived. This was urged by the Officer Commanding of the 4.5 Howitzer battery, as he wished to get his guns away. Accordingly we set off to get at the Hun at about 12.30 to 1 o'clock. Two Companies, B and D, were in the front line with C in support. [Our] A Company was on detached duty at Templeux. We had considerable support from our faithful 18 pounder battery and of course the 4.5 Battery in front, and somewhat to my surprise the attack was quite successful although we had a number of casualties.

Gordon MacReady wrote after the war: 'It seemed, however, that insufficient attention had been paid to the reports previously received of an imminent attack on this front, and reserves, scant as they were at this time, were not correctly located.'[2] MacReady skirts the issue of reserves in his autobiography but hints that the reserves were not well managed and could have had an earlier decisive effect if managed better by General Headquarters, who were lacking in foresight.

MacReady, a sapper in the army before the war, was mobilised in 1914 and saw action at Le Cateau, where after sleeping behind a wall a mile behind the front at Nery woke with German Ulhans all about. This was the famous incident of L Battery, Royal Horse Artillery, which won it two Victoria Crosses.[3] Luckily for MacReady the war mostly settled down after that and he held a series of exciting posts testing dangerous prototype guns and setting up the expanding Royal Flying Corps. He was soon offered a position on the staff of 55th (West Lancashire) Division, with which he served for twenty-two months. He then gained a position on the staff of the East Lancashire Division.

To the north of 66th Division the 16th (Irish) Division was in a bad way. Part of Congreve's VII Corps, it also faced the bulk of the German attack. General Gough had ordered that the front line be held strongly, against the objections of Major General Hull, with the result that the front line battalions suffered very heavily in the initial bombardment. This and the resultant German breakthrough led to the flanks being turned and the back areas of the Irish being taken before the front line redoubts had fallen. By clever use of the valleys and fog the Germans funnelled troops through to where they were least expected. It was in the valley on the southern flank of the Irish where it bordered the East Lancashire Division that the Germans made most progress, coming up to the Irish battle zone defences before the defenders realised they had arrived. They penetrated at the spot to the north of the East Lancashires that was hardest to defend and this is how the flank of 66th Division was turned.

The Irish were rapidly being destroyed:

> The enemy attack was pushed northwards so as to roll up the front of the Irish division; posts in a wood to the north of Ronssoy and a factory just to the west of the village were held by 1 o'clock. A counter-attack by two battalions of the 47 Brigade, in reserve, was ordered but subsequently cancelled by divisional headquarters. This order did not reach the 6/ Connaught Rangers in time. This battalion, with two tanks, moved forward towards Ronssoy about 1.30 p.m. There was no artillery to support it, the field batteries nearby having been captured or being engaged in trying to bring out the guns under machine gun fire, thus worried by low flying aeroplanes and receiving heavy enfilade fire from the right, the counter-attack failed.[4]

This enabled the Germans to roll up the front of the Irish Division and turn south as well, rolling up the flank of the East Lancashire Division and gaining a penetration in the valley of the Cologne river, threatening the depot at Roisel, and protected by the high downs either side.

The position by noon that seemed less than desperate in the East Lancashire Division was threatened by the fall of its northern neighbour, rent like a tear in a piece of paper. This is when General Gough sensed a greater problem of his own making. The difference in situation was extreme when compared to that of 21st Division north of the Irish, where the initial German attack failed. This appears to have been the result of the closeness of the battle zone to the forward zone, so at least somewhere on this front there were adequate defences, with machine guns sited to take full advantage of the terrain. This is worth noting as evidence that it was the site and quality of the defences that were important not just the overwhelming nature of the attack. The lie of the land had enormous effect on the defence, sometimes to British advantage, others to that of the attacking Germans.

The battle to the north was pushing the Irish Division back but it was defending stoutly where it could. The Official History describes the fight put up by Hull's Irish Division:

The Germans, having gained a footing in the upper part of the Cologne valley in the front of the Battle zone of the 66th Division had proceeded by about 10 o'clock to envelope the defences of Ronssoy from the south west, south and south east. By 11.30 they had forced an entry and shortly after noon had gained possession of the village, although some posts held out until the evening, by which time all the men of the Fusiliers had been killed or captured.[5]

Major General Malcolm at Nobescourt farm was confident at this point that the Germans were being slowed down. The infantry battle was continuing and although his northern flank was threatened his battle zone was coherent, if only it had been built more competently, for as we have noted the wire was good but the trenches were inadequate. His major problem was lack of communications and his ability to control the battle. He sent one of his staff, Lieutenant Colonel Gordon MacReady, on horseback with his orderly on a motorbike, to a front line brigade headquarters, quite probably that of 197 Brigade. MacReady remembered:

> The Division, like others on the flanks, was holding a frontage at least twice as broad as it could hope to defend successfully against a determined attack, and there were no reserve Divisions in the immediate vicinity.
>
> At daybreak a heavy bombardment started. Communications were soon disrupted and I rode off to one of the brigade headquarters to ascertain the situation. Losing myself several times in the fog I eventually reached my destination which was in a state of some confusion. Parties of men were straggling in, saying that the Germans had broken through, but no one was sure where they were, or where our front, if any, now was.
>
> I left the Brigadier sorting out his troops as best he could, and manning a rear line of defence, and started back to divisional headquarters. I soon found that the enemy had in fact broken through very deeply, and with my Irish orderly had to do a great deal of circuitous galloping to get round the enemy machine guns which were already some hundreds of yards behind Brigade H.Q.[6]

The red tabs of staff officers on cavalry mounts and motorcycle messengers were riding around the battlefield trying to find out what was happening in the thinning fog, without care they would easily be captured or killed.

Tanks were also on their way to reinforce 66th and 24th Divisions in the form of 5th Battalion Royal Tank Corps (formerly E Battalion). This battalion was to be split between Hervilly and Nobescourt Farm. This much needed armoured support consisted of up to thirty-six tanks and three support tenders from the 5th Tank Battalion. The 9th Cavalry Brigade, with the 15th (King's Own) and 19th Hussars, 1/1 Bedford Yeomanry, Y Battery Royal Horse Artillery and 9th Cavalry Machine Gun Squadron were also on their way.

Captain H. Saxon of 9/ Sussex Battalion was in place with his eighty men in Trinket redoubt, where they had been since 9.15 that morning. As corps troops they were now in the East Lancashire Division area of operations, digging in as best they could:

The redoubt had been made from part of an existing partly dug trench line. It lay across a small road leading from Hesbécourt to Hargicourt, just on the reverse slope of the highest ground which this road crosses before it drops down to L.10.a [map reference]. It allowed a field of fire to the immediate front of about a dozen yards beyond the wire, I have noticed that the men always disliked such positions. It was very strongly wired in front, which was undoubtedly all that had been considered when the original trench was marked out. There was a partly completed 'single apron' on the right front but no wire on the remainder of the right or on the rear or left flank. Only in one small portion was the trench so much as a yard deep. There was a supply of small arms ammunition, bombs and rifle grenades, iron rations and water. We had nearly two hours digging before we heard any news from the front. The mist began to clear before 11 a.m. and the sun to shine through.

Shortly after the mist lifted sergeant Greenfield was on lookout, came back waving his rifle cheering, and calling 'Johnny's coming'. Sergeant Greenfield was always a fighting man!

Soon after Greenfield's warning men of the 2/6 Manchesters began to fall back through us, these men were not in touch with the enemy, two platoons under their company commander Captain Collier afterwards came forward again and joined us, holding the right front of the redoubt – they fought splendidly to the end, staying with us when the rest of their battalion retired from Carpeza Copse.

Before noon we could see the Boche advancing in large numbers from the direction of Cote Wood. There was no sound of machine gun or rifle fire being used against them and as they advanced there was no sign of resistance. I was informed by an officer of 66th

Division that the main line of the defence in Hargicourt had not been manned – this was later confirmed by another officer. The only artillery directed against the enemy visible to us came from a field battery a short distance to our right rear (this battery or at first two and later one gun remained firing at the Boche while they advanced along Fervaque Farm ridge).

The artillery battery was the remnants of 330 battery Royal Field Artillery under the command of Major Cuncliffe. Tom Hardman was in the divisional ammunition column at Templeux. His short letter to his wife said succinctly: 'It is so rumoured that our line has been pierced and Germans are at Templeux. We are standing to, expecting to have to hop it.'[7]

At Nobescourt Farm, Major General Malcolm was receiving more urgent messages that confirmed the fall of the forward zone and the danger on the left flank. At 12.16 that afternoon Bobby Quarry and the Priel Woods was confirmed as having fallen and 16th Division confirmed that Ronssoy had been lost. It was hoped that Irish troops who had the advantage of underground dugouts were still holding out. While the left was causing concern the right was not unfavourable as the confident defenders of Le Verguier were holding out. The Germans were working around the west of Fervaque Farm, as seen by the Sussex defenders of the redoubt. Indeed, they saw and heard the last stand of Fervaque Farm. 'We heard the sound of Boche machine guns from Fervaque Farm and for about ten minutes [British] Lewis Guns and bombs, then silence from the farm.' The men of the 2/7th Manchester Regiment in Grand Priel Woods had ordered up their reserve company to reinforce their right flank, which was obviously under pressure. The 199 Brigade had similarly ordered up a company reinforcement of 2/6th Manchester Regiment from brigade reserve.

The Irish to the north had lost their battle zone already, so Malcolm's flank had to conform to this loss. On Malcolm's left the enemy were in Sherwood Trench near Templeux quarries. It was obvious at headquarters that the thrust of the German assault was against the valley of the Cologne river, with a bridgehead on either side of this valley.

While Ronssoy was being captured from the south, a very severe struggle was raging in and around L'Empire, on the top of the ridge around Ronssoy, where there was practically no break between the houses forming the two villages. The front line of the Battle zone formed a sharp Salient round Lempire, so that the garrison of 2/

Irish, exposed to attack on three sides was eventually cut off by the fall of Ronssoy and the wood nearby. After a desperate fight, most of the battalion was killed or captured but the enemy was not able to establish himself in Lempire until towards 2 o'clock.

Between the Lempire defences and those of Malasisse Farm, about one mile to the north west, the enemy gained a footing at some points in the Battle zone between 10 and 11 o'clock, and the farm held by the 2/ Royal Dublin Fusiliers was captured about 11. Local counter-attacks were then delivered and it was not until nearly two o'clock that this line of defence was lost. The front between Malasisse Farm and the left of the division held out much longer.[8]

On the right flank the German attack was remembered by Malcolm:

> The attack around Fervaque Farm appeared irresolute and disorganised.

German losses caused by several important actions nearby may have contributed to this disorganisation of command around Fervaque Farm, where the German advance seems to have slowed. However, to the left the

> attack was gaining ground on both sides of the valley and its success on the high ground of the north of the river around F.25 [map reference to the North West of Templeux] was directly threatening the communications of our Templeux defences.[9]

The situation was potentially critical with such a breakthrough to Malcolm's left flank and Watts at Corps HQ quickly allotted him cavalry reserves. The 200 men of 15th Hussars and two machine guns were to be given to Malcolm to stem the tide on the left and brought up to readiness about a mile behind Templeux Woods. This appears to be a small but potent reinforcement, but this was all that was available so soon in the afternoon. The remainder of 2nd Cavalry Brigade was kept at Hervilly to be used should the situation worsen.

At 12.25 it was reported that the stand made by Captain William Beaumont and his men was over and the Hankey quarries that they held had fallen. A quick order was given for a barrage on this area as the men were presumed dead or captured. At this same moment, the 9th Manchesters were driven out of Higson quarries nearby. This meant the end of resistance in the centre of 66th Division's defences. It was a matter now of holding the Hargicourt Switch and the battle zone where the Sussex Regiment had been viewing the last survivors of the fighting pulling out:

> It was at the appearance of the Boche that the spirit of the men seemed to break through their Sussex reserve, a spirit that remained in evidence throughout the next 24 hours. They were in the best of spirits and seemed delighted that they had not marched up there without cause. I was continually greeted with the remark that 'my' push seemed to have come. Within half an hour of our first sight of the Boche we heard a Lewis firing and later saw two men retiring and occasionally stopping to fire, this gun belonged to the Manchesters and was the only form of resistance we saw offered forward of our position, they retired to our left, shouting a cheery message that it was 'all right'.[10]

Several hours later the Sussex Regiment was involved in the fight for the battle zone; Colonel Hill's men were on the front line as the Lancashire men in the front lines were dead or prisoners, some few had pulled back through the battle zone to reorganise. Some fighting details such as that under Captain Collier joined forces with the reserve forces. They were then shelled heavily by German 5.9in howitzers with the intention of destroying the wire. At least they had had time to dig in.

At 12.37 the silent battery in Roisel was given the order to commence firing so another twenty heavy guns entered the battle. This provided cover for the other batteries to continue retiring as they were disposed close to the front and were vulnerable to the German infiltration.

At one o'clock news came through to the walking wounded post at Montigny Farm that the flanks had been turned, threatening the advanced dressing station at Templeux. Montigny Farm was located just to the south of Jeancourt Station to the east of Nobescourt Farm. The medical team at the Templeux dressing station battled on with saving the wounded, but back at headquarters it was decided that the doctors there should not be imperilled and Captain Bounds was sent forward to bring back Captains Berry and Chapman to the reserve dressing station at a crossroads between Roisel, Hesbécourt and Templeux, behind the redoubt line.

> The journey of Captain Bounds and the Transport men who accompanied him is one that is not likely to be forgotten by any of the party, for over shell swept roads they passed through an almost continuous barrage. Arriving in the ADS at a few minutes after 3 pm they could see small parties of the enemy advancing over the high

ground of the quarries. The work of loading up the wagons with medical stores and equipment was done in a time never previously approached on parade ground practices, and we have since been told by one of our men who was taken prisoner that as the Transport officers and 20 stretcher bearers got away at 3.20 pm from one side of the ADS the enemy entered on the other side and captured eight men who unfortunately were unable to escape. For this work Captain Bounds was awarded the Military Cross.[11]

The battle zone was becoming increasingly unhealthy for all troops as the German forces pushed forward now that the forward zone had fallen. In the south the main forces of 24th Division were still offering heavy resistance in the well-built defences of Le Verguier. In the north the position of 16th Irish Division was becoming untenable and the East Lancashire Division was falling back to the redoubt line to begin the second stage of the defence.

Fifth Army commander General Gough received somewhat tentative reports from his corps commanders, which he sent on directly to General Haig at Montreuil. He told his corps commanders to fight a delaying action without committing to a decisive struggle for any one particular position. Gough then set off on a 60-mile round trip to visit to his corps commanders, starting with his new corps commander Butler in the south, then a confident Maxse, and then to Watts where he learnt that the situation was serious as the two under-strength divisions were in difficulty. Gough's advice to Watts was to hold on to the defence in the centre where the Le Verguier defences and redoubt positions were offering steady resistance, while bending back his left to allow for the breakthrough at the border of the East Lancashire and Irish Divisions. The 50th (Northumbrian) Division was being brought up as reserve to Watts' XIX Corps. On Congreve's front, except for the loss of Ronssoy, the situation was 'very satisfactory' as the 21st and 9th Divisions were giving good resistance. The 39th Division was being brought up to bring reserves to the VII corps of Congreve. Gough was back at his headquarters by supper time, although he does not state when this was; he was always in intermittent telephone contact with the other corps commanders.

Gough had acted quickly in getting 50th (Northumbrian) Division at readiness. Such was the effectiveness of this action that the 50th was brought up by train from near Villers-Bretonneux to Boucly, west of Roisel, by trains via Péronne (usually around twelve trains were required for a division) much more quickly than was expected. Advance elements of this division were arriving by the evening of 21 March.

Ralph Frost and the 2/7 Manchesters had been fighting the Germans all day and had managed to pin down the attackers, despite being machine gunned by aircraft and attacked by massed formations of Germans. They were aided by the field artillery: 'It was the close range fire of B battery, 330 Brigade, Royal Field Artillery, which beat off all attacks.'[12]

A small part of the battalion under Captain E.A. Smirke succeeded in breaking through and, thanks to cool leadership and disregard of the dangers, made its way back to the crossroads to the south-west of Templeux, where it attached itself to the 6/ Battalion. However, the order to retire did not reach most of the men, who made no attempt to escape and surrendered at about 5 o'clock. Ralph Frost was among those who held on all day:

> I must have led a charmed life, for a bullet went through the left sleeve of my tunic, on a level with my heart without so much as scratching me. Round about 5 p.m. we retreated about 100 yards to a small quarry, but the end was near, for all our bombs had gone and we were down to fifteen rounds between us. Second Lieutenant Fox, a corporal and fifteen men were all that remained of our company. Fox was wounded. It wasn't long before Fritz surrounded us … I will never know why he did not wipe us out, our corporal wanted us to fight it out, but we told him in no uncertain terms that he would be shot unless he surrendered. My first thought when Jerry came right in was will he shoot us or use the bayonet and then I said 'I shouldn't get that parcel from home' as I had received a letter to say there was a parcel on the way. There were only 16 men and one wounded officer left of A company. I grabbed my water bottle which was full of rum, which I had been saving in case I was cut off at any time.[13]

For the men of B battery and the Manchesters capture was inevitable as they were surrounded. Ralph Frost survived until the Armistice and was demobilised in March 1919.

Captain Feetham and the Border Regiment Pioneers were still holding on:

> Sniping was very heavy from all sides and he also brought up trench mortars. We did a lot of good shooting in return from the top of the quarries until about 3 p.m. when a battery of our own 18 pounders started shelling us in horseshoe trench [and] we had a lot of casualties from these guns. The Boche got into the quarries at about 3.30 p.m. and they attacked Graham from the rear, he fought until 4 o'clock when he was obliged to give in having practically no men left.

German troops on the move during the Kaiser's Offensive in March 1918. (US Library of Congress)

Two of the key commanders of the March Offensive – the German Chief of the General Staff, Paul von Hindenburg, on the left, and his deputy, General Erich Ludendorff. (US Library of Congress)

An abandoned British trench which was captured by the Germans; in the background, German soldiers on horseback view the scene. (US Library of Congress)

Above left: General Herbert Lawrence. (Bury Fusilier Museum) Above right: General Neill Malcolm. (Bury Fusilier Museum)

Below left: Ralph Frost. (IWM). Below right: Colonel William B. Little. (LWC)

Above: Norman Dunkerley (seated far right) and his colleagues in Malta. (IWM)

Above: An ammunition dump burns as British troops hastily pull back to new positions in the face of the German onslaught. (Historic Military Press)

Private Thomas N. Booty (back row, second from the left) and his squad at Colchester. Few of these lads would have survived the fighting in 1918. (Joan Marshall)

Above: The problems of the railway bridge at Péronne; repaired by the French in 1918, blown up in March 1918, the trestle to the left is a 1918 German bridge, that to the right a later British one. (IWM)

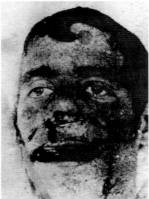

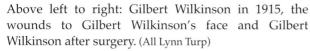

Above left to right: Gilbert Wilkinson in 1915, the wounds to Gilbert Wilkinson's face and Gilbert Wilkinson after surgery. (All Lynn Turp)

Right: Gilbert Wilkinson showing his better side. (Lynn Turp)

Below: A wounded soldier of the British 66th Division helped through the streets of Péronne after returning from the Battle of St Quentin during the German Spring Offensive, 23 March 1918. (IWM)

Below right: General Hugh Bethell. (Bury Fusilier Museum)

Captain Potter, General H. Lawrence and the Curée of Passchendaele at the 1928
Passchendaele ceremony. (Bury Fusilier Museum)

 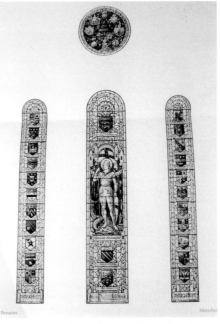

Above left: The unveiling of the Passchendaele memorial window in Passchendaele
Church. (Bury Fusilier Museum). Above right: The detail of the Passchendaele memorial
window. (Bury Fusilier Museum)

Above: The dedication of the Le Cateau Memorial. (Bury Fusilier Museum)
Below: Buglers alongside the Le Cateau Memorial. (Bury Fusilier Museum)

IN MEMORY OF THOSE OF THE 66TH DIVISION
OF THE BRITISH EXPEDITIONARY FORCE
WHO FELL IN THE LIBERATION OF LE CATEAU
FROM GERMAN OCCUPATION IN OCTOBER 1918

Above: The hole that failed at Rastatt. (Bury Fusilier Museum)

Below: The Midland Hotel Manchester circa 1905. (Mary Evans Picture Library)

Just at this time I saw the Officer Commanding of the Lancashire
Fusiliers and we considered the situation, we had only fifty men left
and over 200 wounded in the tunnel and all but one of the entrances
had fallen, we gave in about 4.30 p.m.

The 6/ Battalion, strengthened by Captain Smirke and his men, held a
position on the outskirts of Templeux. The village fell at 6 o'clock that
evening. The German advance had halted that afternoon, but came on
again and they crept into the village. In the Brown line Peter Hall was
quickly overrun, but he found the experience of being a prisoner of war
a short one as he was able to escape, only to be recaptured until the
Germans were not able to keep tabs on their prisoners in the mist and
shell fire. There must have been a large number of such waifs and strays
across the changing battlefield.

I took a chance again as we approached a small hill on our left, ran
to the other side of this hill, found the main body of 5th Manchesters
and persuaded them to ambush the Germans, take them prisoner
and release our men. Then they told us where the main body of the
6th Manchesters were so we caught up with them just before they
reached Péronne.[14]

The cavalry was at last within striking distance of the front and at 4.15
pm the horses and men of 9th Cavalry Brigade were brought forward
to hold the Brown line. By early evening the tanks of 5th Battalion,
Royal Tank Regiment were starting to reach the front. In this case four
tanks of 13 Company arrived at Nobescourt Farm and Smallfoot Farm,
the headquarters of 66th and 24th Divisions. The rest of the tanks,
twenty-eight in all, were still slowly moving up. These were mostly
salvaged from previous battles and were therefore affected by battle
damage, leading to mechanical problems. They were based in the Bois
de Buire near Roisel and the slow progress was due to further
mechanical problems exacerbated by heavier traffic on the main roads
to the battle front. The new commander of 5th Battalion, Major A. W.
O'Kelly, must have been frustrated by the tanks allotted to him as they
clanked their troubled way to the front, their commanders keeping their
eyes peeled for German aircraft that pestered them from time to time.

The day drew on for the Sussex Regiment in the four redoubts. Even
its headquarters at a Nissen hut was not spared a healthy shelling, a
mule standing with the mess cart suffered a direct hit from a 5.9in shell
that 'wounded two valuable [human] runners'. C Company reported
that the enemy was in L.10.a. and British troops retreating, these were

William Beaumont's men. The same company reported that the enemy were working round them and they were firing to their right rear as well as to their front.

At 4 o'clock C Company reported that the Germans were all around Trinket redoubt and in Carpeza Copse. The redoubt had reportedly fallen and the afternoon was much quieter after this. Colonel Hill managed to get some reinforcements from 66th Division, which added to the men under Captain Collier mentioned earlier, these being sent to protect the left flank of A Company, Sussex Regiment, and watch the north from the high ground south of Roisel [see map 7].

At 8 o'clock that evening Colonel Hill was able to visit Trinity and Trinket redoubts: 'The line between them was filled with details of 66th Division also the sunken road on left of A Company leading to Templeux. Got some details of 66th Division to dig in on right of C Company and cavalry [15/ Hussars] were going to patrol from them to Carpeza Copse which was held by [the] division.'[15] The Suffolk men were doing a grand job of holding, but elements of the East Lancashire Division were aiding them by holding their flanks.

Captain Collier pulled together his men and decided to move them to join the rest of the Manchester Regiment in Carpeza Copse, putting out a line of men to link the two positions. Captain Saxon went out to try and find Collier and his men and,

> was astonished to find the Commanding Officer [Colonel Hill] walking up the road. He told us that there were rations for us in Hesbécourt and that he had arranged for the artillery to lengthen by 200 yards as we had complained that they were dropping on us, he seemed to find nothing wrong with life except that 'there was too much retiring going on', he apparently paid things up with the Manchesters who returned to their original position. The Boche retired to about 50 yards in front of the redoubt but they must have been much further forward on our right – we took two prisoners in our rear during the night. We feared that the C.O. might have walked into some of them, but then we heard that he was back at H.Q..

Colonel Hill seemed to have led a charmed life for his tender years, for he was only aged about thirty. The men settled down for the night, sentries took turns to watch for the enemy and Captain Saxon went out and found that:

> The first part of the night was rather anxious work, it seemed likely that the enemy would just walk over us from the rear. We could hear

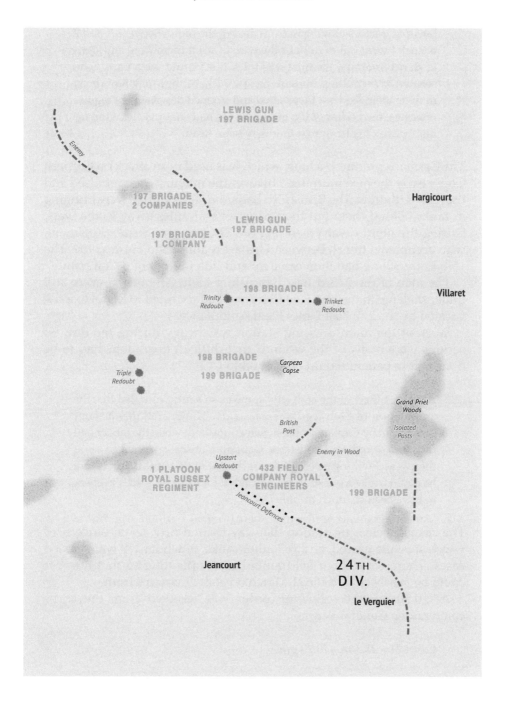

Map 7: Situation, 7pm, 21 March 1918.

tanks or tractors moving in front during the night. Between 1 and 2 o'clock I went out in front of the wire to see if there were any signs of trench mortars, the mist was thick but I could see a party who seemed to be putting up wire on low pickets, they may have been moving their dead but they halted and stooped down at very regular intervals, the bodies of the men who we had shot put the wind up me! I didn't realise at first that they were dead.

The Germans produced a tank, which was used in an attack on Carpeza Copse early the next morning, however the infantry were repulsed and the tank withdrew. The British 5th Battalion, Tank Corps, were bringing in tanks behind them but they were several miles away to the west. During the night cavalrymen relieved D Company, Sussex Regiment, who occupied a trench between Upstart redoubt and Hesbécourt. The 15th Entrenching Battalion came up and dug in front of B Company.

The men of the 2/3rd East Lancashire Field Ambulance were still under shell fire in their new quarters and had retreated to Roisel to a site vacated by the 2/2 East Lancs Field Ambulance.

Work at the main dressing station was heavy during the day. So serious were many of the wounds that difficult operations had to be done before patients could be sent on to CCS:

> A young officer of the 66th Division was so badly wounded that the amputation of both legs was necessary. The operation was later carried out by Captain Dobson. Some time later when the officer had fully recovered consciousness, Captain Dobson returned to see if there was anything he could do for the patient's comfort, but before he could frame a question the wounded Lancastrian said 'I'm sorry to have been so much trouble Doc.'

The casualty clearing station that day treated fifty-seven officers, of which six were gassed, and 769 other ranks, of whom 278 were gassed cases. There were three field ambulances operating so that number could be nearly tripled for 21 March on 66th Division's front.

At 10.20 pm the following order was received from the corps commander, General Watts:

> G.684 21 – 21.3.18 – 10.20 pm.

> Every effort must be made to retain the Redoubt Line. No withdrawal to be made from this line. Tanks when available should be used to counter-attack if necessary.

Addressed 24, 66 [divisions] repeated
Army Flank corps and G.O.C. Royal Artillery
XIX Corps

During the night several small attacks occurred on the Divisional line:

> German patrols were active and were evidently anxious to find out
> if the British were retiring under cover of darkness. The post held by
> Second Lieutenant Skene (6/ Battalion) was attacked during the
> night by a party of Germans but had little trouble in driving them
> off. Another German patrol tried to slip past the southern end of
> Templeux but was turned back by A Company of the 6/ leaving an
> officer and two men dead.[16]

NOTES:
[1] IWM Department of Documents, papers of Colonel Little.
[2] MacReady, G., *In the Wake of the Great*, London, 1965, p.24f.
[3] ibid, p.13.
[4] Edmunds, E., *Official History, 1918*, Vol. I, p.191.
[5] ibid, Vol. I, p.191.
[6] MacReady, G., pp.24–5.
[7] IWM Department of Documents, papers of Tom Hardman 84/1/1.
[8] Edmunds E., *Official History, 1918*, Vol. I, pp.191–2.
[9] TNA, WO95/3121.
[10] TNA, WO95/2219, 9th Royal Sussex Regiment.
[11] Francis, A. *History of the 2/3rd East Lancashire Field Ambulance*, 1930, p.95.
[12] Farndale, M. *History of the Royal Regiment of Artillery, 1914–1918*, p.265.
[13] IWM Department of Documents, papers of R.C.A. Frost 09/6/1.
[14] IWM Department of Documents, papers of P.R. Hall 87/55.
[15] TNA, WO95/2219.
[16] 'The Annihilation of 197 Brigade', article in Latter, J.C., *The Lancashire Fusiliers 1914–1918*, Vol. I, p.288ff.

Chapter 10

Never Retreat

22 March, Friday, Dawn

At 4 o'clock the peace of the dawn was again shattered by a heavy bombardment of the British positions that lasted three hours. In the front line further support for the infantry was organised and in place. By early on the morning of 22 March the twenty-eight remaining tanks of 5th Battalion, Royal Tank Regiment, under Major O'Kelly had taken up their positions to help 66th and 24th Divisions. The disposition of the tanks was set that seven were to attack Hervilly wood, one tank each to support Vixen and Viper redoubt, seven to Roisel to act as a reserve, and seven in Hervilly itself. In itself this mass of tanks was a valuable addition to the defence of the front, however the tactical use of the tanks was to cover the infantry retreat as mobile pillboxes: it was to be a misuse of a valuable asset. This would have been a decision made by the corps commander, Herbert Watts.

In the early morning light the beleaguered positions of the East Lancashire Division and its neighbours in 24th Division sent out patrols to reconnoitre German positions and attempt to make contact with friendly forces. Colonel Lloyd of the 9/ Manchesters sent out several patrols, which reported that the Germans were not going to advance as they were digging trenches in the thick fog. The Germans were not sticking to their plan of continuous advance and it was the stiff resistance of the redoubts and heavy losses, particularly of officers, that had brought this about.

Encounters in the fog were likely to be strange, individual affairs, such as that of Lieutenant Hunt who recounted to a senior officer that he:

> Met a German officer in Ruelles Wood, and that he had a parley with him; both being in overcoats were not able to get at their weapons

to finish off the encounter. However Lieutenant Hunt finished him off in the end in [a] hand to hand encounter and returned rather badly mauled. This gallant officer was unfortunately afterwards killed. Ruelles Wood was now occupied by the enemy so the left flank of the Hesbécourt Switch was in the air. Another officers' patrol went out to Carpeza Copse and reported all the trenches round there filled with our dead. Machine Guns were firing into the back of our trenches from the direction of Hesbécourt which were still taken to be ours, who were under the impression that the Switch had been evacuated; patrols were sent back to endeavour to stop them but they were met by sustained fire and had to return.

The battlefield was very uncertain, with no one unit sure of the placement of another, and the fog and general disruption meaning that the enemy seemed to be behind every bush and tree. Those units in fixed positions were more confident of their front but many 'friendly fire' incidents must have occurred. Patrols missed each other and may even have seen each other as the enemy. This was no place to fight a decisive battle and it was General Gough that saw this clearly.

The Germans were pressing their advantage in the valley of the Cologne river, which was the short cut to Péronne just 7 miles away, and were knocking on the door of Roisel. This was where the gap between 16th and 66th Division had appeared. The necessity was to counter-attack to regain the Hesbécourt plateau.

For the infantrymen of the Sussex Regiment under Captain Saxon it had been a long night. Again the mist was thick and Saxon recorded that a morning patrol had reached Carpeza Copse, which was found to be in the hands of the enemy, and no sign was found of the Manchesters or the cavalry screen between the redoubt and the wood. The morning was quiet, and Saxon and his men felt isolated and alone: 'If it were anyone but the battalion behind us we should have felt that they had cleared out and left us.'[1] The Germans had worked their way round the Sussex men during the night, and although they were not visible, they could hear them all around. Soon the rifle fire followed by machine gun fire started. In response, British artillery fired at extreme range, straddling the positions and causing casualties both to friend and foe alike, but particularly among the Manchester Regiment men, who occupied the flank of the redoubt.

The cavalry had their own problems to deal with as it was soon reported that Hervilly was captured, and therefore the Brown line had been penetrated. The redoubt line was outflanked and would be unlikely to be held, and it certainly could not be reinforced. The German artillery had started again at 4 o'clock and the infantry assault again at 7 o'clock.

At 7.35 am the 15/ Hussars were ordered to retake the Brown line east of Roisel with a dismounted attack.

> Owing to the very unfavourable situation in other parts of the line, it did not seem likely that the attack even if successful could effect any material change, as it appeared that the party making it would become quite isolated. Nevertheless as the situation was desperate, the counter-attack was ordered to take place, in spite of the almost hopeless conditions under which it had to be carried out.

The attack was to be made by A and C Squadrons with B in support.

> Roisel itself was under very heavy shellfire and on both flank large numbers of the enemy could be seen advancing in considerable numbers. Major Godman, who led the attack, took with him A squadron and four machine guns. B Squadron covered the advance on the left or northern flank, whilst C squadron remained in reserve. By 9.30 a.m. the attack was in progress. It was Major Godman's intention to secure the high ground east of Hesbécourt, and having secured the high ground to turn east and attack the Brown line.
>
> In spite of the heavy hostile fire the attack succeeded and A squadron occupied the Brown line, but as was anticipated they found themselves isolated. By this time it had become quite manifest that any attempt to hold the Brown line was doomed to failure, as north of Roisel the enemy had overwhelmed our positions, and was already well established east of the railway. Meanwhile both sides had concentrated their fire into the village of Roisel, which had become untenable.[2]

The horses of the dismounted cavalry were in a laager behind the lines at Hesbécourt. The mass of horses was spotted by circling German aeroplanes and attacked. No attempt had been made to conceal them and they suffered accordingly from the German strafing attacks.

Major Godman and his men held on for hours that morning. They linked up with men of 2/6th Lancashire Fusiliers and made a good account of themselves. General Gough later wrote of this stand: 'In one case forty men of the 15/ Hussars and 2/6 Lancashire Fusiliers held out until fifteen only were left; eventually these were surrounded and overwhelmed.[3] In this way many small units holding out were overwhelmed in the battle and gave their lives heroically.

A separate counter-attack was ordered by Watts by 15/ Entrenching Battalion. However, with communications being bad, the runners sent with the order failed to find the battalion where they thought it was and so the counter-attack never took place.

The news got worse as now Le Verguier in the 24th Division's area fell after twenty-four hours of defence. The defence of this front line village by Colonel Piers of the 8/ Queen's, despite being attacked by five battalions and the artillery of two German divisions on three sides, was a great deed. Colonel Piers also managed to withdraw the remainder of his forces to a new position where they continued the fight, although he disobeyed orders by undertaking this action.[4] The thoroughness with which the defences had been prepared at Le Verguier compared badly with the defences in the East Lancashire Division front.

The Sussex Regiment men holding on in their redoubts were now aware that the battle had moved on. Colonel Hill in Hesbécourt was rallying stragglers, his D company had reported at 8.18 am that Upstart redoubt had fallen, and the scene was rapidly descending into disorder, as is evident from Colonel Hill's report:

> During the morning many troops of Y division [66th] and cavalry came through Hesbécourt, these were rallied and held the line to the north. But our artillery barrage came down in the midst of them, which was supposed to be defending Hervilly which had been reported to have fallen at 10 a.m. I sent my orderly to tell the artillery that Trinket redoubt one mile ahead was still held by C Company. Went on trying to rally troops, which were quite 200 in number, but I found it difficult as there was no line to hold. Tried to do the same thing at Roisel where I found a Colonel and 300 men who I told to hold Roisel and I would try and do the same at Hervilly and high grounds to south of it. (A squadron of cavalry turned up at 10.30 who had been told to retake Hervilly!)[5]

Good news was brought to headquarters that 50th (Northumbrian) Division, brought up from reserve, was in position to the rear of XIX Corps between the villages of Caulaincourt and Boucly to cover the retreat of the corps between the rivers Cologne and Omignon. It had been brought up by train and road and although the men were exhausted by the move up they were a fresh defence against the fall of the two divisions scrabbling to hold on to the redoubt line. Added to this their commander had been removed just before the battle, so they were also leaderless. They were spread thinly over 12,000 yards of front with two brigades forward and one concentrated to the left flank in the Cologne valley.

This was unknown to the men cut off in the redoubt zone as communications were impossible; runners sent out were captured, as were wounded who tried to filter back to the aid posts. The Germans pursued the attack on the East Lancashires' front in an attempt to break through. They even brought up a tank to attack the stout defenders of Carpeza Copse, which fell that morning.

For Captain Saxon and his men of C Company, Sussex Regiment, in Trinket redoubt, their ammunition was running low and their fellow Manchester defenders faced the same situation:

> Boche trench mortars opened fire from the front and at the same time machine gun fire from the rear increased greatly and more guns fired from the rear. The mist was still fairly thick. Corporal Anderson and his rifle grenade squad tackled the trench mortars, only one gun of which was actually landing in the trench. We heard shouted orders from the rear and the machine gun fire ceased. We fired steadily to the rear. Either the Boche hadn't put their trench mortars under cover or the rifle grenade firing at a target that couldn't be seen was very good. The mortar's fire started to slacken and stopped. The Boche to the rear just seemed to lack the pluck to make the last few yards. The men's blood was up and it certainly would have cost them more than our men in numbers to get into the trench, but if they had made a rush enough would have got in to finish us, but as soon as they got into view from the dead ground and a few went down, they funked it. Just after this attack I served out the last of the Small Arms Ammunition, the Manchesters to our left were using a great deal.[6]

With the redoubts cut off every effort was made to reach them again and counter-attacks were now in progress. The 5th Tank Battalion was at Nobescourt Farm and heavy artillery had been brought forward with heavy batteries XXI and XXII Brigades, Royal Garrison Artillery, in the rear of the Green line. There were now 112 heavy guns in rear of XIX Corps and 217 field guns. The corps still packed a punch and could deliver a devastating fire on any targets identified. The 1st Cavalry Division provided 124 guns of H, I and Y Batteries, Royal Horse Artillery, and the East Lancashire Division LXXXVI, 250, 330, and 331 Artillery Brigades, Royal Field Artillery. In the early morning mist men of the Hussars and artillerymen had rescued four guns of 24th Division that had been abandoned in the previous day's fighting.[7]

Colonel Lloyd and his 9/ Manchesters were on the receiving end of some of this artillery as at 10.30 am a barrage was put down to the rear of their positions

> which at first was taken to be that of the enemy, but it increased in volume and two direct hits came on the battalion headquarters killing one company commander who was there and severely wounding the adjutant. The remainder of the runners and signallers were scattered but moved further up the trench. A pigeon basket was luckily found and a message dispatched to ask our artillery to cease fire. The enemy now began a retaliatory barrage on the Eastern side of the trench so the situation became a little more uncertain especially as the slightest movement brought machine gun fire from the rear. Two messenger dogs went past which it was not possible to stop and it now seemed tolerably certain that the position was surrounded.[8]

Overnight the headquarters of the brigades of 66th Division had moved with Divisional Headquarters under Major General Malcolm, retiring from Nobescourt Farm to Doingt along with 199 Brigade. In addition, 198 Brigade went to Courcelles and 197 Brigade to Buire. All four headquarters were within a few miles of one another, huddled on the north bank of the Cologne river near Péronne but with adequate communications to what remained of their forward units. This was a concentration of the remaining units of the division on the east bank of the Somme around Péronne with a view to defend the town. At least by having the headquarters near one another they would be able communicate, something that had been increasingly hard in the last day under constant barrage and with misty conditions and new positions for the units under their command. Major General Malcolm at least was able to command, send out orders and be visible to his subordinates, something that had not been possible on 21 March under such attack.

Now an attempt was made to counter-attack and the dismounted men of the 8/ and 9/ Hussars with six tanks attacked and pushed the Germans into Hesbécourt, and for a time stayed their advance. On the left 16th Division was beginning to retire and Watts asked permission to withdraw his XIX Corps behind the 50th Division line.

Gough talked to Hubert Lawrence, who was now at General Headquarters (G.H.Q.) at Montreuil. Lawrence had thought it unlikely that the Germans would attack again on 22 March: he was proved wrong as the weight of the offensive had pushed the British back and despite the stout defence of the British army several dangerous gaps had appeared. One such was that in the northern flank of the East

119

Lancashire Division. The Germans were pushing towards Péronne, one of their primary objectives. The orders for the East Lancashire Division now were to retire west of the Somme at Péronne and dig in. There was no panic here, just an orderly withdrawal.

The remnants of the 9/ Manchester Regiment were now preparing to retire at midday with no hope of relief. Colonel Lloyd heard the sound of artillery become

> fainter and further away. I decided to endeavour to break through to the Brown line and hold that. Orders were given and the retirement began successively from the left. Bodies of Germans were now seen advancing on the flank the same way as we were retiring. They were finished off about 300 yards east of Hesbécourt village. We ran into four German machine guns firing inwards from the right. Thinking that they must be our own they were signalled to but this only added zest to their endeavours and there remained only one thing to do, to get through at all costs to the Brown line, i.e. the line east of Hesbécourt, and fight a delaying action there. I regret to say very heavy casualties were incurred from their machine guns and not many escaped their attention but everyone knew it was either capture or get into the Brown line and they carried on in their endeavours.
>
> I unfortunately got hit at this juncture, and was perhaps not able to control the remnants who succeeded in getting through as I got a bit behind and had no officers left, but the men were quite undismayed and ready to do anything they were asked to. To add to their discomfort a German machine gun had established itself in the northern end of Hesbécourt village and the Brown line was also turned. The sunken road between Hervilly and Roisel was made a rallying point and here I handed over the remnant of the battalion to Lieutenant Oppenheimer, the Intelligence Officer. I regret having to go but was unable to get around properly.[9]

For the 9/ Manchesters the fight was over, those surviving men breaking out about the same time as the Hussars attacked Hebescourt from the other direction. That the only suitable officer left was a lieutenant shows how decimated was the battalion.

There had been a determined defence in the East Lancashire Division front. None more so than the stricken infantry garrisons. Decorations were few as so few officers survived to tell the tale, and visibility was so bad that few could report actions of which they were not part. Yet one man won the Victoria Cross on the front here. This was twenty-four year old Private Herbert George Columbine of 9/ Squadron, Cavalry Machine Gun Corps. Columbine was from Walton-on-the-Naze in Essex.

> For most conspicuous bravery and self-sacrifice displayed, when owing to casualties, Private Columbine took over command of a gun and kept it firing from 9 a.m. till 1 p.m. in an isolated position with no wire in front. During this time wave after wave of the enemy failed to get up to him. Owing to his being attacked by a low-flying enemy aeroplane the enemy at last gained a strong footing in the trench on either side. The position being untenable he ordered the two remaining men to get away, and though being bombed from either side, kept his gun firing and inflicting heavy losses. He was eventually killed by a bomb which blew him up and his gun. He showed throughout the highest valour, determination and self-sacrifice.[10]

Columbine and the 9/ Squadron were under the command of 1st Cavalry Division, but both Columbine and Sayer were under the command of XIX Corps. That these two VC actions happened on the same flank, within 3,500 yards of each other, may well have dampened considerably the German resolve on this flank. Both demonstrate the loyalty of the fighting British soldier to the cause and the fact that they were willing to give up their lives in action. There were no doubt many such actions by men on the front, but many were not seen by officers or other survivors and therefore no award could be given. The two actions no doubt had considerable effect on the German advance in this right flank of the East Lancashire Division. This may explain the slow advance on this flank when in the north the Germans were already pressing down the valley to Roisel.

The division and all its units were mauled: 'No perfectly accurate figures of the casualties sustained in the stricken division during the first thirty-six hours of the this battle – The Battle of St Quentin – are available but it is computed that so terrible a mark had been made that the rifle strength was reduced by more than one half.'[11] And this was from the men who had manned the field ambulances, and were in a position to describe the casualties they had seen.

It was not just the British who had been mauled by the German offensive, the German Second Army in the attacks had suffered high casualties as well. At the same time that the British were pulling out the remains of the Irish, East Lancashire and 24th Divisions, the Germans had stalled as well, and were bringing in a fresh division, the 13th, to replace and reinforce the shattered 18th. All three German corps that affect this story, the 23, 14 and 51, were suffering high casualties. This interlude meant that both forces could bring up fresh forces to the fight. It was also a sign of just how shattering the fighting had been for both sides.

General Gough had ordered the 8th Division to move down from the Ypres Salient the evening of 21 March and he had seen the commander, General Henneker, at 6 o'clock that morning. The rest of the division was on its slow, laborious way by train late that morning. The general and his staff officer, Colonel Armitage, had set out on a personal reconnaissance that morning. 'But before they completed their reconnaissance found themselves in the fighting zone. The roads along which they passed were a distressing sight – stragglers, wounded, guns, transport, and vehicles of all descriptions all moving westwards, while the roar of battle drew nearer every moment.[12]

Lieutenant General Herbert Watts received orders at 10.45 am to pull his corps back. He informed his divisional commanders to carry out a fighting withdrawal to the Green line 'as soon as it should become evident that the Battle Line position could not be held without danger of the capture of its defenders'.[13] The soldiers of the East Lancashire Division knew they had been mauled, but this was not the case everywhere. At midday on Friday the news came to the soldiers of 24th Division to the south that they were to retreat:

> At twelve noon the withdrawal was begun, much to the surprise of the troops, who were in the highest spirits and felt themselves quite capable of holding off any attack. The 11th Hussars, 13/ Middlesex and 19th Entrenching Battalion covered the retirement. They fought a continuous rearguard action, but the last parties did not leave their position until about 2 o'clock after the engineers had blown up three bridges over the Omignon to prevent any attack on the right flank, now exposed by the withdrawal of the 61st Division.[14]

There was plenty of time for engineers to blow bridges and stop the Germans outflanking several key positions. In the East Lancashire Division to the north the northern flank had been turned and the Germans were flooding down the line, and there was very little they could do about it except retreat, and so the division was to be moved behind the Somme river, the next great natural barrier to the west. For the moment the soldiers of 50th (Northumbrian) Division would hold the front. As an advance post the 1/5th Battalion of the Durham Light Infantry, a territorial unit itself, was brought up to hold Roisel.

The officers in the rear assumed that the enemy had seized most of Hervilly Wood near Hesbécourt at 11 that morning and four tanks of the 5th Battalion, Tank Corps, now were ready to counter-attack the wood. They assembled at Bois de la Croix (Cross Wood in some documents), south of Hervilly with elements of the 9th Dismounted Brigade, the dismounted remains of 9th and 19th Hussars. They attacked Hervilly Wood at 12 noon, and although some of the tanks were disabled they managed to drive the enemy out of part of the wood. Colonel Mort sent a report that 'his attack had been successful, he had [met?] up astride the Hervilly road and in cooperation with the tanks had brought off a successful attack, thereby regaining Hervilly and relieving a very critical situation'. This was the only offensive use of armour in XIX Corps area of operations and it seems to have been of limited use and only effected a temporary setback to the Germans.

However, reading the brief summary of the actions of the tanks of 5/ Battalion, Royal Tank Regiment, this appears far from the case. The tanks went into action where possible and although of limited use in the mist and fog, fired extensively. The details are sketchy and unfortunately do not mention the commanders by name, so only the serial number of each tank is recorded. A summary of the war diary gives the following highlights of the tanks that fought with the East Lancashire Division. Tank 2033 was in action for four hours and drove 4 miles, firing fifty rounds of 6-pounder and 2,000 machine gun rounds, three of the crew were wounded and the tank successfully retired. Tank 4571 was in action near Roisel for two hours, where the enemy was closely supported by two field guns; it drove 12 miles and fired 900 machine gun rounds, after which it broke down and was captured. Tank 4661 was also in action near Roisel, where it also came up against field guns; it drove 15 miles and fired 2,000 machine gun rounds, before it broke down and was burnt out. Of the other tanks, 2083 started for Roisel but had to turn back due to mechanical trouble and the commander was wounded. Tank 2808 and its commander and all crew went missing and the vehicle was burnt out. Tank 2811 drove 20 miles, fired 300 rounds from its machine guns and was in action near Roisel, where its commander was wounded but the tank was successfully recovered. The last tank, 2961, drove 6 miles but then broke down. The success of the tanks was varied; they certainly fired off their machine guns and presumably caused a number of casualties among the enemy forces while under considerable fire themselves.[15]

Further north-east of Bapaume a full-scale tank attack was prepared by the 2nd Tank Battalion that afternoon and I include it as an illustration of the way tanks could be used. These tanks

at 5 pm were advancing northwards from Beugny. One battery of the 256/ Brigade Royal Field Artillery covered their movement with smoke shell, helped out by grass fires which the Germans had started in the hope of dislodging the defenders. Scared at the sight of the tanks, the leading German infantry retired in disorder, as a spectator said, 'demoralized', carrying with them the larger bodies concentrated in rear. The four batteries of the 256th Brigade R.F.A. did great execution among them, and were able to catch the German artillery struggling to come into action in close support of the infantry. Unfortunately the tanks remained out too long, slowly cruising around firing at the Germans. They were unaccompanied by infantry to make good the ground gained, except one tank on the right, which two companies of the 11/Cheshire followed, and they soon became the targets of guns in position a few miles away on the higher ground near Lagnicourt.'[16]

Even the efforts of IV Corps further to the north were not textbook in their use of tanks, but they mounted a temporary attack that thoroughly demoralised the enemy infantry, which had few tanks.

Lieutenant General Watts had thirty-four tanks at his disposal in XIX Corps area and plenty of infantry, but chose to use them as mobile pillboxes or 'savage rabbits'. The exception was the limited attacks at Hesbécourt and Hervilly Wood. This was borne out of the fact that most of the tanks had mechanical problems and were of little use, Watts knew this and sacrificed them along with any thought of recovering them. The use of any horse cavalry in this area was limited by the amount of belts of barbed wire and the low visibility, hence the use of dismounted cavalry as infantry. The Germans had no armoured back up to note and very little cavalry at this stage, so it appears that a sustained cavalry attack might have had a chance of routing a part of the German forces had conditions been right, however this was still an infantry battlefield, and major use of cavalry and tanks would have to wait for the open country around Villers-Bretonneux in April 1918.

The moment had come and gone for counter-attacks on this part of the front. Now the infantry slogged back to the Somme bridges and let the men of 50th Division to the north and 24th Division to the south fight rearguard actions. The divisional artillery was to stay to cover the

Northumbrian Division, so part of the division at least was to remain in action. What remained of Malcolm's division held the ground between Jeancourt and Hervilly Wood; the remnants of what had been a fine division twenty-four hours earlier were mostly marching back to Péronne. Those left behind were either dead or prisoners of war, although the majority were 'missing'. It was still hard for Major General Malcolm to even assess what was left of his division. His counter-attacks had failed and now the Germans were pressing forward again from the north.

For the men of the division caught in the enemy advance, quick decisions were necessary:

> A private of the division saw a party of the enemy advancing over a little knob of ground in front of him. Having no desire to be killed or taken prisoner, he turned and ran like [expletive] until he was close to battalion headquarters. On the way he overtook a pal who was carrying an important dispatch to the Brigadier. Hearing from the private that he had quitted his post, the runner suggested the grave offence should be covered up by both men delivering the message at headquarters. A month later both men received Military Medals for carrying a dispatch under heavy shell fire.[17]

Lieutenant Tom Hardman of the Royal Artillery was almost caught with the German onslaught:

> Fritz broke through. Had to run. He got in our Observation Point and took one officer and two signallers prisoner, but the officer got away and killed two German officers, wounded another and so got away, but the men were captured. We also had one officer and one driver wounded.[18]

Among those falling back was Gunner John Gore, who recorded in his diary:

> Reinforcements were brought up from somewhere but it was hopeless. The Fifth Army was well whacked, with a German division facing a battalion of our lads. Hopelessly outnumbered. Had to keep on retiring. Reached Brie where we slept in a chalk pit. On the River Somme Royal Engineers are mining the bridge.[19]

The XIX Corps of General Watts was just holding its line. Further away in Fifth Army more momentous events were taking place that would have far-reaching consequences. The southern neighbour of Watts' corps, the XVIII Corps of General Maxse, had retired to the Crozat Canal and the XIX Corps would have to also retreat in order to maintain the front. This had left a gap in the line south of Caulaincourt with potentially disastrous results for the army. The III Corps of General Butler to the south was still holding the Crozat Canal and therefore placed in a dangerous salient should the Germans break through in the area of Ham.

With the position of Watts' corps holding the Péronne bridgehead perilous at best and the Germans streaming down the valley of the Cologne River, a very dangerous situation was being created. General Gough realised this and ordered Watts make a withdrawal to the Somme river. To the north Congreve would defend the line of the Tortille river. The strategic picture now dictated the tactical withdrawal for Watts, and indeed for the East Lancashire Division commanded by Major General Malcolm. In fact, both Watts and Congreve had held their ground longer and more effectively than most of Maxse's divisions to the south, despite the depth of the German penetration, but had lacked much-needed reserves.

That same day the sun broke behind the low clouds of the northern Lakelands and the water lapped on the shore of the lake. It was so quiet in the Lake District, near Keswick, only the whistle of steam launches broke the silence. Lieutenant Colonel William B. Little relaxed in the lounge of the hotel on the first few days of his well-earned leave. Fellow officers graced the hotel, some with a wife in tow. All were up early, making the most of their leave from the front. Soon the papers arrived and Little read with mounting horror the continuing news of a great offensive on the Western Front. News was becoming more urgent and revealing the large scale of the offensive, however he was due leave and wanted to enjoy it to the full. He noticed then the headline 'Fighting at Hargicourt'. That was his sector of the front, and he knew his Border Regiment pioneer battalion were divisional troops in reserve for the front line. News of the German break-in was enough to rile his senses; for the second time in this war he was in the wrong place at the wrong time. After a quick discussion with a couple of fellow officers, he returned to his room, booked out of the hotel, much to the disdain of the landlady, and motored to Penrith station, left his motorbike with the station master and consulted the railway timetable for the next express to London. This was the big battle that had been anticipated and he was not going to miss it for the world, as his men needed their commander.

Soon he was on an express train passing Warrington and Crewe, joining fellow officers including Captain E.L. Higgins of the 2/7 Lancashire Fusiliers racing to the Channel ports. Once there the same fog that hampered the battle also stopped Colonel Little crossing, impatient though he was to get to the fighting.

William Benjamin Little was a keen horticulturist who originated from Carlisle. At the age of fourteen he became an apprentice gardener and was a student at the Royal Botanic Gardens at Kew in London. He taught at Armstrong College of the University of Durham, and travelled all over Northumberland and Cumbria teaching at schools. A keen motorcyclist and a trophy winner and veteran of the Isle of Man TT, he was about to take part in the international motorbike trials in the south of France when war was declared. He was stranded, forced to abandon his Triumph motorcycle and had to return to England by train as all petrol was seized by the French government. The consul at Lyon put him in charge of a theatre troupe who were also returning to the UK. On his return he joined the cyclist battalion of the Durham Light Infantry and was gazetted as a lieutenant. In the north-east Little was in charge of the first armoured car to be used in the area for coastal defence. During fighting at Ypres in May 1915 he was gassed, absconded from hospital and voluntarily returned to his unit in France. Despite, or because of, this Little became a staff captain in 151 Brigade, an acting brigade major in 1916 and second in command of the Border Regiment. On the sudden and untimely death of its commander, he took over himself. On a higher command course at Aldershot he was regarded as:

> An officer of great energy and determination. He is cheerful, conscientious and reliable. He learns readily and is good at imparting knowledge and has great application and considerable imagination and initiative. Handles troops well and has considerable military knowledge. [He] is fitted to command a battalion.

NOTES:
[1] TNA, WO95/2219.
[2] Lord Carnock, *The History of the 15th Kings Hussars*, 1932, Gloucester, p.162ff.
[3] Gough, H., *The Fifth Army*, 1931 (reprint Bath), p.275.
[4] Quote on: www.queensroyalsurreys.org.uk.
[5] TNA, WO95/2219.
[6] TNA, WO95/2219.
[7] Edmunds. E., *Official History, 1918*, Vol. I, p.282.

8   TNA, WO95/3121.
9   TNA, WO95/3121.
10 *The London Gazette*, 50720 Private Herbert George Columbine, 8 May 1918.
11 Francis, A., *History of the 2/3 East Lancashire Field Ambulance*, p.97.
12 Boraston, and Bax, *The Eighth Division 1914–1918*, 1926, Eastbourne, Naval and Military Press, p.175.
13 Edmunds, E., *Official History, 1918*, Vol. I, p.282.
14 Edmunds, E., *Official History, 1918*, Vol. I, pp.282–3.
15 Online source, 5th Battalion March 21–23, 1918.
16 Edmunds, E., *Official History, 1918*, Vol. I, p.310.
17 Francis, A., *History of the 2/3rd East Lancashire Field Ambulance*, p.98.
18 IWM Department of Documents, private papers of Tom Hardman.
19 IWM Department of Documents, private papers of John Gore.

Chapter 11

Péronne

Friday

In peacetime the quacking of ducks and the croaking of amphibians is the main sound on the marshes of the Somme. It is here that Péronne lies, an ancient fortified town dating from the seventh century. It sits at the point where the river turns from south–north to flow west towards Amiens. This position at the hinge of the river and the battlefield gave it significance not only as the bridging point of the Somme but also in controlling access to Amiens and the land to the south of the river. Flowing into the Somme here is also the Cologne river.

Previously besieged by the Spaniards in 1536 and the Prussians in 1870–71, the town was no stranger to war, previously destroyed only forty years before the Great War. Taken by the Germans in 1914, the main destruction to the town started in 1916 by artillery bombardment, accelerated by the German 1917 retreat when it was systematically destroyed with every partition, wall, door and piece of woodwork destroyed. Not only that but the Germans mounted vitriolic signs applauding their own destruction. Every house was looted and ransacked and every object stolen.[1]

It was at this vital bridging point that communications flowed and a key point of the fight was to occur. Péronne was served by four railway lines and it was a local communications hub. This remained so in 1917 and 1918 and it would become a flurry of activity in the wake of the German offensive [see map 8].

Marching in the other direction to men such as John Gore were the soldiers of 50th (Northumbrian) Division, who were to hold the line now that the East Lancashire Division was retiring across the Somme. One battalion of the Northumberlands in particular, the 1/5th Battalion,

129

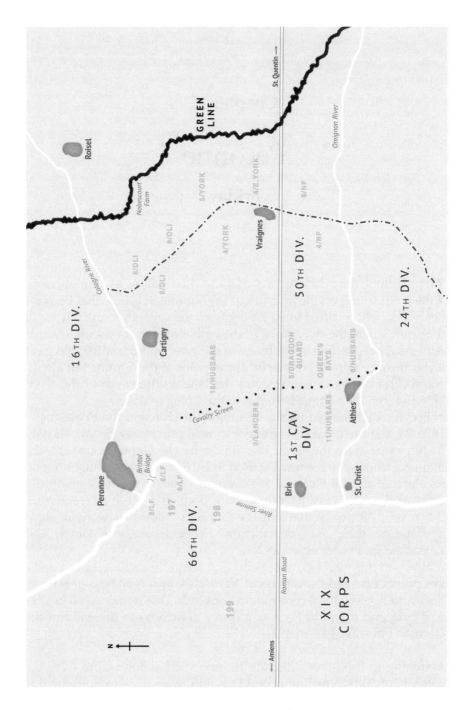

Map 8: Péronne bridgehead.

Durham Light Infantry, was to hold Roisel against the German attacks down the valley of the Cologne river. This deployment would take time and it is not possible here to include all the actions of the Northumbrians, apart from that which is essential to our narrative:

> In the early hours of the morning the battalion detrained at Brie and to huts [sic] between Hancourt and Tincourt. At 9 o'clock the battalion moved to the trenches near Nobescourt Farm and was attached to 198 Infantry Brigade. With following dispositions. A & B Companies were forward between Roisel and Hervilly, C Company in support and D company in reserve in the Green Line. Battalion headquarters was at Nobescourt Farm. About 2 o'clock the 66th Division had orders to retire through our line and A, B and C Companies covering their withdrawal.

The Durhams occupied several lines of trenches at Nobescourt Farm, which faced north-east, which as it happened was from where the threat was forthcoming. As illuminated earlier, Nobescourt Farm was the nucleus of the British defences, and for that reason it was used as divisional and now a battalion headquarters of the Durhams. The line was held so that the East Lancashire Division could retire from its defence of the Péronne Bridgehead. However, at 2 o'clock the remnants of this division were to be pulled out to west of the Somme. The defence of Roisel was a necessity as the line to Hervilly was being abandoned and all wagons, horses and soldiers were moving out along the valley of the Cologne river to Péronne or over the high ground of Hancourt, Bouvincourt and Vraignes to the Roman road to Brie. The direct route to Péronne was threatened by the German push to the north and not suitable for transport purposes, having been assigned to Congreve's VII Corps.

The failure of the counter-attacks had meant the loss of Hervilly Wood, into which the Germans placed machine guns that raked the trenches of the remnants of 9/ Sussex Regiment in Hesbécourt. The machine gun fire inflicted casualties upon Colonel Hill and his men cowering in trenches that had been wrecked by artillery fire. Those who could get out of the enfilade fire made their way to Nobescourt Farm. The Sussex Regiment had offered more than twenty-four hours of resistance in several areas and paid for their courage in casualties. That evening their roll call only mustered 120 men in the whole battalion. According to German sources, the 'fire spouting village of Hesbécourt' had been attacked by three battalions, an artillery battery and an infantry bombing squadron.[2]

A withdrawal on such a large scale was sure to cause problems for the men of the Army Provost Marshal. One of these was Captain Westmacott (Deputy APM 24th Division) on his way to the bridge at St Christ-Briost just south of Brie. He noted dryly:

> As I passed Brie bridge I saw that both up and down bridges were blocked by a broken down lorry and a damaged 60 pounder gun respectively, but as the DAPM XIX Corps was supposed to be controlling the bridge I did not interfere. I pushed on to St Christ bridge which I found quite clear, and I sent Fenwick to the main road to divert all traffic to this bridge. By this means I got two brigades of cavalry and three batteries of Royal Horse artillery to cross at the trot, and I had all my wheels over by 11 o'clock, the enemy having never shelled us once.[3]

Scenes like this were enacted up and down the Somme valley as units endeavoured to pull out and reorganise behind the river, having held the German offensive for more than twenty-four hours, they were desperate to rest and reorganise.

For the engineers of 432 Field Company the scene was repeated. They remembered:

> During the late afternoon the 66th Division was ordered to withdraw through the 50th Division, which had come up to man the Green Line. The enemy was advancing in great numbers, quite like a football crowd on our heels. Each field company was again concentrated, and after a hasty meal moved each with its brigade group into billets on the main road from Roisel to Péronne.[4]

The Germans had not yet realised the measure of the British retirement and were still concentrating on the battle for the Péronne bridgehead. In the early afternoon the troops of 24th Division were just pulling out. The front was moving back to the general line of Boucly, Nobescourt, Bernes, Poeuilly, Caulaincourt, held by 24th and 50th Divisions under their Generals Daly and Stockley. It had been intended that the East Lancashire Division would rest in the Péronne bridgehead, but no one had factored in that the Green line was not very advanced in completion. It had been started; but despite the work of thousands of Italian labourers the wire was woeful and the trenches were a mere scratch on the surface. It took the whole afternoon for the message to get through to headquarters that this line was in the open on forward slopes and offered no protection and no hope of withdrawal once occupied.

More reinforcements were on the way, in the form of 8th Division, which was brought up overnight with the intention of concentrating at Athies to form the southern flank of the defence of the Péronne bridgehead, reinforcing 24th Division. The three brigades of this division were de-trained at Chaulnes, Nesle and Ham. It was expected that they would have a day to dig in on the new line, which would enable them to vastly improve the position on the east side of the Somme river. Given that they were dumped in the middle of the night into the devastated zone, and no maps could aid them, the result was chaos and it soon became obvious that the division would not be able to reach its new line with the roads being so full of withdrawing troops and the men were instead sent west of the Somme.

This was the last straw in the defence of the Péronne bridgehead. The only option was to withdraw the whole corps to the other side of the Somme river, the Péronne bridgehead was but a notion, hardly more than a line on a map. The reinforcements of the men of 50th Division had been in place in the Green line since 8 am. The men of 66th and 24th Divisions withdrew through the fresh ranks of the 50th Division and 'soon streams of men, horses and limbers were coming through and the Green line became the front line'.[5]

The last remnants of the front line of the East Lancashire Division were to withdraw fighting through the Northumbrian Division:

> The behaviour of the Germans on different parts of the front varied. On some parts they permitted the troops to walk back across the open undisturbed, being too tired to follow; on others they endeavoured to sweep forward in large numbers. In the rear guard actions which ensued heavy casualties were inflicted on the enemy: but some forty men of the 15/ Hussars and the remnants of two companies of the 2/6th Lancashire Fusiliers were cut off and the fifteen unwounded survivors captured.[6]

The southern flank of the East Lancashire Division at Jeancourt was defended by men of 432 Field Company Royal Engineers. To their south was the 7/ Northamptonshire Regiment, part of the corps reserve who had been holding the battle zone defences and had followed events that day with interest:

> At about 8 in the morning news was received that enemy had renewed his attack and had succeeded in taking Le Vergier. Troops on our left and right were falling back steadily. At About 1 o'clock the Commanding Officer went over to 17 Brigade to get news of the

situation but found that they had retired and also the troops to our right, leaving our right flank in the air. Our left Company reported the enemy advancing on their left flank. At 1.25 in the afternoon a message was despatched to 73 Brigade at Bernes stating that both our flanks were in the air and that we were apparently isolated and that if compelled to retire we should take up a position on the Vendelles-Hervilly Ridge. At 1.35 p.m. owing to the rapid advance of the enemy on our flanks and to avoid being surrounded, the CO ordered Companies to withdraw. This withdrawal was effected in good order but with some difficulty due to our isolated position. The Battalion withdrew through 50th Division who had been brought up and were holding the Green Line in front of Bernes. After concentrating at Hancourt we proceed to Meraucourt and rested there for the night.[7]

At 3.30 pm the inevitable happened. The Germans were close on the heels of the withdrawing 66th and 1st Dismounted Divisions, just coming up to the brigades of the 50th Division. It became now a story of the defence of 50th Division.

By 4.30 pm 149 brigade which was on the right, on the spur north of the Omignon in front of Caulaincourt, was heavily attacked. And the enemy, coming on in eight waves down the Omignon valley, broke in on the right front. A desperate resistance was offered, every available man being put into the fight, and two counter-attacks were made; yet by 6 o'clock Caulaincourt was definitely lost and the right of the brigade swept back.[8]

The men of 150 Brigade in the centre were not attacked until 5.30 that evening, although this varies slightly in different accounts. At Nobescourt Farm the resistance still held, now being occupied on the right by the 1/4th Yorkshire Regiment (Green Howards) under the thirty-two year old Colonel Bernard H. Charlton. Here 150 Brigade had 'a good field of fire and being well supported by their artillery, they had no difficulty in holding their line'. On their right were the East Yorkshires and the 5th Yorkshire Regiment in reserve.

At Nobescourt Farm on the left the 5/ Durhams were in support of 198 Brigade. The Germans attacked

the line on our right causing our Battalion to be withdrawn to the outskirts of Nobescourt Farm. B Company being moved into support behind the farm. Captain J K M Hassler was killed and

Second Lieutenant H J W Scott wounded here. Battalion hung on here until orders were received from Brigade that at 3 a.m. a withdrawal was to be made and a new line dug in front of Cartigny.[9]

The failings of the Green line defences had reached headquarters and orders came back to retire further back. The retirement was made successfully and the brigade dug in at Cartigny, where it remained for just a few hours. It was now made known that the men would retreat over the Somme. This was to be a rearguard action and the battalions of the Northumberland Division made the necessary arrangements. One company of the Green Howards held the hill top knoll of Le Catelet farm, commanding Cartigny, until the other units had pulled out to Le Mesnil. The 8/ Durham Light Infantry withdrew through it to Eterpigny, the crossing point of the Somme.

It was not all retreat and it was reported that the 5/ Northumberland Fusiliers counter-attacked with the 6/ Battalion in support at 5.15 pm. An immediate attack by the Germans threw the Northumbrians out again, only to be beaten out again by a single company of the 5/ Battalion. The 24th Division to the south had been pushed back and this exposed the right of the division. To the north across the Cologne river the flank was in the air, having lost touch with the 16th Division.

The Green line position was vacated and at 3 am the Northumbrian Division was ordered to move back over the Somme. The bridge at St Christ was to be used by 149 Brigade, that at Brie by 150 Brigade and that at Eterpigny by 151 Brigade. 'The whole movement will be carried out as rapidly as possible consonant with steadiness and control.'

The story of the withdrawal is told extensively by the war diary of 6/ Northumberland Fusiliers:

> The retirement from the Green Line was carried out in perfect order along the whole battalion front, and at 4.30 in the morning the troops arrived on the new ground, and after being supplied with hot tea and rum from one of the Battalion cookers, commenced digging in on a line of posts running south from the Mons [en Chaussée] to Vermand road. In a couple of hours our troops had dug in sufficiently to secure the line, and orders were made to hold it.
>
> At 8.30 a.m., however operation orders were received to commence a retirement at 9 o'clock to which the whole line would conform. By the time these orders could be repeated to companies,

the front line had become involved in close contact with the enemy, who also advanced in large numbers and in mass formations.

The 150 Brigade, on the left, counter-attacked along their front and commenced a retirement, but on the Battalion front A and C companies were too involved with the enemy to get clear, and three platoons of A company and part of C company were unable to free themselves and were afterwards missing. Lieutenant Balden with part of A company, was last seen fighting in a hand to hand encounter with the enemy. Lieutenants Oswald and Hamilton were both seen wounded and were afterwards missing. In the meantime B company covered the retreat of the remainder of the battalion, and fought a brilliant rearguard action as far as Mons [Estrees], where it was relieved by another company.

Throughout the whole retreat the battalion had withdrawn in perfect order, although the enemy pressed forward with machine guns, artillery and aeroplanes, and kept up a gruelling fire from all these weapons. They continued west to Brie and there passed a welcome line of infantry of the Eighth division.[10]

Brie was an important stores depot and railhead as the line from Chaulnes to Péronne passed under the west side of the river bridges here:

In and around Brie enormous fires were burning and ammunition dumps which could not be removed were blown up. Huts, camps, aerodromes etcetera on the eastern side of the Somme canal were also burning during the retirement. The bridges over the Somme were prepared for demolition.'[11]

Watts sent the following order to his divisional commanders:

All concerned. All bridges may be destroyed at discretion of divisional commanders, 50th, 24th, 1st Cavalry, according to circumstances and as soon as all troops have crossed. All such demolitions to be reported to Corps.

The assistant director of light railways was meant to blow the light railway bridges at Brie but had neither the explosives nor the men to do so.

Lieutenant MacKenzie of the Royal Engineers visited XIX Corps Headquarters to make sure he had verbal and written orders in person as to his duties. The officers and men of 281st Army Troops, Royal

Engineers, were detailed to place demolition charges on the bridges on the previous day, 22 March. The men stood to by the bridges and put in charges while Captain Kentish did a round of the bridges and inspected the charges. The bridge at Brie was, as we have seen, hit by a shell at 5.10 in the afternoon that affected its use. This bridge was demolished at 11.10 am on 23 March, only on direct orders from the corps commander of Royal Engineers. Their next move was to assist the evacuation of the remains of the Péronne bridgehead by cutting the remaining bridges over the Cologne river at Cartigny Mill, where Lieutenant MacKenzie and men spent the whole night wiring the bridge and making sure all British forces were across before blowing it. At Doingt a tank crossed back across the bridge at 10.30 and the bridge was blown just over an hour later at 11.45 that morning of 23 March. The approaches to Péronne were destroyed when the bridge at Flamicourt was blown at 3.15 in the afternoon.[12] There was no great haste in the moves of the Royal Engineers to demolish the bridges as the German advance was steady.

The German attack, however, had gained momentum, and the weaknesses on the left and right flanks meant the whole line had to give, so the Green Howards retreated 800 yards west, Nobescourt Farm was lost and the companies of the regiment became separated in the mist. Colonel Charlton and his adjutant, Captain J.S. Bainbridge, went out to rally the men and unfortunately were killed in the confusion. The enemy attack was held, though, and stopped short of any further advance.

The field ambulances were on the move again and were awoken:

> Turning out tired at 1 o'clock [at night] was not pleasant, but our faithful cooks supplied us with a good breakfast, thus our route march through the night was robbed of much of its discomfort, but ten kilometres during the night is at any time far worse than an equal distance during daytime. During the retirement we had not taken into consideration that we should be kept at it during the following day.[13]

The artillery were also on the move. The corps artillery started to move back across the river at 7.15 that evening with 21 Brigade moving first and 22 and 23 Brigades at 9 o'clock that evening. Colonel Bayley was ordered to move his headquarters at midnight, and this was established later that night at Foucacourt-en-Santerre with the guns that could saved (but without the counterweight sand boxes that would have to be emptied before they could be withdrawn).

NOTES:

1. Michelin, *Bygone Pilgrimage, Guide to the Battlefields 1916–1917*, p.96f.
2. Edmunds, E., *Official History, 1918*, Vol. I, p.285n.
3. IWM Department of Documents, private papers of T.H. Westmacott.
4. Anonymous, *History of the East Lancashire R.E.*, pp.240–1.
5. Online source, 1/4th Battalion, Alexandra, Princess of Wales Own Yorkshire Regiment, p.52.
6. Edmunds, E., *Official History, 1918*, Vol. I, p.286.
7. TNA, WO95/2218.
8. Edmunds, E., *Official History, 1918*, Vol. I, p.287.
9. TNA, WO95/2840.
10. Wyrall, E., *The Fiftieth Division 1914–1918*, p.206.
11. Wyrall, E., *The Fiftieth Division 1914–1919*, p.205f.
12. TNA, WO95/547.
13. Francis, A., *History of the 2/3rd East Lancashire Field Ambulance*, p.98.

Chapter 12

No Supports Remained

23–24 March, Saturday and Sunday

After a few hours' sleep the men of the East Lancashire Division were set the job of guarding the bridges over the Somme. They were digging in on Watts' new line covering the river crossings. Among these men was Peter Hall:

> The 5/ and 6/ Manchesters were given the job of holding the bridge from the town of Péronne, where the wine was running in the gutters as the French tried to get rid of it. We crossed the bridge and dug in on the west bank, guarding the bridge.

Stores were being destroyed in Péronne and the bridges were being prepared for evacuation. The minor wooden bridges and gangways across the Somme and its marshes were being prepared for demolition by being covered in petrol prior to being set alight, petrol being more in abundance than explosives and easier to use.

Captain Bounds of the 2/3 Field Ambulance was one of the last to visit Péronne. As the ambulance had run short of dressings, Bounds went to the Advanced Depot of Medical Stores located there and under direct German artillery and rifle fire, passing the retreating men of 66th Division, he successfully carried out and brought back 'such stocks of shell and other dressings as to suffice for all needs until [they] were withdrawn out of the line'.[1]

The division had by now a brief amount of time to concentrate and sort itself out for the first time since 20 March. The new alignment was 198 Brigade from around 0.20 central to 0.8.d.6.2 [map reference] covering 197 Brigade from there to La Chapelette. 199 Brigade and the machine gun battalion, and further, the pioneers of the 1/5 Border

Regiment at Barleux. The divisional artillery was still forward under command of 50th Division to give maximum support to the retirement. For the infantry it was its first chance to rest for days. The East Lancashires formed a line to the north with 117 and 118 Brigades of the fresh 39th Division at Biaches just near Péronne (116 Brigade was just to the north of the Somme) [see map 9].

A different story was told by some units of the Eighth Division arriving in the middle of the withdrawal. The newly arrived division was in the line but confusion had reigned and more than one unit found itself in the wrong place. Other units were 'stolen' by anyone with enough authority to pull rank on the officers in charge; a machine gun company was taken by XVIII corps and not seen again until after the battle. 'No opportunity was given to the infantry commanders and staffs to choose their defensive positions and dispose their troops to the best advantage.[2]

The billeting party of the 2/ Northamptonshires, arriving in the village of Athies, east of the Somme, allocated billets, but then found that they were surrounded by Germans and had to fight their way out and return to Licourt, on the other side of the Somme.[3] This shows the confusion that was rife and the impact of the German advance that was shrinking the Péronne bridgehead.

One of the less fortunate soldiers of the division that day was James Jessiman, the machine gunner from Cornhill, Banffshire. He was manning a rearguard position and was captured after the gun was damaged or ran out of ammunition and the next we hear from him he was in a prisoner of war camp at Mainz in Germany.

Major General Malcolm was worried about the crossings from Péronne, which were hard to defend. A special force under Brigadier General Hunter, 199 Brigade, was reinforced to defend this sector, which seemed an obvious area for the Germans to form a bridgehead across the Somme and its canal:

> The position was strong, but not as impregnable as appeared on the map. Péronne itself afforded an ideal covered approach to the river, and trees and undergrowth on both sides of the river materially limited our field of vision; moreover the situation on our left was extremely doubtful and to guard against eventualities in this direction the divisional commander at 9.30 a.m. ordered the machine gun battalion to move with all available guns to about the Orme de Barleux to cover our left at La Chapelette and to watch the crossings at the Faubourg de Paris and Biaches. The 199 Brigade was also ordered to extend its front with one battalion to the Fauborg de Paris

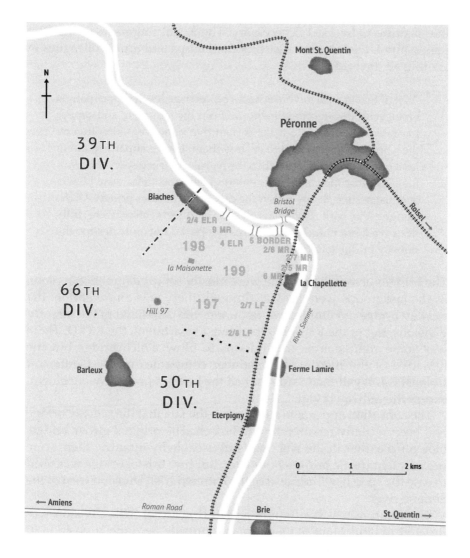

Map 9: Somme River line.

inclusive and patrol the river to the north as far as Biaches and the crossing at H.24.b.9/0. The Pioneer battalion was placed under the orders of Brigadier General Hunter to form a reserve and was placed in N.11 and N.17.[4]

The Border Regiment Pioneers were still under the command of Major Rigg and, now somewhat depleted in numbers, were resting behind the

141

line waiting to be used if necessary. The Royal Engineers of the East Lancashire Division were assisting their corps and army colleagues in visiting all the bridges:

> A bit of breakfast at daybreak and a conference: result sapper patrols on bicycles through Péronne to find out the situation, and sapper parties to all bridges to make certain that none were forgotten by the Corps troops detailed to destroy them. Each company found at least one uncared for, and when the patrols returned soon after with the news that the enemy was entering Péronne, these were blown, and just in time, at any rate in the case of the Biaches bridge. All the bridges the 66th Divisional Royal Engineers blew were fully destroyed, but unluckily the Corps troops did not quite destroy the railway bridge into Péronne.

The bridges across the Somme were mostly set for demolition as soon as the last troops were across, although there was an exception: the railway bridge at Péronne was not under the command of the infantry divisions, but of the Railway Operating Department, the R.O.D. There was some confusion as to who was to blow which bridge but the initiative of the men of the Engineer companies under Lieutenant Colonel L.J. Wyatt made sure that all the bridges possible were blown, except the railway bridge.

The confusion appears to have due to the fact that the railway bridge had been recently repaired by the French. The original girder bridge, blown up earlier in the war, was still useable by infantry; there were replacement trestle bridges built later. But first Bristol bridge was used to ease the speedy withdrawal of the battered Irish Division west of the Somme river.

The fighting was continuing as 118 Brigade of 39th Division was ordered to hold Mont St Quentin, just outside Péronne, a position of greater strength than the town below it. The Official History tells the story of the withdrawal through Péronne:

> By one o'clock the enemy attack was becoming very heavy all along the line and a retirement of both of the 16th and 39th Divisions was ordered. Thanks to the 1/ Royal Dublin Fusiliers, whose position covered the Cologne defile, and to a particularly fine rear-guard action fought by the 157 Field Company R.E. and the 11/ Hampshire, holding the 48 Brigade sector in and around Doingt, the enemy's advance was for a time checked so effectively that the 16 Division, the length of its columns of march sadly reduced by the

previous fighting, was able carry out its withdrawal through the southern part of Péronne. Crossing the Bristol Bridge between 3 and 6 p.m., it took position behind the river about half a mile west of Biaches, with a brigade stationed for a while east of the village, in touch with the 66th Division.[5]

The British were now on the west side of the Somme, back into the old French battlefields of the 1916 Battle of the Somme. Overlooking the bridges out of Péronne was the Chateau of La Maisonette, known by its height to the Allies as Hill 97. In 1916 this had been the site of vicious attack and counter-attack to take this commanding spot. Prussian artillery had shelled Péronne from here in 1871, and the whole area was much ruined from the 1916 battles. 'The pretty Maisonette château had been reduced to a shapeless mass of ruins, while the beautiful park in which it stood was so devastated as to be unrecognisable.'[6] Ringed with old trenches and strongpoints, and deep cellars, it still afforded the British a defensive line more extensive than that of the Green line had to the east of Péronne. This was a strong position for the men of the East Lancashire Division to hold. The artillery men would have been expecting an artillery duel between themselves and German guns on Mont St Quentin, the other side of Péronne.

The East Lancashire Division, nominally formed of three brigades, was battered and broken. In reality it had two composite brigades of hurriedly re-formed survivors. From north to south the brigades were aligned 197, 198 Brigades in the front line and 199 Brigade in reserve. The nominal battalions north to south were 5/ Border, 2/8 Lancashire Fusiliers, 6/ and 2/7 Lancashire Fusiliers, 4/ East Lancashire, 9/ Manchester, 431 Company R.E. and 2/5 East Lancashire, with 2/5 Manchester Regiment and 2/6, 2/7 Manchester Regiment in reserve. This list gave a fuller picture than actually existed of the battered remnants of the division. The battalions that had occupied the front lines were barely a company strong.

The Northumbrian Division still held the line east of the Somme and was pulling back. A cavalry screen was formed behind the Northumbrian Division of the 1st Cavalry Division, which also screened the open flanks. This was a rear screen for the infantry on the Green line and a forward screen for the infantry on the Somme bridges. The 8/ Hussars held the right flank, with the Queens' Bays, 5/ Dragoon Guards and 18 Hussars to their north on a line from Athies to Le Mesnil [-Bruntel]. The flanks of the East Lancashire were held by 24th Division to the south and a single brigade of 39th Division to the north.

The Somme river proved more of an obstacle now. A German shell had damaged one bridge and the Hussars were unable to use it and so rode to St Christ bridge instead. However, on hearing that the bridge there was also broken, they rode to Falvy, where they had tremendous difficulty crossing on the low planks. They attempted to swim their horses across, only becoming bogged down under shell and machine gun fire, with increasing equine casualties. The dismounted cavalrymen took cover and defended the crossing until relieved. Also at Falvy, a company of the East Surreys was cut off and had to swim across the river. Those still east of the river were in great danger of being cut down as the Germans attempted to capture a bridge and the engineers determined not to let them. At Pargny explosives were sent for from the cavalry and the job was finished at 6 pm by the 19/ Hussars.

The tanks that had played a part in the counter-attacks and survived were pulled back to the bridges over the Somme. A few of the tenders were sent to Moislans to the north-west but when this village was found to be in the hands of the enemy, they were destroyed. Other tanks moved to the bridge at Brie, where two heavy bridges had just been completed by American engineers. German forces were closing in on the bridge and one tank actively held back German forces advancing on it. The tanks were unable to cross because their crews did not have time to take the sponsons off before crossing, and these were also burnt. Thus E Battalion had lost all but three of its tanks since 21 March. Large amounts of tools and supplies were destroyed by the men under Major Henshall but Staff Sergeant Trigg concealed some of his tools in expectation that he might someday return. The men were redeployed as Lewis gun teams and continued to play an active role in the withdrawal under Colonel O'Kelly.[7] The bridges were then destroyed. It was then found that the rearguard of the 1/4 Green Howards had been left on the east bank of the river. They were able to scramble across the remains of the bridge, although the fear was that the Germans would also be able to cross this way.

The final elements of 16th and 39th Divisions were west of the Somme or west of Mont St Quentin by the early evening. At Bristol bridge outside Péronne three officers spent the afternoon attempting to demolish it with explosives. Captain Barker and Lieutenants Bowden and Mead were busy at this all afternoon until at 6 o'clock the 180 Tunnelling Company finished the task.[8] Men were increasingly lucky to get across at all and further south Sergeant Monty Watson was ordered to cover the retreat of 151 Brigade of 50th Division to the west bank of the Somme and after the infantry had crossed, the bridge was blown up. One span had actually been blown when he and his section withdrew; Watson threw his Vickers machine gun in the river and waded and swam across with his men at 3.15 that afternoon.[9]

Artillery was engaging the enemy as they came over the ridges east of the river. The guns of I Battery, Royal Horse Artillery, engaged them that afternoon, 'some good targets engaged during afternoon as enemy came down ridges towards the River Somme'. This was the experience of the field and horse artillery. This was open warfare the like of which had not been seen since 1914. The heavy artillery of the Royal Garrison Artillery had been in a new position by 10.25 am and then was ordered to move to a another position further back.

This was agreed to but with the proviso that:

> the batteries would probably be out of action for the rest of that day. Reference your order to retire batteries further west of [Somme] canal. Most of them are in action or just getting into action – communications with brigades is very difficult and delays in getting tractors and lorries cannot be helped. The brigades expected to move cannot be expected to be in action today'.[10]

The demolition of the bridges was a wide-ranging affair and as we have seen there was often an appreciable difference between what could be achieved with the explosives available and what this represented in the mind's eye of higher command. Many of the bridges were quite substantial and did not just vaporise, but still offered a route for determined infantry to clamber across. Thus for the moment infantry had to cover the ruined bridges to afford some kind of defence. The Somme is often a slow and sluggish river and easily crossed with rafts. For the time being the Germans were moving up to the line of the river and occupying their new positions. The bridges on the front of 66th Division were blown up at 3 o'clock in the afternoon on the orders of Major General Malcolm with the exception of Bristol bridge, which as we have seen was left for 16th Division to use.

The last soldiers were trudging through the empty town of Péronne when General Haig issued the following order to his third and Fifth Armies:

> Fifth Army will hold the line of the River Somme at all costs. There will be no withdrawal from this line. It is of the greatest importance that the Fifth Army should effect a junction with the French on their right without delay. The Third and Fifth armies must stay in closest touch in order to secure their junction and must mutually assist each other in maintaining Péronne as a pivot.

145

Gunner Tom Hardman reported that:

> Fritz pushed us back right over the Somme but he must have lost a
> very large number of men as he came over each time in massed
> formation.

It was these massed formations that the infantry and artillery was firing
on. The effect on the Germans when they expected an easy victory was
to destroy their discipline. Despite the orders, Péronne was vacated that
evening after a fighting rearguard by the men of 11/ Hampshire
Regiment, the Pioneers of the Irish Division. After that the town was
empty, although the Germans presumed that it would be defended and
laid down a furious bombardment on it.

The Germans pushed down to the river that evening but did not
attempt to cross on the front of Malcolm's East Lancashire. The main
effort was further south:

> During the rest of the afternoon there were artillery duels across the
> river, but no determined effort was made by the enemy to force a
> passage. During the night ... several attempts were made by the
> enemy to force a passage of the Somme on the front of the 8th
> Division. About 9 o'clock a party succeeded in rushing the ruins of
> the canal bridge at Pargny and occupying the village. An immediate
> counter-attack by about seventy of the 1/ Worcestershire and 2/ Rifle
> Brigade, in three parties drove the Germans back with the loss of
> many killed, twenty prisoners and four machine guns. For
> organising this counter-attack their Commander, Major Roberts, was
> awarded the Victoria Cross.

In the early evening the Germans started to make concerted attempts to
cross the Somme river. This started in the area guarded by the 8th
Division outlined by the action above. Another attempt was made at St
Christ and was driven off by the Sherwood Foresters. In the sector
opposite Péronne not much occurred.

Peter Hall, guarding the ruined bridge at Biaches, recounted:

> I shall never forget that night. In spite of the efforts of the French to
> get rid of the wine, the German advance had been so rapid that they
> had not been able to destroy all their stocks completely and the
> Germans were soon roaringly drunk, singing and shouting, and by
> midnight setting fire to buildings all over the town.[11]

It was a moment out of a Wagner opera, as the Götterdämmerung of the German army, and signified a subtle change that would come over the advance of the Germans from the rank and file to the High Command.

The Germans had finally occupied Péronne, originally an objective for the first day of the battle, but it had cost them heavily, their casualties were much higher than expected, and when the Guards Division attacked they had expected a walkover similar to the attack in Italy at Caporetto: the British had showed them otherwise. The men of Malcolm's East Lancashire Division and the soldiers of XIX Corps had delayed them for two days and all the time had not broken, showing a steadfastness and an apparent willingness to lay down their lives.

It was not all steadfastness in the British army: as Peter Hall was dug in on the west bank of the Somme, a gap opened up between 39th Division to the north or left of the East Lancashires. Hall volunteered on Sunday to go back to headquarters and round up men to fill the gaps.

> There was another incident during the struggle to hold the bridge. Colonel Maxwell of the 5th wanted reinforcement and as our Colonel was not about Major Brookfield asked for volunteers to go down the road to a Headquarters establishment and ask for assistance. Charlie Percival and I set off and when we got there found the whole place a shambles. Most people had moved on except some who were drunk and fooling around pinning medals on each other! I lost my temper and said that the Germans were a quarter of a mile up the road or less and what help could we have.
>
> We were told to do whatever we liked. So we rounded up everyone we could – cooks and bottle washers and all sorts auxiliary people and marched them back to our lines. Some of them would not have expected to fight and I felt sorry for them but it was the luck of war.
>
> When we got back the Colonel said 'I'll see you two get mentioned in dispatches for this' a statement that proved an embarrassment because the sergeant overheard and went back to Manchester wounded soon afterwards and told everyone we would be mentioned. However the Colonel was taken prisoner and the Major killed so nothing came of it.[12]

The Germans now threatened Pargny to the south. The German plan originally had been to take Péronne and then pivot to the north and wrap up the British Third Army to the north to Arras, with the Somme held to guard the flank of this movement. The relative success of the attacks in the south and the retreat of Butler's III Corps and the retirement of Maxse had lured the German High Command to make a change of strategy and decide to attack and seize Amiens, a vital cog in the British line of supply.

General Ludendorff now came to the conclusion that the original concept, to drive up north-westwards from the start line, could not be sustained. He issued orders on 23 March for his most northerly formations to continue in their attack, but the Second German Army was to head west towards Amiens and the Eighteenth Army to work alongside on its left. The major effort was thus an assault on a line from Noyon through Montdidier to Amiens. He had decided that Amiens was a prize worth reaching out for.[13]

The requirements of the East Lancashire Field Ambulance were more rudimentary, as the exhausted medics established their ambulance in a hamlet to the west of Barleux and an A.D.S. was formed in a quarry on the north side of the road between Barleux and the Somme. Bearer posts were established on the main Péronne road, between La Chapelette and Eterpigny, two posts in the right sector and two in the left sector. For the moment each side took stock and the Germans waited for their artillery to come up. The British gunners dug in and reinforced their positions. The main problems facing the soldiers were hunger and thirst. Some form of scavenging was necessary to get the requisite supplies. The men of the 2/3 East Lancashire Field Ambulance were lucky to have a good ration corporal:

> The magnificent work of Lance Corporal Wells in bringing up rations during the whole of the retreat is worthy of special mention. As soon as he had delivered his day's rations he at once set off again to get in touch with the Royal Army Service Corps and never once during the whole retreat did he fail to find the Field Ambulance in its various wanderings, and deliver safely the quartermaster's supplies. Colonel England of the R.A.S.C. said of him that his work was outstandingly good, and that he was the best ration Corporal in the Division. Colonel England's regret was that the Ration Corporals of the other units were not so efficient.[14]

The heavy artillery had been repositioned that afternoon as we saw earlier and at 7.10 that evening was able to open a concentrated fire on Brie and the approaches. This village was the point at which the Germans were currently pressing their attack in an effort to cross the Somme river.

It was reported on the morning of Sunday, 24 March that Germans were trying to cross the canal in the area of Biaches with a pontoon bridge. Aircraft were deployed to bomb the locality, although no pontoons were spotted, and artillery shelled the area as well. Communications were established with 39th Division on the left and 50th Division on the right. Part of this reorganisation involved the 6/ Durham Light Infantry pulling out of its positions and leaving a gap in the front that was quickly filled by another Durham battalion, the 7/ D.L.I. (Pioneers).

Headquarters seemed to be a little unsure of the general strategy. Official policy was to hold the Somme river line 'at all costs', and this had been imposed on Gough by Haig. The reality of the situation was a little different and the whole front had to be taken into account, rather than individual corps or divisional sectors. At 9.20 am a wire was received from Watts at Corps H.Q. that laid down 'although there was no intention to withdraw, unless absolutely necessary. Yet, should the position become untenable, the Division would fall back on the general line, Assevillers inclusive to Estrees, and the 39th Division on our left from Herbecourt to the Somme'.

The Germans, meanwhile, were also reorganising and instead of pushing north-west were now re-forming to follow the order to attack across the Somme and west, gaining them the valuable prize of Amiens to the rear of XIX Corps. It was not until the evening that it was reported again that the Germans were crossing the Somme on Malcolm's divisional sector. The 2/5 Manchester Regiment reported at 6.31 pm that a post was being established at the bridgehead at I.33.d [around the railway bridge] but that it was reinforcing its own position to contain the enemy post. 'The bridgehead and the unbroken railway bridge at Péronne had enabled large bodies of Germans to cross on the left of the new line.'[15]

General Malcolm recalled that:

> The situation was well in hand, but serious inconvenience had been caused by the short shooting of our British artillery, which appeared to be firing from the direction of Frise. Many casualties were caused by this shelling which, added to exhaustion and strain, was highly detrimental to the morale of the troops, and caused considerable disorganisation.'[16]

At 7 o'clock that evening a company of the neighbouring 6/ Durham Light Infantry was brought up and counter-attacked the German bridgehead, but the Germans were now in sufficient strength that two attacks by the battalion were both unsuccessful in taking the position and throwing the enemy over the river again. That evening the 149 Brigade of the 50th Division were placed under General Malcolm's command and the 5/ and 6/ Northumberland Fusiliers placed under General Hunter of 198 Brigade. The flexibility of the divisional system under the corps commander Watts is shown here as commanders could increase or reduce the number of soldiers under their command depending upon the situation.

Tiredness was setting in across the army and General Malcolm reflected with hindsight that it would have been better to have

> extricated the field companies of the Royal Engineers and the pioneer battalion from the line and withdrawn them to reorganise in divisional reserve. There had been a lull in the attack, our infantry reorganisation had been more or less completed, the troops had had a fair night's rest, and our numbers with the addition of the troops of the 50th Division in close support should have been sufficient to repel any attempt of the enemy to force the crossings. This course had been suggested by [Malcolm] to General Hunter in the early morning, but in view of the fact that most definite orders from the higher command had been received that the river line was to be held at all costs, that the situation round the Péronne bridgehead was causing anxiety, and that the supporting troops of the 50th Division were more or less earmarked for the Eterpigny sector and were ... not considered available for reinforcing the Biaches sector.[17]

For Gunner John Gore it was a tiring time having spent the previous day at Faye:

> There were a few dugouts, very poor ones. We had a fire but as I was looking after the ammunition I got no sleep all night. The men were loading up the limbers and waggons in reliefs. We stayed there until all the batteries had drawn out and retired down the road. Then we went. The DTMO leading us on horseback. All the roads were heavily shelled so he took us across country to Chouings. [25 March] At Chouings there is a big ammunition dump. We found an old deserted house, Clarke, Ford, Dyer, Hampson, and self slept in the cellar on straw with a good fire on. Slept well. Everybody on fatigues in reliefs except myself.[18]

The result was that these units remained in the front line and were not used to strengthen the line, and were caught up in the general withdrawal. In the rear of the German lines, in a prisoner of war compound, R.C.A. Frost was hungry and cold: 'We had no food at all from the 20 March until the 24 March and then it was about half a pint of oatmeal water and salty at that.'[19]

Both British and Germans had used Sunday to reorganise their own forces and on Monday, 25 March the Germans had moved their direction of advance to resume offensive operations in the direction of Amiens. The right flank of 24th Division had been pushed back on Sunday and this required a reorganisation of the line, and the pulling back of certain units. Brigadier General Hunter's 7/ Durham Light Infantry withdrew from Eterpigny and the enemy under cover of an intense machine gun barrage and a certain amount of artillery fire crossed the river in large numbers. The G.O.C. 198 Brigade, however organised an immediate counter-attack with two companies and by 12.30 pm the enemy had been pushed back and the former line was re-established, though the 7/ D.L.I., who had become very demoralised, could not be stopped and retired in groups through Barleux on to Assevillers. Tiredness was affecting the troops and morale was sinking as the German thrust began to take its toll. The Germans were getting the upper hand, pushing along the Eterpigny–Villers-Carbonnel road. General Hunter pushed out a line with his 197 Brigade to the north of this road in order to contain this movement. At the same time 149 Brigade sent forward two battalions to hold the spur south-west of Barleux.

The soldiers holding the positions around La Maisonette now came under fire from German artillery, machine gun and trench mortar fire as the Germans obviously meant to cross at Péronne and push eastwards.

> Forward positions at Ferme Lamire and La Chapelette causing considerable casualties to the troops occupying this area, a portion of which withdrew to the high ground between the Orme de Barleux and La Maisonette, the majority were holding on and our supports were occupying the front or rear of the slopes of the crest line according[ly] as the enemy fire decreased or increased. Fighting continued through the afternoon although the situation remained unchanged.[20]

Peter Hall was caught up in this fighting and remembered:

> Somehow we held onto this bridgehead, resisting every attack and under heavy artillery bombardment and, worse still, large numbers of trench mortars from the troops in the town on the opposite bank,

151

not only the minenwerfers but the very heavy ones called flying pigs, which on landing dug in deep before exploding and thus produced a large crater. One of these exploded just in front of the parapet, killing two other men in the same bay with shock and with flying metal from the bomb itself. Although I was nearer to it than they were it just pushed the parapet on top of me, burying me face downwards with only my left hand showing where rescuers came running from the next bay. They saw the hand moving and that I was alive and shouted for stretcher bearers.[21]

Despite this it took fifteen minutes to dig him out as he was pinned in by the weight of sandbags:

Many times since those days, if I have gone to bed overtired I have woken up dreaming of that crushing weight trying to bury me.

It was not a healthy place to be and pitiful deaths were suffered. Hall remembered a trumpeter

was very seriously hurt. Before dying he propped himself up against the trench and put his trumpet to his lips and put all he knew into playing the trumpet voluntary. The sound even penetrated the bombardment and the mortars stopped firing and the Germans started cheering. At first we thought they were showing their appreciation of the music, but as we looked round we could see that their troops had succeeded in crossing the river on both sides of us and were closing in behind us.[22]

This fighting was an odd affair and strange things happened in those days of tiredness and fighting.

Hall and what remained of his battalion saw no sense in being cut off, and made for the ridge behind their position, unseen by the Germans they ran up a gully and were making good their escape until they came to a road with a culvert underneath that was their only means of escape. 'There was no alternative but to dash out of the gully and across the road and into the gully again. An enemy Machine gun got onto us and about a quarter of our men were killed in that dash across the road.' He was hit by shelling and flying stones, knocked unconscious and it was only the appearance of the cavalry of the 17/ Lancers, who attacked over his unconscious body, that saved him from capture or death.

At 5.45 that evening the order was received to withdraw to the Assevillers line. This withdrawal was to be covered by the 149 Brigade, after which it would return to its own division. In the East Lancashire Division the 197 and 199 Brigades were to share the sector with 198 in support at Becquincourt. The new line, roughly on the line of the modern motorway, was reached by 10.30 that night. Clever use of artillery also meant that the Germans did not realise the withdrawal had been made until the early hours of the next morning. 'Two single 18 pounder guns which had previously been given a roving commission to demonstrate in front of our outposts during the night, were handled with great boldness and it is improbable that the enemy suspected that we had retired before several hours after dawn on the 26th [March].'

Casualties were continuing to mount and it was decided that the brigade level of command was working sufficiently well to continue its use.

> Since the total effective strength of the Division was now considerably less than that of an ordinary infantry brigade it was decided to continue the system of grouping all the forward troops under the command of one brigadier. Brigadiers were to take this turn in order to avoid over fatigue to themselves and their staffs. This system worked well and was continued with few interruptions till the Division was withdrawn.

This was the beginning of the smaller 'forces', such as Carey's Force, which fought the withdrawal at the brigade level but were comprised of anyone who could hold a rifle and might come from a wide variety of battalions or regiments as men were amalgamated from whatever was left of their original unit. The manpower shortage was being adapted to and the command structure evolving to give commanders a rest and becoming a modern flexible structure.

Gough visited his corps commanders that evening, and of General Watts he said: 'As I passed near his headquarters I looked in about 5.30 pm and found the general so weary that he could hardly keep his eyes open. I do not think he had had four hours sleep in three nights and days.' Gough arranged with Watts' A.D.C. to make him lie down and rest and later to have some food to eat. It was not just the infantry who went without sleep and food.

NOTES:
[1] Francis, A., *History of the 2/3 East Lancashire Field Ambulance*, p.99.
[2] Boraston and Bax, *The Eighth Division, 1914–1918*, p.175.
[3] ibid.

4 TNA, WO95/3121.

5 Edmunds, E., *Official History, 1918*, Vol. I, p.359.

6 Michelin, *Bygone Pilgrimage Guide to the Battlefields 1916–1917*, p.109ff.

7 *History of 5/ or E Battalion Royal Tank Corps*, The Tank Museum, Bovington.

8 Murland J., *Retreat and Rearguard – Somme 1918*, p.162.

9 Crutchley, C.E., *Machine Gunner*, 1973, p.95.

10 TNA, WO95/198.

11 IWM Department of Documents, papers of P.R. Hall.

12 ibid.

13 Marix Evans, M., *Somme 1914–18 Lessons in War*, p.187.

14 Francis, A., *History of the 2/3 East Lancashire Field Ambulance*, p.99.

15 Latter, J.C., *Lancashire Fusiliers 1914–1918*, 1949, p.293.

16 TNA, WO95/3121.

17 ibid.

18 IWM Department of Documents, papers of J.W. Gore.

19 IWM Department of Documents, papers of R.C.A. Frost.

20 TNA, WO95/3121

21 IWM Department of Documents, papers of P.R. Hall.

22 ibid.

Chapter 13

We Have Won The War

26–27 March, Tuesday and Wednesday

Infantry of the 149 Brigade, Northumberland Division, were to cover the infantry withdrawal and 66th Divisional artillery were to give artillery fire with the 86 Australian Field Artillery brigade, 250 R.A. Brigade and C, K and G Batteries, Royal Horse Artillery. This withdrawal was carried out in good order and command passed from General Hunter to the general commanding 149 Brigade at 7.30 that evening. This was carried out in accordance with the flanking 118 Brigade. The new line had been reconnoitred in daylight and subdivided into sectors and dumps of ammunition and various stores provided. The divisional commanders held a conference with General Watts on the advisability of further retirement as

> both flanks of the corps appeared to be thoroughly exposed and the enemy's Very Lights seemed to form a semicircle around us. After some discussion and reference to the Army command [General Gough], it was decided that we were to hold on to the Estrées – Assevillers – Herbecourt position until strongly attacked, but not to fight decisively. Further orders were subsequently issued as to the next line to be held.

The night passed quietly in both front line and rear echelons. Rear headquarters were in Warfusee-Abancourt and brigade headquarters in Harbonnières.

The East Lancs Division was in position now on an old 1916 trench line, with 39th Division on its left and 50th Division on the right. At 8.30 in the morning 198 Brigade began a move from Bequincourt to Foucaucourt to cover the withdrawal of 197 and 199 Brigades, which

155

were on the Assevillers line. The Germans attacked the front of the 39th Division at Hesbécourt, which was taken by them. This was an important loss as the village was on high ground and enfiladed the ground to the south where the line continued. On the right of the division pressure was mounting on the Northumberland Division, which was forced to withdraw at 11 o'clock from its line, and the recently placed 198 Brigade, which was in position to cover this weak spot. 'Had it not been for the troops of 198 Brigade, our line of retreat would have been seriously jeopardised [see map 10].'[1]

This ongoing pressure by the Germans forced General Borrett, who was in command at that time, to take the decision to withdraw to the Vauvillers to Foucaucourt line, which was reached by around 2 pm. The general movement and momentum was towards the new line and later caused a large amount of congestion on the roads, which 198 Brigade avoided. At that moment it was discovered that no communication was available with 39th Division on the left when Rainecourt was reached. The enemy were pressing forward on the right (of the 39th Division). It was important that Rainecourt village should not be lost before the division arrived and accordingly 198 Brigade of the East Lancashires was placed there to defend the location against enemy incursion. The battle was taking on a fluid and open nature now that no natural obstacles were available to defend, and the German General Staff change of plan to attack Amiens instead of north of the Somme was giving momentum to the battle in XIX Corps sector. The men of 198 Brigade were in Rainecourt village when they had been destined to be in reserve in Harbonnières.

The scene was set for the battle of Harbonnières. It was at this point, crucially that Lieutenant Colonel Little arrived via the divisional training camp near Corbie on 25 March. Again taking the initiative, he raised four companies from among the men there, put them under officers and marched them forwards towards the fighting. At this very moment when reserves were non-existent, Little was arriving with more than 600 much-needed men and marching them up to the line. In the meantime the battle developed, somewhat worryingly for East Lancashire Division and XIX Corps commander Watts. The four companies of Little's force were under Captains C.H. Potter, G.W. Fox, N.D. Robinson and E.L. Higgins.

The earlier heavy fighting that engaged the left of the corps and disrupted the rearguard of 39th Division had far-reaching effects for the placement of 198 Brigade.

It upset the subsequent withdrawal of 197 and 199 Brigades. In their turn they were being heavily engaged and slowed by enemy forces pestering their heels. The British had slipped ahead of the Germans too

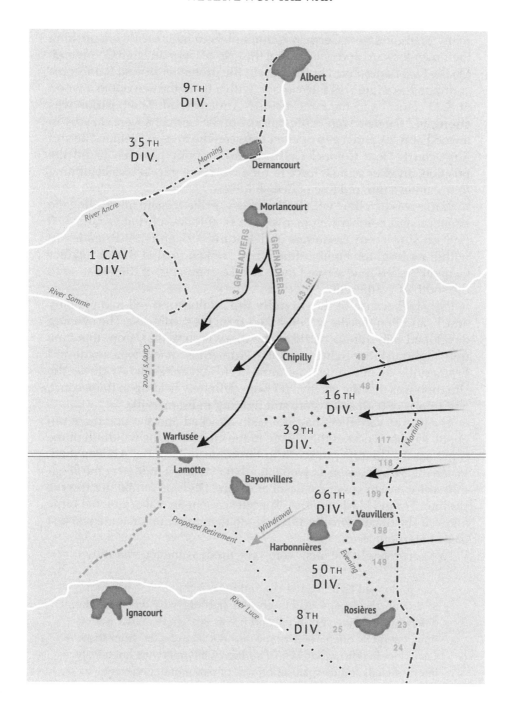

Map 10: Between the Luce and Ancre, 27 March 1918.

many times and now German commanders in their turn were pushing their men forward and one can feel the grip of German High Command. On the East Lancashire Division's left, the problems around Rainecourt continued as a line was thrown out, with a flank thrown out to a wood at X.33 central and the Foucaucourt–Amiens road. The position was strong and the men were reorganised, but the Germans were close by in a wood at R.29, and a gap opened between the lines at Framerville and Rainecourt. Here Colonel Gell organised about 100 men to fill the position, another scratch force to fill a worrying gap. It was beginning to resemble a thin red line of British forces.

Worse was to follow with British heavy artillery again misreading the situation and bombarding its own forces at Rainecourt at around 3.30 pm, causing more casualties and leading 197 and 199 Brigades to withdraw from the bombardment to a sunken road at R.33. Brigadier General Borrett now arrived there to take command of the situation to the south of Framerville.

Perhaps because of the 'friendly fire', Rainecourt fell to an enemy attack, and Framerville was attacked from the north-east. The evening developed into quite a battle as the diary reports that 'from this time until nightfall bitter fighting ensued. Numerous attacks were made and Framerville at one time was almost entirely retaken. At dusk, the situation was that the enemy had been definitely held up in Rainecourt, and troops of both sides were still fighting in Framerville.'

The line at Vauvillers had not been attacked and the line there ran about 300 yards east of the village in the vicinity of the windmill of the same name. The line ran north to the sugar mill on the Amiens road. When the 39th Division arrived later that evening it took over the sugar mill sector and forces of the East Lancashire Division retired to a reserve position around Harbonnières. The subsequent arrival of Colonel Little allowed the mixed force of 198 Brigade men to retire for some rest just east of Harbonnières.

Not surprisingly the men were very tired, as the records show:

> The prolonged fighting and continuous marching were beginning to tell on the troops. Although still fighting well when on the defence, they were very tired, and it was evident that after a short time, energetic offensive action could not be expected from them. Casualties in officers had been very heavy, all units were hopelessly intermingled, and reorganisation was of paramount necessity.

Peter Hall was also tired: 'I was so disgusted with this muddled war and felt that the army of the future would be more dependent on air support so I [later] applied for a commission in the Royal Flying Corps.'[2] He was indeed ahead of his time for just four days later the R.F.C. would be reborn as the Royal Air Force, and a new breed of men would be needed. But for the moment Hall fought on, as many of the infantry searched the sky for friendly air support.

John Gore had spent the previous day or so moving ammunition and delivering it to the forward dumps on the new lines. It was not popular work, as ever for Gore, but it played its role in delaying the Germans as good organisation played its part in the retreat. 'All the roads were being heavily shelled so we went across country to Chuignes.' On March 26 Gore recorded: 'Jerry still advancing, had to buzz off very quickly and managed to get an ammunition lorry to Villers-Bretonneux, passing through Lamotte and Warfusee-Abancourt.'[3]

Another welcome relief to men at the front was a force under Major Kingham, who also arrived from the corps reinforcements camp with 300 men. So all in all that evening the division received more than 900 reinforcements, new commanders with fresh and willing minds, replacing worn and hungry men who were losing the will to fight on. Some had been in battle for five days and nights. Major Kingham's men were put in reserve to the north of the railway station at Harbonnières. These welcome reinforcements gave the British a boost and fresh troops were crucial in any situation as grave as the one faced by General Watts and his divisional commanders, including Malcolm and the East Lancashire brigadiers. The line from right to left was now held by forces under the Northumberland Division, Norton, Hurlblatt and Gell, Colonel Little's force and the 39th Division with Whitehead, Hill and Kingham in reserve.

The nature of the ground was now in the favour of the British defenders, as it was a

> bare, level plain [which] afforded an exceptional field of fire, and from Harbonnières station to the cross roads Q.3.d.9 ran a very good system of trenches, protected by excellent wire. This line was reconnoitred in the early morning, and divided into sectors with a view to reorganising on it all oddments [of different units] at present in support.

Lieutenant Colonel Little's force arrived during the afternoon. He found General Malcolm with some of his staff in a cellar in Lamotte and was welcomed. 'Right glad he was to learn that a battalion in fresh condition had descended upon him. God is good. Malcolm said: "You will be able to take over the front line from Brigadier General Hunter at dusk and give him and his weary troops a night's rest." This I did.' Little kept the slips of paper that reported the relief of his four company commanders, Potter, Fox, Robinson and Higgins: 'Relief complete'. The front line covered some 2,000 yards from near the sugar factory on the Amiens road to south-west of Framerville. Little's description of his command is clear and shows his determination to lead and make a difference to the military situation.

Little was in his element. Captain Feetham reported:

> Well, between 10 and 11 o'clock, as you know, the Hun attacked and that day's fight I shall never forget. It was great. The Division on our left fell back out of sight. Then the troops on our right did the same. My two forward companies I decided to bring back about 200 yards as they were in a position in which enfilade fire could do a lot of damage from the left. They were being heavily shelled and machine gunned, but they fought back splendidly and took up their new positions in fine style. One company I used to refuse the left flank.
>
> Then some troops – I think Colonel Whiteheads (ELR) came up and these I used to refuse my right. My line now ran on the line on which you [Colonel Little] saw me. I saw the position might now become serious if counter-attacks were not launched on the flanks, so went back (incidentally turning troops on the way with my revolver). And met a Brigadier, I think of the 50th Division, east of Harbonnières. I told him the situation and he went off to get a counter-attack going on the left. Then I saw some of our men assembling on the right and ran over to tell them exactly where they were wanted. The left went well up to a certain point but they never reached my line by some 5 to 600 yards. I think they must have come under fire from the Proyart direction.[4]

Colonel Little's papers reveal the way the battle unfolded:

> The 4/ Northumberland Fusiliers (50th Division) have withdrawn from my right flank leaving a gap of four hundred yards between my front and the left flank of the 197 Brigade. At 3 a.m. I received a message from Lieutenant Colonel Gell to the effect that he and Lt-Colonel Hurlblatt were withdrawing to Vauvillers. At 9 o'clock Higgins reported three Very lights having been put up west edge of Framerville and two Bosch machine guns suspected in the church. Then from Lt Colonel Whitehead (East Lancashire Regiment) came 'enemy troops advancing down slopes x.4 and x.10 apparent direction Framerville. I send you this information as General Officer

Commanding 66th Division informs me you have to deal with this front and I have to support you.'

Then from Robinson 'party of enemy appeared outside village and retired on being fired on'.

From Fox 'enemy advancing x.9 and x.10 few of our troops on left flank falling back.'

From Higgins 'Enemy moving in mass north of Framerville.'

From the 6/ Cheshire (39th Division) 'Troops on our left are falling back.'

Higgins 'Cambridgeshires on left of Amiens road are retiring.'

From Colonel Whitehead 'My orders are to get and hold Framerville. Can you tell me if any of your troops are in or in front of the town?'

My reply was in the negative and quite rightly this counter-attack never developed. During this time things were livening up and there was considerable rifle and machine gun fire with occasional shelling. At 11.40 a.m. I sent the following message to Colonel Whitehead, 'General Malcolm has been here and states that our present line is to be held at all costs and wishes you to ensure that the commanding Officer of the battalion on your left clearly understands this order.' A battle then developed all along the front and men of my composite battalion had good shooting. But troops on our left were falling back rapidly.

I managed to stop some of them and under a Captain and subaltern of a Cambridgeshire Regiment placed them facing north along the Amiens road. Two forward companies I withdrew about two hundred yards to obtain a better field of fire, and right well did they take up their new positions. My left flank was now being enveloped and I ran back for help. I met a brigadier and told him of the position. He got men together for a counter-attack and this was pushed forward but never reached any line. Towards the gap I saw the enemy approaching and running back again I found men of the 22/Durham Light Infantry digging in north-west of Harbonnières. These men I extended and in rushes went north towards the Amiens road. Several prisoners were taken and those of the remainder who could, fled. My left flank was now quite secure.

161

The counter-attack on the right went exceedingly well for a time, in fact they actually passed my line, but no sooner had they halted than the old Hun attacked again and instead of our people sticking to their ground, they turned about. In the meantime the sight of the counter-attacks on both flanks had cheered up my fellows no end, but when they saw the right falling back again those on the right felt a little bit shaky. However they soon pulled themselves together again and got some good shooting at some Boche who tried to get round them. My front was now running at right angles about 1,000 yards facing north and 200 yards east. Thanks to the freshness of my own officers and men the enemy could make no headway on our immediate front, but those in Vauvillers on our right gave way, and falling back towards Harbonnières, left our right flank exposed.

Going back again I found two or three guns of the Royal Horse Artillery under a subaltern, who had been firing manfully in the direction of Proyart. I told him the danger spot was now Vauvillers and that I wanted him to protect my right flank by preventing the enemy from entering this village. He was glad to have a definite order and there and then switched his guns round.

I then went over to the right and near Harbonnières station found troops with more than one 'red hat' assembling for a counter-attack on Vauvillers. To them I explained where my men were.

This counter-attack went well and oncoming waves of the enemy were driven back and Vauvillers retaken. But the village could not be held and our troops were once more driven back by a fresh onslaught. It was, I believe, in this counter-attack that Lt Colonel Hurlblatt was killed and Lt Colonel Gell taken prisoner.

I still have a message from Captain Bond, Brigade Major, timed 11.45 p.m. 27 March 1918, addressed to poor Hurlblatt. It contains various instructions and finishes with a personal note. 'The General wants you to come back to Brigade Headquarters at once and have 24 hours rest so that you can take over from Colonel Little tomorrow evening.'[5]

Such were the fates of war. Colonel Little was forced to withdraw due to the failure to keep Vauvillers and the evacuation of the Harbonnières Station position by other forces in the area [see map 10a].

At six o'clock in the morning one company of the force under Major Kingham was ordered forward into close support of Colonel Little. Major Kingham was also ordered to reconnoitre the divisional front with a view to taking over the line with his men, fresh as they were. What remained of the East Lancashire Division was due to be pulled

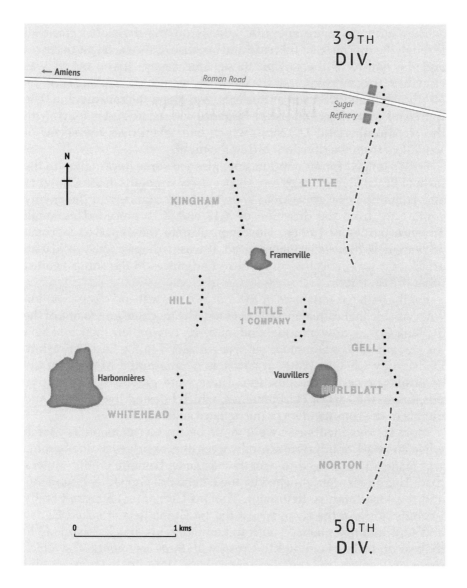

Map 10a: Harbonnières.

back into Harbonnières so the men could be rested and reorganised, as it was evident how exhausted they were. General Malcolm visited Colonel Whitehead, Colonel Little and Major Kingham. He arranged artillery support and ordered that full support was to be given to Colonel Little in case of an attack on his position.

The Germans made sporadic attacks on the divisional front all through the morning; in this case and because of the excellent defences and the nature of the terrain these were easily driven off. It was elsewhere that morning that the Germans were successful, against the Northumberland Division at Rosières, and along the railway line. The right flank of the East Lancashire Brigades was secure and in touch with the Northumberland Division, which had taken over the sector of Vauvillers from the division during the night.

Frost's longed for air support now gleaned some information in the form of Royal Flying Corps reports of enemy strengths in the Chuignes and Fontaine-Les-Cappy areas showing large numbers of the enemy coming up from the direction of X.12 and X.18 preceded by small advance parties of troops. However, despite the expected German advance here this never materialised. It was perhaps a feint, or just an attack that was cancelled in favour of advances to the south against other British forces.

For the battered remnants of XIX Corps some rest and reorganisation was possible in the area of Harbonnières. The machine gun teams of the 5/ Tank Corps, now an independent force, having left their tanks on the east side of the Somme river, were attached to the East Lancashire Division by General Watts at corps as he attempted to increase the defensive power of the position. These were placed in a defensive position to the east of Harbonnières, which boosted the position and morale of the commanders of the defence substantially.

More serious incursions were made by the Germans on 27 March when an attack south from Chipilly over intact bridges on the Somme was made and managed to penetrate as far as Lamotte on the Amiens road. This attack was launched by the 1st and 3rd Grenadier Regiments and the 43rd Infantry Regiment. The 3rd Grenadiers attacked Sailly Laurette north of the river, whilst the 1st Grenadiers attacked Cerisy and 43rd Infantry pushed south to Lamotte. This attack was made to the rear of the line held by XIX Corps with three regiments. The attack more or less cut off the remnants of the 16th Irish Division and threatened the defences of three more divisions, the 39th, 66th and 50th.

The attack that reached the main Roman Road at Lamotte-Warfusee forced swift action to avert a crisis. Gough ordered a major withdrawal by elements of the Irish Division and the 39th pushed a flank to the north. A battalion from the Northumberland Division and the 2/ Devons were rushed up to cover the northern flank, a counter-attack was organised and pushed north across 39th Division's front. The Devonshires, after heavy fighting and considerable casualties, succeeded in driving the Germans back and linking up with the left flank of Major Kingham. This was the Battle of Rosières. The effect of the attacks on Malcolm's East Lancashires was to make him also push a flank out to the north. A force under Colonel Cope of the Northumberland Division counter-attacked and put itself in position between the 39th and 66th Divisions just in time to fend off a German attack.

An overt threat remained to the British defence that was achieved by the attack across the river, pushing back the remnants of the Irish Division, threatening the flank of the 39th Division, and by default the northern flank of Little's force. The remains of the East Lancashire Division suffered so many casualties in their exposed positions that they were thoroughly depleted. General Malcolm thus moved Colonel Little to the north and pushed a flank back to cover the crisis using his brigade staff to man the line. These were extreme measures, but there was no one else left. Orders were issued to fall back on the line held by Carey's Force to the west. This was the decisive battle of the campaign as far as Watts' corps and the East Lancashire Division were concerned. Still the most determined German attack had not broken the British line, so an organised withdrawal south-westwards was allowed. The German pincer down to Lamotte had not cut off the British to the east, and was not strong enough to do this. Had the Germans had cavalry, tanks and enough infantry they could have forced a decisive battle here, surrounded XIX Corps and opened a gap in the line, pushed on to Amiens and won the battle, even the war. However, they did not. General Malcolm reaction's was: 'It is quite good Gentlemen, we have won the war.' This was a view that was echoed in the headquarters of General Watts and General Debenney.

A similar attitude was taken by the German High Command on a strategic scale, and led many Germans to see this day as the failure of the offensive. The German Seventeenth Army was not progressing and the Second Army had not progressed as much as had been hoped on the previous day. Crown Prince Rupprecht tried to influence his generals to support the attacks against Amiens with three divisions. German Headquarters refused his request and he exclaimed: 'Then we have lost the war!'[6] The Germans had been held once again and although months of battle and deadlock would follow, this was the moment that the commanders could see the German offensive had failed. This was not apparent to the men on the ground and thousands had given their lives and would continue to die to give the generals their moment of enlightenment. Foremost among them were the fallen of XIX Corps and the East Lancashire Division, still being wounded and killed. General Gough had prophesied that if they could be held for eight days that would be enough and it would appear he was correct; even the German commanders were aware of the failure to break through and take Amiens, that the British had held their line.

NOTES:
[1] TNA, WO95/3121.
[2] IWM Department of Documents, papers of Peter Hall.
[3] IWM Department of Documents, papers of John Gore.
[4] IWM Department of Documents, papers of Colonel W.B. Little.
[5] Lancashire Bury Archives, *Clickety-Clicks*, 1937–38, pp.20–30.
[6] Edmunds, E., *Official History, 1918*, Vol. II, p.41.

Chapter 14

Front Line Generals

28–31 March, Wednesday to Sunday

On 27 March Tom Hardman was caught up in the withdrawal, retiring through Dompières to what he decribed as 'valley positions':

> Fritz shelled us heavily and from 4 o'clock till I was hit he must have had a number of guns ranged on us for shells came over like a shower of rain. About 8 o'clock he dropped a shell amongst me and my horses and blew them to pieces out of my hands, still nerves hit me [sic], overcame another which blew my horse's back off killing him also wounding my Major. Me and another seven men wounded, wandered around all night looking for a dressing station. Found one at Guillacourt where they dressed my wounds. The men made some breakfast and gave me some bacon and bread. I had had nothing for two days and nights and was very hungry.

Tom was evacuated by ambulance to the rear areas. For the men of the East Lancashire R.E. the withdrawal was a sad affair as they had to destroy installations along the Amiens road:

> A stand in each place, in which some of the R.E. assisted, was made to cover the retirement and delay the enemy's advance. During this part of the retreat, parties of engineers were told off to set on fire the many huts, rest camps, hospitals, etc., that had been built along the main Amiens–St Quentin road during the winter of 1917–18, and a heartbreaking task it was to see some of the better cared for YMCA and Church Army huts that had served many a weary soldier as a haven of rest, thus sacrificed before the advancing enemy and sent up in flames.[1]

Somewhere in the withdrawal Peter Hall came across a group of fifty men looking lost and bewildered. The young officer had a map that he was too shaky to read and the sergeant major could not read a map after twenty-five years in the army. They asked Hall to help and

> could [I] guide them to where they had been instructed to re-join their battalions. I saw that it was only half a mile from where I hoped to find mine [unit] so much to their relief I agreed. When we got there the Colonel was a real old army type blimp reeking of whiskey and in a flaming temper he tore strips off the younger officer then turned on the sergeant major and then on me; 'As for you, you must be a deserter. I shall court martial you in the morning.' That really got my back up. I was exhausted, hungry and had got his men back. I said 'I thought you were an officer and a gentleman and I expected at least a thank you for getting your men back.' That steadied him and he started to cool down and turned away and said, 'Don't forget if you are still here in the morning it is a court martial'.

After that the sergeant major congratulated Hall on his handling of the colonel and gave him some coffee, a meal, and sent him on his way. He got back in time for the battle of Harbonnières. Hall had a different take on the counter-attack:

> There was a stupid blunder. We had dug-in in front of the village and between us and the enemy was a strip of cultivated land about a mile or more wide and nearly half a mile in depth, as flat as a table and without any cover whatsoever. A splendid defence position and we could have held out there for a day or two or until the tanks came up. But some fool of a brass hat said that this was no time for defence, we must attack. When our officers pointed out that we were short of ammunition he said 'never mind, fix bayonets and give them a taste of cold steel, they'll never stand for that.' They didn't need to, they were not that stupid. I estimate that we lost 2,000 men in less than thirty minutes. There were thirty survivors of our battalion when we got back to where we had started from and no officers. The others were dismayed. Nothing like this had happened before and there seemed to be nothing for it but to break and run, especially after the awful and unnecessary carnage we had just seen.[2]

To the south a new crisis developed as the Northumberland Division was pushed back at Rosières. There were no reserves available to aid the defence as a critical situation developed against the southern defenders. A battalion of Northumberland Fusiliers was found to be digging in to the rear after being misinformed that their division was pulling back, and the battalion was ordered forward again to the former position. In Harbonnières a further crisis unfolded as it was reported that the Germans were advancing. Now General Malcolm in person rounded up the last reserves he could find there, Royal Engineers who were survivors of the three field companies and the signallers of the 199 Brigade were collected and taken forward to man the defences of the village. A counter-attack was organised and the men who had been pushed back from Framerville, the aforementioned battalion of the Northumberland Fusiliers, did attack and restore the original line. This was the bottom line, as the divisional commander was almost leading his men on the ground and using his last available forces to stem the tide.

The counter-attack was not recorded by the East Lancashire Division, but to the south the Northumberland Division also joined the counter-attack and left a record of its success. The men of the Durham and Northumberland Battalions formed up ready to attack:

> There was no panic, and on receipt of orders, we quietly took up our position, and watched with interest the counter-attack which we could see developing a mile or so away from us on the left [East Lancashire Division] … We accordingly pushed on, platoon by platoon, and section by section, in quite the old field day style, the men firing freely at the Germans who could be seen advancing towards us five or six hundred yards away.
>
> We came under machine gun fire, and the bullets were kicking up dust all along our line. We had many casualties, and as we looked back over the level ground behind, we could see the forms of men who had fought their last fight, while here and there there were wounded trying to make their way to the rear. After a while it became very exciting, as we could see the halt and turn back through the trees near Vauvillers. Our men gave a sort of grunt and advanced ten times as quickly as before. Eventually the resistance of the enemy broke down.[3]

The XIX Corps' attack including the two battalions saw them reoccupying their old line, having launched a partly successful counter-attack. However, it was never intended that they would hold the line, it was a spoiling attack in order to cover the retreat. The line was held there during a quiet night, the enemy having been broken by the attack.

Changes to the command were now occurring. General Gough was visited by Haig's Military Secretary, General Ruggles-Brise. He asked Gough if he was tired and said he and his staff would be replaced by General Rawlinson, to which he could only manage an 'all right', beyond requesting when this would take place, the answer being the next day, 28 March. In the meantime he had to extract XIX Corps from a difficult situation in which they were almost cut off. Tired commanders could not always muster the energy to contradict their senior officers, and he had resolutely stuck with Foch's order to 'hold at all costs', when earlier in the campaign he had ignored the order when he thought it suitable. In his memoirs he acknowledges his mistake, but that was the effect of tiredness on senior commanders:

> Similar positions had been met before by the commanders in the Fifth army during the course of the battle, though not in so pronounced a degree, but we had withdrawn in time and extricated many units from dangerous positions, while keeping the line intact. We could also have done the same in this case also if we had been left to our own initiative and military knowledge, alarming as was the situation, without the heavy losses which compliance with the order of Foch entailed.
>
> Watts recognised the situation here as quickly as I did, but out of a misplaced desire to be loyal to Foch and our allies, and having received no qualifying instruction or support from G.H.Q. [i.e. Haig], I hesitated to ignore Foch's order to 'hold on at all costs'.[4]

The commander of Fifth Army blamed his higher commanders and the Anglo–French command system that came into place on 26 March. There is nothing personal about changing commanders in such a long battle, but Gough took it to heart and was ostracised until approximately 1927. He was really only brought back into the fold with the death of Sir Douglas Haig.

This left breathing space for General Malcolm to pull back his divisional headquarters to Gillaucourt at 1.30 in the morning of 28 March so as to be in the same place as the new commander of the Northumberland Division, Major General Jackson. The northern flank at Lamotte was proving worrying as rumours were confirmed that the Germans held it. Watts at Corps H.Q. confirmed that Lamotte had fallen to the Germans but there was hope of a counter-attack to restore the situation there. Bayonvillers was also in German hands and now Watts gave his authority to a counter-attack of forces from the whole corps, men from 39th, 66th, 50th and 8th Divisions were to carry out the corps plan and then withdraw from the salient around Harbonnières and re-form on the line Rosières–Gillaucourt–Wiencourt–Marcelcave.

A conference was organised between the three divisional commanders, Major Generals Henneker, Jackson, and Malcolm, for that night:

> All three officers were of the opinion that, unless Lamotte could be retaken and the situation on the left restored, the greater part of their divisions would be in danger of being cut off; and they reported their view to the XIX Corps, Major General Henneker speaking on the telephone. Lieutenant General Watts had, a few hours before, made much the same report to General Gough, but had been told that in accordance with General Foch's directions, there must be no voluntary withdrawal. It was evident that a rigid adherence to this decision would enable the enemy to achieve a breakthrough on a considerable scale and envelop a large part of XIX Corps.[5]

Watts rang Gough, who in turn telephoned Foch during the night to confirm permission to withdraw. During the conference of the commanders of 8th, 50th and 66th Divisions they decided to hold the Marcelcave area and sent forward orders, which were received at 4.15 am. The village was found to be manned by the men of the Army Field Survey Company, intending to provide a defence if they could. The Royal Engineers and machine gun parties were immediately sent forward west of the village to provide cover for the division. The village would be part of a slight salient but this was found to be acceptable to the strategic plan. The tactical withdraw would not be towards Amiens as this route was now blocked but counter-intuitively south-west across the Amiens road and cross country towards the river Luce.

The orders did not always arrive in the proper fashion and the withdrawal turned into something of a rout. Demoralised troops reported between 10 and 11 o'clock on Thursday, 28 March that their flank had been turned and, falling back through Caix, attempts to organise these troops failed as their extreme tiredness and indeed low morale was breaking after a week of battle:

> They were very badly in need of a rest, there was no such thing as a Platoon or Company, and junior officers were for the most part incapable of dealing with the situation. In short the men were no longer fighting, and it appeared absolutely necessary that if the Division was to be of any further use, it should be withdrawn from the line, and given an opportunity to reorganise and pull itself together, even if only six hours could be allowed.[6]

If the Germans had been in better fettle, with artillery and cavalry ready this was the moment that they might have won the battle. In stark reality the Germans 'were tired, and possibly hungrier; there was little artillery support for them, and without it the German infantry did not seem inclined to face fire'.[7]

Peter Hall and his comrades now fought their exhaustion as well as the Germans, got themselves back into fighting spirit and, upon finding some ammunition, they carried as much as possible and hid the rest. Then,

> as soon as we were clear of the village we were on ridges of moorland. I divided the men into three groups of ten, and spaced the groups out left and right over nearly a mile. When we were in position the centre group, in which I was stationed let the Germans see us retreating, moving rapidly and making as much use of all the moorland roughs and banks of heather. As soon as the Germans started to pursue us they came under enfilading fire from the groups left and right. This made them hesitate. Group by group we retreated a few hundred yards in turn, each group being covered by the other two. These tactics confused the Germans and slowed them down. We then dug in for the night and the Germans did the same perhaps thinking that we were planning a night attack.[8]

Hall was showing considerable initiative and went on to continue his fighting retreat, changing tactics and generally making a nuisance of himself to the Germans. Elsewhere other men were holding the ground outside Amiens. A detachment of 5/ Battalion Tank Corps, still without tanks but remaining as machine gun units, was to hold the main road at Villers-Bretonneux for two days. Under Lieutenant Pitt they were part of Carey's Force, and upon Pitt being wounded they came under the command of Second Lieutenant Whyte. The Tank Corps' history explains that:

> A Vickers Gun section was already in place on the north side of the road and so Whyte placed his guns on the south side. The infantry holding the line at this point were all low category men and not more than twenty men had any experience of holding a rifle.

Nonetheless, Whyte and his men held the line there for two days. The British army was now reduced to men mostly without front line experience and rear echelon men. The Official History states that 'from 27 march onwards until reorganization the infantry of 66th Division was so weak that brigades ceased to exist, and the three brigadiers took it in turns to command the infantry'. Carey's Force was holding to the west as the divisions of XIX Corps retired. It was by such small measures that the line was held that Thursday and Friday.

The situation was explained to Watts at corps headquarters, who had to reply that they could not be withdrawn and would have to hold for the moment. An army line of defence was established on the line Demuin to Hamel, largely garrisoned by tunnelling company personnel who had improved the line and put barbed wire on it. The scratch force also included American railway troops without any military training. It was here that a force under General Carey was established, the latest of the 'Forces' to be improvised from men of the Royal Engineers and stragglers from XIX Corps. This line was occupied by allied forces from 11.40 that night.

The men of the East Lancashire Division now were moved in a south-westerly direction to occupy the flank at Ignacourt on the river Luce. The forces available to General Malcolm in the front line posts were 400 men under Colonel Heseltine, Major Gracey, and Captain Grey of the East Lancashire Regiment, with Colonel Little's remaining force of 300 men in reserve. Captain Grey had taken over command that morning of the remnants of the East Lancashire Regiment from Colonel Whitehead. The forces of the division were divided into five positions, one of eighty assorted men, another of eighty men of the Border Regiment, and two parties of soldiers south of the river [see map 11].

To their north Carey's Force was holding the line at Marcelcave, which had been partly occupied by German forces. Malcolm requested that the remnant division be withdrawn through Carey's Force and concentrated at Domart Wood. Some of the divisional artillery was established south of the river, although touch with the adjoining 20th (Light) Division was never obtained. The batteries were eventually ordered back into the divisional area to support their own troops. News was heard of men approaching from the high ground and that the French forces to the south were falling back. At 11 o'clock on Friday morning the Germans attacked Ignacourt. Malcolm's forces were withdrawn with artillery support bombarding the village as the soldiers covered the exits from the village. At 1.15 that afternoon Malcolm was wounded by German shrapnel, and was evacuated, his command being taken over by Brigadier Hunter.

At 6.40 the next morning, Saturday, 30 March, the Germans put down a heavy barrage on the British positions. Not surprisingly, under this amount of pressure parts of the army line were broken by the German attack at 8.10. Generals Borrett and Williams went forward to bolster

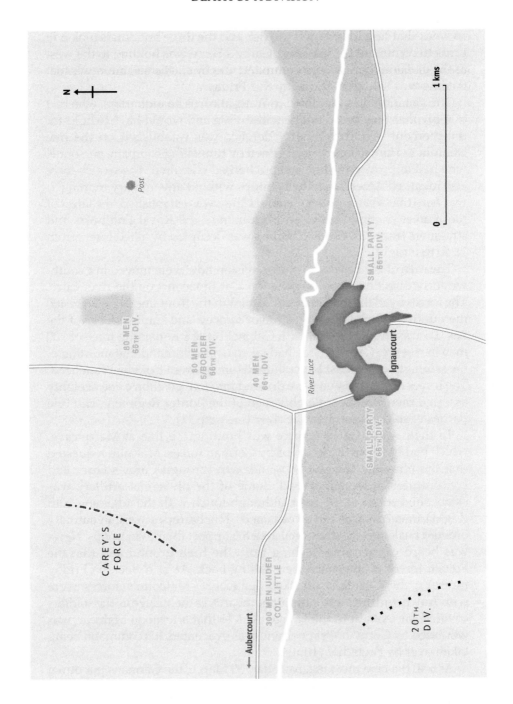

Map 11: Ignacourt.

the soldiers and hold the line, and moved their H.Q. to Gentelles Wood. At about 10 o'clock Brigadier General Borrett was wounded and it was left to General Williams to command the line. The situation was so crucial now that generals were in the line commanding what was left of their divisions, and becoming wounded alongside their men.

The soldiers under Colonel Little and Major Gracey were holding out in Aubercourt, but to the south 20th Division was withdrawing from Demuin, which was immediately occupied by the enemy:

> About 10 o'clock Colonel Little finding his position in Aubercourt untenable, unless the situation around Demuin was restored, ordered a counter-attack with about 140 men on this place, and drove the enemy back with the bayonet as far south as the church. The enemy however still held the southern outskirts of the village and the high ground to the south and we could not get any further.[9]

This was the first of three counter-attacks launched by the division that day as a final attempt to stem the advance. The East Lancashire historian recorded:

> About noon these troops, exhausted as they were, took part in a counter-attack in an effort to retake Demuin. But gallantly as the counter-attack was led and taken part it failed – as was inevitable in the circumstances – and the troops were forced back to the line from where they had started from.
>
> The divisional reserves under Captain Grey were then ordered to defend the western edge of Demuin, which they took up at around 6.30 p.m. Whence they fought a rearguard action to higher ground north of the village. Thence he withdrew to Gentelles where Brigade Headquarters was situated whilst a strong German attack on the right flank forced back the mixed troops back to Hangard.
>
> At about 3 o'clock in the morning on [Sunday] March 31 the remaining troops were relieved by troops of the 18th Division.[10]

This had been the final act of the East Lancashire Division in the withdrawal to Amiens. Now the men could start to recuperate. After some food and rest, at a pace that was steady enough for the exhausted soldiers of the East Lancashire Regiment, they were moved back east of Amiens for a complete rest and refit. It is to the soldiers' everlasting credit that on being asked to undergo a 12-mile march to their final destination, not a man protested, nobody fell out and the soldiers of the East Lancashire Regiment under Captain Grey staggered singing into the village of Pissy. Of the men of this battalion, only eleven officers and 265 men answered roll call. Similar rest was arranged for the remainder of the division, much to the objection of French commander Foch, except for the artillery that remained in action.

The division was to have a final role in the October campaigns, but that was months away. For now it rested and recuperated behind the lines.

197 Brigade alone recorded casualties as following:

	Killed	Wounded	Missing	Total
Officers	8	40	61	
Other Ranks	78	326	1,575	2,088

The battalions of 197 Brigade recorded casualties of 665 in the 6/ Battalion Lancashire Fusiliers, 681 in the 2/7 L.F. and 742 in the 2/8 L.F..

On relief of the East Lancashire Division in Longeau the men who were counted numbered as follows:

	Officers	Other Ranks
197 Infantry Brigade	22	627
		(includes Brigade
		H.Q. personnel)
198 Infantry Brigade	26	601
199 Infantry Brigade	24	526
5/ Border Regiment (Pioneers)	8	201
66 Battalion M.G.C.	16	243
Field Companies R.E.	11	178
	107	2,376
		Total 2,483

On 1 April about 2,376 men of the 9,000 men who had manned the division on 21 March still stood, more were wounded and many were dead or prisoners of war. There were some 7,368 casualties, of whom 431 were officially known to have died, 1,668 were wounded and 5,269 were missing. The high level of missing is inevitable as they were unaccounted for; killed, missing or prisoners of war.

Of the protagonists we have followed with the East Lancashire Division, General Malcolm was in hospital, as was Tom Hardman. John Gore was brought back with the divisional transport on 28 March and soon was asleep in a pile of straw behind the lines. Poor Peter Hall and his men, who had been congratulated by officers for holding off an entire German brigade for more than a day by his intuitive tactics, were

held as deserters by the military police and placed in a former prisoner
of war cage. The only result of their protestations of innocence was a
sign placed on the barbed wire of their stockade declaring 'the survivors
of the 2/6 Manchester Regiment'. James Jessiman was next heard of in
a prisoner of war camp in Mainz, Germany, where he remained as
servant to the British commander. His one consolation was that he was
able to get his sister, Meg, to send him a copy of the medical *Grey's
Anatomy* to study until the war ended. He was repatriated in November
1918 and given two months' leave before being demobbed at Grantham
in March 1919. Also enjoying a rest were the men of the 2/3 Field
Ambulance, sleeping in a barn in Cottenchy to the south-west:

> In Cottenchy we found billets of a better class than we had enjoyed
> for a week past, and though we made a belated arrival at 2 o'clock
> on the morning of the 29th March, we certainly valued the
> opportunity of sleep. At first we were a little hampered by a noisy
> gun behind the billets, but eventually we found slumber, and in the
> morning no Sergeant-Major or orderly sergeant came round to call
> us to the stern requirements of the beastly war until noon was fast
> approaching.[11]

Overseeing the withdrawal of units were the red hats of the Provost
Marshal, acting as police and sorting out stragglers, deserters and the
lost. At one of these collecting posts initially at Demuin was assistant
provost marshal Captain Westmacott 'on the 28 March moved back to
Demuin where I found things in a very critical condition as the 66th
Division on our left had run like stags and we (24th Division) were
obliged to move back our left so as not to be left in the air.'[12] He had
caught up men such as Peter Hall, men who had become separated from
their units, or more probably had no officers left. There is a disparity
between the provost's assumptions and that indicated by men such as
Hall. Westmacott stated that the main reason for the large amount of
stragglers 'was that sufficient maps were not issued to the men and also
because troops were not told clearly enough where they were to halt,
with the result that they lost themselves and kept on walking until they
met a stragglers post'.

On the German side of the lines, Captain William Beaumont was on
his way to Germany as a prisoner of war:

> The same day I was taken on a train of open trucks to a big hospital
> at Bohain. Here I was put in a room with about two hundred
> stretcher cases packed like sardines, and a wounded Tank Corps

177

Officer and I helped them as much as possible during the night, though many died, and I managed to get some coffee for them from the Boche doctor. More wounded officers turned up next day, and after another night we went by train to Hautmont, near Mauberge, after a long halt at a junction. I met a Boche N.C.O. at the junction who before the war was head waiter in the dining room of the Midland Hotel, Manchester. I had known him quite well then. He was inclined to be chatty, but I was not liking Boche at the time.

In the front lines units that were part of the make-up of the division were still involved in the fighting. A unit of the East Lancashire Regiment under Captain Snailham was attached to 18th Division and involved in the fighting at Hangard Wood. This comprised seven officers and thirty-eight other ranks. After fighting a rearguard action from Demuin they held a position in an orchard south-east of the village of Hangard and under orders to the 18th Division. They re-joined their unit on 2 April at Clary.

Gunner John Gore woke refreshed and remembered that:

> on all this retirement I had carried with me a 1000 franc note which was intended for the battery's pay but as we had to skip in such a hurry I put the money in my pocket and said nothing. I now reported this to one of the officers and we had a pay day. With our G.S. wagon Sergeant Sutherland and one or two men we went to Villers-Bretonneux and came back with a wagon full of loot. Champagne, wines, tinned fruit, sardines, etc. very acceptable. Made three journeys but were shelled on the road so went no more.

The fighting was still progressing and although it was over for the East Lancashire Division, the fighting continued with the Australians facing the Germans at Villers-Bretonneux. The risk of death was not all gone for John Gore as on 10 April:

> Corporal Ford mad drunk again. Threatened to shoot Sergeant Manning. Pointed his revolver at my chest and told me my last hour had come. Scared to death but didn't move. Told him to go and have a sleep. Staggered away and told the DTMO who put him under arrest.

Today this might be ascribed to Post-Traumatic Stress, but at the time there wasn't much that could be done as men tried to cope with stress and tiredness after the long retreat. 'Ford was awarded a severe reprimand as there was no time for anything else. For the artillery to which Gore was now assigned there was no rest as they remained in action, moving to near Proven.[13]

There was bound to be some letting off of steam after such a long period of battle, and the only recompense offered in those days was sleep and rest away from the battle zone. The East Lancashire Division had come through, but only just and much reduced in strength. What would the future offer such a noble gathering of survivors? They had managed to blunt the German offensive, the German commanders had changed their objectives and then failed to win the battle and the campaign had ground to a halt in front of Amiens. This was crucial and we have noted how they achieved this, through individual courage, leadership and refusing to give in whatever the circumstances might be.

NOTES:
[1] Anonymous, *History of the East Lancashire Royal Engineers*, p.241.
[2] IWM Department of Documents, papers of Peter Hall.
[3] Wyrall, E., *The 50th Division 1914–1918*, pp.294–5.
[4] Gough, H.. *The Fifth Army*, 1930, pp.318–9.
[5] Edmunds, E., *Official History, 1918*, Vol. II, p.26.
[6] TNA, WO95/3121.
[7] Edmunds, E., *Official History, 1918*, Vol. II, p.27.
[8] IWM Department of Documents, papers of Peter Hall.
[9] TNA, WO 95/3121.
[10] *History of the East Lancashire Regiment*, p.309.
[11] Francis, A., *The History of the 2/3 East Lancashire Field Ambulance*, p.105.
[12] IWM Department of Documents, papers of Westmacott.
[13] IWM Department of Documents, papers of John Gore.

Chapter 15

Spirit Unbroken

1 April–November 1918

On 1 April 1918 General H.K. Bethell took over 66th Division. To say he took over an actual division in light of the fierce fighting that had taken place is to be overly optimistic; he was in charge of the fragments of the division that had suffered fifty per cent casualties in ten days. The infantry battalions were shattered and some just ceased to exist. Most of the remainder were lines of communication men, the headquarters, field ambulances and so on, that had remained at the front of the retreat. It was replaced in the front by Australian forces and other British divisions such as the 8th and the largely complete 58th Division. These would fight the two battles of Villers-Bretonneux and hold the Germans at the gates of Amiens, denying Ludendorff his regional objective.[1] For the East Lancashire Division, or what remained of it, it was now time for the men to rest, lick their wounds and re-form, so they were marched off to Longeau and trains running west brought them to countryside not ravaged by war. Instead, peace and quiet reigned despite the thunder to the east.

General Gough lost his command of Fifth Army. He had made several crucial mistakes in his military command and had made more political errors. The 66th Division had gone down fighting, but due to Gough had survived, which it certainly would not have done if left to the High Command and politicians, who would have sacrificed it for ground saved. Not only did he lose his command, but Fifth Army became part of Fourth Army under Rawlinson.

Bethell brought in his own team of officers for the General Staff, among them Anthony Eden and Walter Guinness. Guinness was a veteran of the Boer War who had won distinction at the battle of Doornkop, where he was wounded while serving in the Suffolk

Company of the Imperial Yeomanry. He Finished the Great War as a captain. Linked to the brewing family in Ireland, he had been MP for Bury St Edmunds in Suffolk since 1907. Guinness was born in Dublin in 1880, the third son of the first Earl of Iveagh and Lady Evelyn Erskine, and educated at Eton College, where he rowed in the eight for three years and was captain of boats. He contested the Stowmarket Division in 1906 and in 1907 sat on the North Paddington district of London County Council.

Bethell had been the man on the spot and had succeeded in delaying the enemy through competent command of scattered units of the British army, but that is not to say he was always the popular choice. However, in times such as this he was the man of the moment. His reward while General Malcolm was recuperating in hospital was command of the East Lancashire Division.

Eden came to the division as brigade major to General Hunter in 198 Brigade. He came from a landed family who lived at Windlestone Park in County Durham; educated at Eton, he was typical of the aristocratic elite. However, by the end of his schooling he was itching to get on in life. In 1915 he volunteered for the King's Royal Rifle Corps, and indeed recruited many local men for the 21st Battalion. He saw action at Ploegsteert (Plugstreet) in Belgium and in France. On the Somme he was ordered to remain at headquarters during the attack on 15 September 1916, where the colonel, the Earl of Feversham, his adjutant and many men of the battalion were killed. He was then appointed adjutant due to his long association with the battalion and he was also awarded a Military Cross. By 1917 he was obviously destined for the General Staff and served as acting G.S.O. with Second Army from October to November 1917 and then was G.S.O. to General Cator of 58th Division before moving to 66th Division in May 1918.[2]

The division was reduced to cadre strength and used to train soldiers destined for the front. The main use to which it was put was to train several American divisions. This was at this stage that politics entered the fray as the American general and Sir Douglas Haig had differing opinions on how American forces in France should be utilised. Haig wanted them to be reinforcements for the British divisions, but Pershing wanted his own command of purely American troops. The chain of command was important, but Bethell ignored orders from his commanders and the Americans refused to be trained by the British. Walter Guinness recalled that,

> some of the American professional soldiers were fearfully zealous in carrying out the orders that no British Officer or NCO was to

command American troops, and they interpreted this to mean that a sergeant instructor couldn't even drill a platoon but had to watch an American officer make a hash of it. Owing to this system it was extremely difficult for the Americans to get the full benefit of their attachment.[3]

They spent most of the time preparing for inspections by High Command, coupled to which it was Pershing who laid down the course of training rather than the British, which failed to prepare the Americans for the trial of battle. Among the staff Bethell was not that popular, but it was his own ideas that were to keep him in check, and they were the reason for his remaining in command of the division as a training division through the summer of 1918. He went around commandeering machine guns with an idea of a division with hundreds of machine guns that would overpower the Germans by firepower alone, however his ambition reached headquarters and he was given a severe dressing down by a superior officer.

Good news was forthcoming that the Australians were being brought forward. These fresh troops had been in reserve since Passchendaele the previous autumn and it was they who resisted the German attacks at Villers-Bretonneux in April 1918. Along with relatively fresh forces of 58th Division and cavalry and armoured units they held the Germans outside Amiens and it was from this springboard that the Battle of Amiens on 8 August 1918 was won and then launched the 100 days campaign that brought about the Armistice. Among the reinforcements coming out from England in mid-April was Herbert Roland Bate.

Bate arrived back in France in April as part of a draft at Boulogne from Ripon, in Yorkshire. He recalled 'a grave situation':

> Owing to the chaos which still prevailed and the losses sustained by the German attack, men have been posted to units in greatest need. With several other officers I found myself posted to the 9/ Royal Sussex Regiment of the 24th Division. They had experienced the full brunt of the German offensive and were now behind the lines, licking their wounds and mourning their dead. Many of the officers and men had been killed, and many more wounded, including their Colonel.[4]

The new colonel was not popular and apparently was shot in the back later, being replaced by a now fully recovered Colonel Hill. Bate himself ended up as a company commander and won the Military Cross in November 1918.

In Germany, Captain William Beaumont had been moved to a punishment camp for no particular reason. Eventually he was moved to a camp at Rastatt, where he was delighted to meet Colonel Gell, Colonel Baillie-Hamilton and Majors Wike and Fisher, all of the East Lancashire Division. It was a pretty poor camp and one day they were served seal meat, which although sustaining was overly fishy.

I had made two good friends in the hospital, McChearly and Stewart, and we generally shared things. We noticed that one of the huts was very near the outside double row of barbed wire. The hut was empty and was used as a card playing room and for reading.

Colonel Gell said one day 'I have noticed you hanging about the hut, have you any ideas in your minds?'

We told him we wondered if it would be possible to tunnel under the wire, and we found out that he and some others had already cut some boards out under a bed and had started digging a hole. Stewart, McChearly, and another Scot named Cameron and I at once joined them and started work. There was about eighteen inches of space underneath the floor joists and when we had sunk a hole about six feet we started to tunnel. We had two coal box shovels and a bent poker. All soil was loaded into old tin hats and handed to a man standing in the shaft on a stool. He in turn handed it to a man lying under the floor who spread it out or handed it to another man to spread.

The tunnel was egg-shaped as we had no way of propping or boarding it, and was about three feet high. By a stroke of luck we found a man who had fifteen candles, so we took him into the company. As the tunnel grew longer we had to take more fellows in as the man working on the face had to hand the helmet back and receive the empty one, and a line of men was required to hand these two and fro and another line under the floor to spread stuff.

Some more prisoners came in and the hut was occupied. The officers in it were awfully decent and took no notice of us as we disappeared under the floor. I think in the end we took too many people in and the news got all over the camp.

One day a Boche sergeant suddenly came to the hut and looked through a hole in the outside boarding. He saw people there and told the sentry to cover the hole with a rifle and went for the Sergeant Major. The alarm was given and we all filed out into the hut through the floor. I was working on the face at the time and so was the last up, just as the sergeant major came into the hut. Several had got away and the rest sat down with the occupants of the hut and stealthily removed the dirty rags from around their knees. The Boche never knew who had done the job.

We had got well under the wire and were a few days from getting out. The tunnel was thirty six foot long and I calculated that we had removed twelve tonnes of soil in tin hats. We should have been out in a few nights.

For their attempted escape the men were moved to Danhölm, near Rugen, an island on the Baltic coast of Germany. They eventually managed to escape from there by paying for a fisherman to take them to Denmark after the Armistice.[5]

The division spent some time on the old Somme battlefields around Montauban and Delville Wood. Walter Guinness describes his time in the division in his memoirs, *Staff Officer.* He was brought into the re-formed 66th Division in the summer of 1918 when the make-up of the division was very different to the beginning of the year. As a staff officer he was very glad of the headquarters it took over from 25th Division, being in deep German dugouts, as the weather turned increasingly cold and wet after 2 October. The division took part in an exercise in open warfare over several days. The main trouble faced by the soldiers on the exercise was the total devastation of the landscape caused by years of war that obliterated all landmarks. Walter Guiness remembered:

It has become very difficult to find one's way by the maps as nothing is left of Mametz Wood and High Wood except by the remains of one or two tree trunks which look in the distance merely like telegraph poles and the mounds which mark the sites of the villages are indistinguishable from thousands of other mounds which have been thrown up by the repeated trench excavations, gun emplacements and bombardments which have scarred the country since the First Battle of the Somme.

However, they were only training and when they moved east they would be in a landscape far less devastated.

The majority of the rest of the battalions attached to the East Lancashire Division were troops brought back from the Middle East, where they had formed part of Allenby's force attacking the Ottoman Turks. They were in much better form than the British troops, who were liable to fall sick to influenza, while the eastern troops were on a quinine course against malaria that seemed to have an effect on their overall health. At this stage of the war advantages such as these would have made a difference to the capabilities of the division.

Walter Guinness was in great admiration of the South African troops now attached to the division.

> Magnificent troops, far ahead of any Canadians or Australians that I ever came across. Many of their officers and N.C.O.s are old British Regulars who settled down in South Africa after the [Boer] War and the result is that in discipline they are in a class by themselves among non British troops besides being splendid men physically.[6]

The South African Brigade had itself been wiped out twice in the war, at Delville Wood in 1916 and at Marrières Wood in March 1918. Now they faced a tricky attack at Le Cateau in 1918:

> The position attacked by 66th Division, and especially by the South African Brigade, requires to be studied on the ground before the difficulties overcome by the initiative and leadership of the regimental officers and non-commissioned officers and by the gallantry of all ranks can be fully realised. None but the very best troops could have attempted, let alone have succeeded in such an enterprise.

The position at Le Cateau was made difficult by the fact that the town lies in a hollow with a railway junction above it, a river and high ground to the north-east. The division had previously captured Le Cateau and the railway, but owing to the high ground to the north-east being held by the Germans were unable to hold the position. A new attack was planned that would bypass the town. The Northumberland Division on the right would attack first as it had further to go. The East Lancashire Division would attack to the north of the town. The attack started at four o'clock in the morning on 17 October in a dense fog that meant rockets to be used for communication were rendered useless and Walter Guinness had to rely on interpreting the walking wounded as they were brought back. The Northumberland attack to the south was reported as being successful and the news was forwarded to 66th Division headquarters.

The barrage started at 7.30 am, with the attack starting twenty minutes later. Little news was heard until 8.30 that morning as telephone lines were cut and the South Africans had met fierce opposition. A thick belt of barbed wire and murderous machine gun fire slowed down the advance but somehow a route was cut through the wire. Guinness was finding it:

a very strenuous day at Advanced Divisional headquarters in intermittent telephone communications forward with our brigades and back with Bethell in divisional headquarters in Maretz. All through the day and most of the night we were trying to co-operate with the changing phases of the attack by the 50th Division and there were masses of orders to be issued. The railway triangle which dominated Le Cateau from the east was only captured by the South African Brigade at 6.30 a.m. on 18 October and by midnight our South African Brigade had made good their final objective and the 198 Brigade had completed the mopping up of Le Cateau. I had a lot of trouble through these operations owing to a misunderstanding with the South African Brigade.

General Bethell had been up to see General Tanner and had shown him the various objectives marked in various colours on his map. When we finally issued the orders these lines were shown in different colours. Tanner, however, still went by the colours which he had sketched on his map at the original interview with Bethell, with the result that he attached a different meaning to the green or red lines as to what I did in our telephone conversations.

On 20 October Guinness made a personal survey of the ground attacked by the division. He found:

> The performance of the South African Brigade was wonderful. They forced their way over the river and cut a line through the wire by hand under the most murderous machine gun fire at short range from a commanding position. They then rushed the railway embankment. This cutting was about sixty feet deep and gave the most perfect protection by the Boche who were holding it. The South Africans captured it by hand to hand fighting and the bottom of the cutting was full of dead Germans. I don't think I have ever seen so many dead as those for which the South Africans were here responsible. From what the inhabitants of Le Cateau said, the Boche expected to hold their line for months and thought that it was practically impregnable.[7]

The assault on the town by 198 Brigade was made easier by the attack of the South Africans, although it had to be taken in house-to-house fighting made more difficult by the number of cellars.

The attacks were eventually successful and the division was rested until 9 November, when it took over from 25th Division in XIII Corps. The division advanced and took the Avesnes road as early as 11 o'clock that morning and by 1 o'clock the road was entirely in the hands of the East Lancashire Division. It was facing a Jäger division that, aided by a sunken road, was able to defend against the Lancashire advance and stop it gaining the objective of the high ground beyond.

On 10 November Bethell's force marched from Solre-le-Chateau with an advanced guard of the 1st South African Infantry, single sections of field artillery, engineers and machine guns. The division had now been changed as open warfare needed specialised units of artillery, infantry, cavalry and machine guns. Damage to a culvert under the road stopped the advance. Reports from 12/ Lancers who were scouting ahead were that the Germans were in strength half a mile ahead. Under cover of the woods, the leading battalion deployed and attacked across a stream, immediately coming under fire from artillery, machine guns and low-flying aircraft, but by three o'clock in the afternoon the high ground beyond Hestrud had been captured. Bethell then stopped the advance as they were under orders to stay in touch with the enemy but not to press forward.

Aerial reconnaissance showed that a German column was moving along a road from Eppe Sauvage to Montbliart. An attempt was made to cut it off through the woods but fading light made this attempt by Bethell unsuccessful. The Royal Air Force instead strafed the column and fought off and shot down fourteen enemy planes. That evening the Germans shelled the station at Solre-le-Chateau, destroying an ammunition dump they had left but not a British ammunition train standing there, which was no doubt their target.

On the morning of 11 November the cavalry screen of the 5th Cavalry Brigade (20/ Hussars and 11th Lancers) found the enemy in the same positions as previously and the South African Brigade reported the same at Hestrud. At 10.15 am an officer of the 66th Division arrived with orders for Brigadier General Tanner that hostilities would end at 11 o'clock. This information had obviously already reached the Germans, who increased the vigour of their artillery bombardment. The Official History notes the final action of the war for 199 Brigade of 66th Division in very ordinary terms.

The 199 Brigade had sent forward two battalions at Clairfays, each with 18-pounders attached, by the available roads, the 18/ Kings via L'Eppe Sauvage on Vieux Sart, with a flank guard on Montbliart, and the 9/ Manchester via Sivry on Renlies. They were to drive off screens of machine guns or infantry, but not to fight a general action. The Kings encountered no opposition and gained touch with the French, whose 51st Division, having taken L'Eppe Sauvage, was also marching on Montbliart. The Manchester met no opposition until beyond Sivry, and was engaged there when the Armistice came into force at 11 o'clock.[8]

The officer mentioned above who came round with the orders for the Armistice appears to have been Walter Guinness. He recalls the morning in his memoirs:

> Besides sending this [order] off by motorcyclist I went round immediately in a motor to prevent any possibility of our Brigades sustaining any further casualties by pushing on. At the moment of the Armistice I was up at Hestrud with General Tanner. Up until the hour of 11 there had been a tremendous noise as if both sides were trying to get rid of their ammunition, and at 11 o'clock it suddenly became very silent. On the front of 199 Brigade north of the road between Sivry and Sivry station at exactly 11 o'clock a very troublesome Boche machine gun stopped firing and the German machine gun crew crept out of their holes in the ground, took their helmets off and made polite bows towards their British enemy, picked up their machine gun and slowly retired.

It is notable how concerned Guinness was to avoid any further bloodshed. And so the Armistice order came into effect:

> Hostilities will cease at 11 a.m. today November 11. Troops will stand fixed on line reached at that time which will be reported immediately to Headquarters Fourth Army Advance Guard. Defensive precautions will be maintained. There will be no discourse of any description with the enemy until receipt of instructions.

John Gore recalled of the Armistice that

> an officer riding by told us the Armistice was to be signed at 11 o'clock. [I] didn't believe him, eventually the news came through and we just sat and looked at one another. There wasn't a drink and I didn't hear a cheer. Everything dead quiet. Can't realise it is all over.'[9]

The East Lancashire Division was by no means finished in its part in the war. Initially it was deployed in reconstructing roads and repairing the damage inflicted by the retreating Germans. The men were told that the division was bound for the Rhine area as part of the occupation forces. For Walter Guinness there was a way out as when a General

Election was held all prospective candidates were given a month's leave to prepare their fight for a constituency. For John Gore he managed to lose the division and make his way to Cologne to join the Royal Field Artillery, where he was gainfully employed.

One undecided officer on the staff was Anthony Eden. In 1919 Eden was as impatient to get out of the army as he had been to get in. The time spent sitting around when, as a staff officer, he would previously have been extremely busy was a difficult period of adjustment. With time to reflect on the war he found the loss of his brother, Nicholas, hard to bear:

> Life is terribly trying here at present and letters mean more now than they ever did. Yet it is your little Nicholas' birthday today. I miss him more ever too darling. There are some days when I cannot believe that I will never see him again. I am afraid that now the war is over and the reaction has set in we shall find the loss of the old life harder than ever to bear.[10]

He could speak for a generation of soldiers and families in these words; not only for the working classes, but for the aristocracy as well life would never be the same again.

Eden was on the verge of demobilisation and as frustrated as every other soldier who just wanted to be home and get on with life. He put his vigour into preparing for the divisional horse trials, when unfortunately he was injured falling under a horse. He really seems to have found a hatred of destruction and wanton violence. His family seem to have picked up the army's enthusiasm for his capability as a staff officer, which Eden reacted to strongly from his hospital bed:

> What is the use of telling me I am making a mistake in not staying in the army. I cannot get a regular commission. So there is an end of it. They have thousands more officers than they require already. Whatever profession I decide to take up I must stick to for life. I could of course sign up for another year in the Army of occupation but that would lead me nowhere and merely waste a year. My present idea is to get into the African Civil Service with a view to going to East Africa. I don't know whether I shall get in or not I don't know but I propose to try when I come back on leave next month. I am up again today but I am not feeling strong. It is a lovely spring day and I have been for a walk, which has made me feel ridiculously tired.[11]

He recovered and spent his time motoring around the battlefields:

> I motored to Louvain [Leuven] yesterday. It must have been a lovely old place. The library of the university has been completely burnt down, over two thousand houses have been burnt down and the town is completely ruined – the Town Hall still stands and the Cathedral has been badly burnt ... As I expect you know there was no fighting whatever in Louvain and the destruction was absolutely wanton. Over two hundred people were shot in the streets and thousands rendered homeless by the destruction of this property.
>
> It must have been a ghastly business while it lasted. I have seen plenty of devastation during the war, Ypres, Arras, Amiens, Chauny, Noyon, Roye, Bapaume, Dunkirk, Armentieres, Bethune ... Albert, but nothing has angered me as much as Louvain. The wanton destruction of so much beauty that can never be replaced stamps the Germans forever as entirely lacking in love of the beautiful and are a brutish master beneath a veneer of civilisation.[12]

In the end Eden was returned to England in May 1919. He was demobilised and spent the summer and autumn travelling in the south of France, Switzerland and Italy. The cleaner air was thought to do wonders for anyone who had been gassed in the war. He then went to Christ Church College, Oxford, and studied Oriental studies with a view to a career in the Foreign Office. He changed this plan again and stood for Parliament in 1923; failing to get a seat in Durham he stood for Leamington Spa and Warwick, gaining a 1924 by-election seat, which he held for thirty-three years. He was in government briefly in the 1920s and then under Chamberlain in the 1930s; sticking to his principles, he resigned over appeasement in the Spanish Civil War. He then served in Churchill's wartime Coalition government and became Prime Minister from 1955–57.

Peter Hall was assigned to the 2/ Manchesters in August 1918. He fought forward over the same ground over which he had retreated in March:

> My commanding officer was an Irishman. Each time we attacked a village he rushed in at the double waving his shillelagh at his right hand and a revolver at his left and shouting like a Red Indian on the warpath and with me a few steps behind him. Often demoralised German fled at the sight. This was a wonderful experience for me after the retreat in March. A day or later we came to a sunken road

cut through the top of a ridge which we had used in March to delay the Germans.

I told him that this would be an ambush but that I knew of a sheep track through a smaller gap only 200 yards away. He reluctantly agreed to use it. As soon as we were through the gap he asked where the ambush was. So I said 'watch this' and let off ten rounds rapid at the spot where I knew the ambush would be. They were taken by surprise and fled like startled rabbits. He said 'My word you know this country – you had better stay close behind me and warn me of other traps.'[13]

Hall had really come of age during the retreat and, refusing a commission, he served until he was wounded in the leg at Misery château and was discharged from Stockport Infirmary in March 1919. He had really shown what an individual could achieve during such a campaign as the March offensive, showing resolute leadership in the face of adversity, as had many of the men of the East Lancashire Division, from privates to the major general, in the best spirit of Tommy Atkins.

NOTES:
[1] These battles are detailed in *Londoners on the Western Front; a History of 58th Division in the Great War*, 2014.
[2] The Avon Papers, AP22/1/265.
[3] Guinness, W., *Staff Officer, The Diaries of Lord Moyne*, 1914–1918, p.218.
[4] IWM Department of Documents, papers of Canon Bate.
[5] Fusilier Museum, Bury, *The Clickety-Clicks*, 1937–38, pp.30–9.
[6] Guinness, W., *Staff Officer*, p.227.
[7] Guinness W., *Staff Officer*, pp.236–7.
[8] *Official History*, pp.552–3.
[9] IWM Department of Documents, papers of J.W. Gore.
[10] The Avon Papers, University of Birmingham, AP22/1/273.
[11] ibid.
[12] ibid, AP22/1/280, the Cadbury Research Library, 20 April 1919.
[13] IWM Department of Documents, papers of Peter Hall.

Chapter 16

Memorial

Westminster Abbey 1920

The East Lancashires had a stake in the burial of the Unknown Warrior in Westminster Abbey. In the search for the Unknown Warrior suitable remains were exhumed from various battlefields and brought to the chapel at St Pol-sur-Ternoise near Arras on the night of 7 November 1920. The partial bodies were received by the Reverend George Kendal OBE, Brigadier Louis John Wyatt and Lieutenant Colonel Edward Gell of the Directorate of Graves registration and Enquiries went into the chapel alone. The remains were laid on stretchers each covered by Union Flags: the two officers did not know from which battlefield any individual had come. Brigadier Wyatt with closed eyes rested his hand on one of the bodies. The two officers placed the body in a plain coffin and sealed it. The other bodies were then taken away and reburied.

On the morning of 11 November 1920, the Unknown Warrior was placed on to a gun carriage of the Royal Horse Artillery and drawn by six horses through immense and silent crowds. As the cortèges set off a further field marshal's salute was fired in Hyde Park. The route followed was Hyde Park Corner, the Mall and on to Whitehall, where the Cenotaph, a symbolic empty tomb, was unveiled by the King. The cortège was then followed by the King, the Royal Family and ministers of state to Westminster Abbey, where the casket was borne into the West nave of the Abbey flanked by a guard of honour of 100 recipients of the Victoria Cross.

The guests of honour were a group of about 100 women. They had been chosen because they had each lost their husband and all their sons in the war. Lancashire was well represented by Gell and Wyatt; Gell of the East Lancashire Division and Wyatt who came from a Lancashire-based lead-milling family in Warrington and served with the Royal Engineers during the retreat.[1]

The coffin was then interred in the far western end of the Nave, only a few feet from the entrance, in soil brought from each of the main battlefields, and covered with a silk pall. Servicemen from the armed forces stood guard as tens of thousands of mourners filed silently past.

Lieutenant Colonel Gell of the 66th Division had played a major role in one of the major events of the post-war years. This was how the nation tried to mourn the dead as they closed an awful decade. Gell had risen in a few years from a lowly lieutenant to command a battalion and then into the Directorate of the Imperial War Graves Commission.

Manchester Town Hall 1924

'At 5 o'clock all those able to attend accompanied General Sir Neill Malcolm to the Cenotaph in St Peter's Square for the laying of the wreath to the memory of old comrades. The wreath is made by disabled ex servicemen under the care of the British legion.'[2]

The Manchester war memorial was unveiled in July 1924 by Lord Derby and a Mrs Bingle of Ardwick, who lost three sons in the war. This is a memorial by Lutyens and is on the approximate site of St Peter's Church. The main Cenotaph is of Portland stone, 32ft high, and surmounted by a bier on which lies a body of a soldier covered by his greatcoat. In front of the Cenotaph is an altar in the form of those in Commonwealth War Graves Cemeteries in France and Flanders bearing the words 'Their Name Liveth for Evermore'. Flanking the Cenotaph are two obelisks 23ft high. At the time of writing this memorial has been fully restored and the area to the west of the memorial incorporating a wall has been expanded and formalised.[3] The unveiling of the memorial in July 1924 in time for the tenth anniversary of the outbreak of war appears to have helped the commemorative events of 66th Division and the expansion of the participation in the annual dinner.

St Peter's Square in Manchester is also the home of Manchester Town Hall, the city library and the Midland Hotel. It was to the memorial that the officers of the Annual Dinner Club of 66th Division and their guests made their annual pilgrimage in January every year between 1924 and 1939 (except 1935 when it was postponed due to the death of King George V on 20 January). They then retired to the nearby Midland Hotel for a reception and dinner.

The Midland Hotel has been acknowledged as one of the most influential buildings in the modern core of Manchester. It was built by Charles Trubshaw in 1898–1903 as the main hotel for the Central Railway terminus, another vast railway station in the heart of the great industrial city. The station was built for the Cheshire Lines Committee, an alliance of three railways serving the North-West, the relatively new Great Central railway, the Great Northern, and the Midland Railway. The hotel is a vast red brick, brown terracotta edifice described as louche and undisciplined yet confident enough to be an essential part of the Manchester skyline. The exterior is clad in polished granite and generous quantities of Burmantofts faïence in which the Wyvern emblem of the Midland Railway features prominently. Built in a flamboyant, confident style, a hotel of this size and status attracted a workforce from far and wide.[4]

Men and women from Lancashire, the Midlands and France, Germany and Switzerland made it a cosmopolitan workplace, far more so than most of England in that period of time. It boasted a German restaurant to support the established community that existed in Manchester at the time, an American bar and a renowned French restaurant. At the centre were the Winter Gardens with palm trees, a contrast to the general climate in Manchester; there was also a massive theatre and banqueting hall, and the Garden café.[5] Guests entering from the Central Railway station would have been able to walk under an ornate iron veranda for the short walk from train to hotel. The main reception was at the railway station end of the hotel, now a bar, and along a further passage they entered the core of the hotel, now the vestibule but then the Winter Gardens.

On entering the Midland on the St Peter's Square side of the hotel guests entered into the carriage court designed for horse-drawn carriages to unload their passengers under cover in Manchester's inclement weather. On walking up some steps they would have come into the Winter Garden and turned left into the Octagon, which survives. Here they would have met for pre-dinner drinks and a smoke to remember former comrades and events before they braced themselves for the dinner down the corridor behind the French restaurant to the banqueting hall in the former theatre. Here every year between 150 and 200 former officers of the division met and dined. It seems to have been quite an occasion and the officers would then drift off back to the Octagon or different rooms, where the units of the division had their own gatherings into the early hours of the morning.

This annual event in the Midland is an interesting social event. This is why I have included it in this history of the division as it forms an interesting occasion that is well documented. The speeches, of course, were of a type and should be treated with caution as a historical source as alcohol did not improve them! Those invited were those of the rank of lieutenant and above. Other ranks were not invited but it does seem that they may have had their own annual reunions on the Saturday following, so that officers could attend their own unit with their men. There is a comment by the officers in the minutes of the dinner club that not many divisions could muster 200 men a year for the reunion, no doubt hinting that most reunions were at the regimental or battalion level. For this reason again it is an interesting phenomenon as an event that made this divisional history different. It is a source of the character of the officers as human beings that rails against the formulaic heroics of the war diaries, which are the main source for the Great War.

It was recorded in the 1930 edition of the Annual Dinner Club that:

> We have to correct a mistaken ideal in various quarters that the 66th Divisional Dinner Club owes its success to the fact that many of its members come from the Manchester District. This is not wholly correct although a substantial nucleus is local. But our members now resident in Scotland, Ireland, Wales and all over England regularly make the journey for the last Friday in January each year, whilst letters and cables of regret come from unfortunate exiles in India and South Africa and fortunate ones in the south of France.

This was the success of the Manchester reunions and the railway network meant that it was quite central for a whole host of former officers. A brief survey of the residences of the 621 member officers of the Annual Dinner Club in 1924 shows that the proportion came from Lancashire with twenty-two per cent, Manchester and London each with sixteen per cent, Cheshire with eight per cent and Scotland with five per cent; other areas make up thirty-three per cent. That thirty-eight per cent came from Lancashire, including Manchester, is not really surprising. Notice that this is post-war and reflects the domicile and workplace of the officers, and most of the officers lived in Great Britain, although a few were overseas, such as Canada with six, three in India, with two on station in China, and two at Singapore. Two lived in France, one of these, Lieutenant Colonel Gell, worked for the Imperial War Graves Commission. Some of the officers were still in the army and many gave a club as their address rather than a home address; others gave commercial addresses.

Due to the losses in the war the result was that those who survived were almost all able to find good jobs, so would spread out to take in the employment where it arose. Those at the rank of officer might be expected to make more of their career opportunities and education.

What is surprising is the low number that went abroad to the Empire (and stayed as members) as there was evidently good employment in Great Britain. What is also evident through reading the annual is that officers were dying relatively young and quite a few were ill each year and unable to attend, through war injuries and general ill health caused by the war.

Passchendaele Church and Le Cateau 1928

On 13 October 1928 a service of dedication was made at the new memorial in Passchendaele church. A hundred representatives of the East Lancashire Division were present, representing a broad swathe of the men of the division and not just officers.

> Passchendaele church was chosen as the site of one memorial, because it was towards the ruins of that church that the Division toiled on that night of mud and rain, October 8–9 1917, and also because it was beyond its ruins that some of our dead were found when the ridge was taken in November of that year.

The memorial in Passchendaele church shows the coats of arms of twenty-four Lancashire towns where the respective units of the division had a depot. These are Leigh, Burnley, Wigan, Darwen, Rochdale, Blackburn, Oldham, Bolton, Ashton under Lyme, Accrington, Bury, Atherton, Clitheroe, Heywood, Bacup, Middleton, Todmorten, Haslingden, Patricroft, Church, Padiham and Ramsbottom as well as Manchester and Salford.

> The Memorial at Passchendaele was unveiled on 13 October last, in the presence of some hundred representatives of the Division and a numerous Belgian assembly. The ceremony was a simple but moving one. On arrival in the church the Town Clerk of Passchendaele, speaking in English, extended a hearty welcome to the visitors. The schoolchildren then sang God Save the King and 'Labranconne'.
>
> Lieutenant Colonel W A Hobbins, who received his DSO for services rendered during the advance on Passchendaele, then called on General the Honourable G A Lawrence GCB, to unveil the window. General Lawrence in a short speech explained the reason for the window and the particular suitability of the site chosen, and then pulled aside the curtain which hung across the arched entrance to the chapel of St Cornelius and disclosed the window, furnishings and decorations which comprise the complete memorial.

In the centre of the window shines the Divisional badge of the blue triangle with transverse yellow bar, and round this are grouped the cap badges of every unit in the division.

In the centre of the middle light is portrayed a life size figure of St George, above the arms of the Duchy of Lancaster, and below the Arms of the cities of Manchester and Salford. In both the side lights are the coats of arms of every Lancashire town in which the respective units of the division had a depot, some twenty-four in all. The general effect is decorative and rich in colour. The window was designed by a Lancashire artist, Mr P Hawke of Messrs Reuben Bennett Ltd, Old Trafford, and carried out by Messrs Bary and Crickx of Brussels.

As we gazed at this wonderful Lancashire Memorial the moving notes of the Last Post, followed by the stirring strains of the Reveille pulsated through the church. (Our buglers were two good lads and sounded splendidly).

After the bugles were sounded the Canon of Ostende accepted the memorial in a graceful speech.

Motor cars then took the pilgrims and some twenty Belgian guests down to Ypres for a ceremonial luncheon at Skindles Hotel. This proved a fantastic little ceremony. Two toasts only were proposed and drunk: His Majesty the King of Belgium by General Lawrence and His Majesty King George by General Herremerre, the Governor of West Flanders. A breezy speech by Colonel Duthoy, Chief liaison officer between the British and Belgian forces completed the proceedings.

This was followed by a night in a hotel in Lille and an early start for Le Cateau:

Shortly before 1 o'clock a reception was held in the salon of the Hotel de Ville. After mutual introductions a procession was formed consisting of the Town Council and local French notables, our noble selves complete with medals and les mutiles et démobilisés de Cateau (the wounded and veterans of Le Cateau) complete with banners. This procession wound its way up to the Grande Place, by way of the Rue des Landrecies to the site of the memorial which is near the horse market.

There the memorial was unveiled in a simple ceremony followed again by the last post and 'stables'.

The horse trough was designed by Colonel William Beaumont MC, a Manchester architect, who fought with the division and [had] been captured in March [1918]. has been excellently carried out in local granite by a Le Cateau mason Monsieur Delviénne-Papon. It is reminiscent of a Florentine trough, and bears on one side in English and the other in French the following inscription

In memory of those of the 66th Division of the British Expeditionary Force who fell in the liberation of Le Cateau from German occupation in October 1918.

After the compulsory luncheon, there were speeches and an evening dance in the illuminated square. The next day the pilgrims departed back to Britain, except for some thirty men who went on the route of the final advance and Fifth Army retreat to Amiens. Spending the night there, they then went over the Somme battlefields and Vimy Ridge and then home via Dunkirk.

Rochdale, Saturday, 30 January 1931

General Sir Hubert Gough attended the annual dinner of 66th Division in 1927, 1930 and 1931. The commander of the Fifth Army was the most senior officer to be invited to the Clickety-Click dinners. That he took part in this officers' reunion is no surprise, it was only in 1931 he accepted an invitation to the mess of the 2/6th Battalion, Lancashire Fusiliers, in Rochdale the next day is more interesting.

As was customary in the army, the distinction between officer and ranks was considerable. Gough had had to fight his corner ever since 1918 when he lost his command, there being an interesting tit-for-tat run of books counter-claiming his reputation, so his attendance at the reunions would have been a consolation for him.

> General Gough replying said that although he had been in the district 24 hours, and that in that time he seemed to have made 24 speeches, each which was the equivalent of going over the top. He said that this was the first occasion since 1918 when he had had the opportunity to thank personally the men who had actually served under him during that trying period and he seized the chance to say how grateful he was to them for the great part they had played during the retreat when Platoons were frequently reduced to the strength of one Corporal and two or three men, with which forces the Germans were held. The retreat undoubtedly brought eventual victory, and there was no questioning the fact, that the Germans there shot their final bolt, lost more than they could afford in men and materials, and that the retreat paved the way for the final advance, which preceded and produced the armistice …

The character of the men who made the retreat should now be applied to the hard post-war conditions, and he thought that the difficulties of the present situation in England, could be overcome by the 'guts' of the men, as shown in that final retreat, and he requested that everyone should make a determination to apply himself to that end.[6]

How this speech went down with the men is not recorded. It ended in the statement that he wished and hoped to be able to attend again, which was cordially met by cheers from the men. Many of the men were no doubt on hard times brought about by the Great Depression, but it was the pull of comradeship and past experience that was the shared attribute of these reunions. Who were the men of the 66th? From the men of the 2/6th Lancashire Fusiliers there were men from Rochdale and many of the towns of East Lancashire who served under its colours. It has been estimated that in total the Manchester and Salford areas alone lost 22,000 men killed and 55,000 wounded in the Great War, an awful price to pay.

The Force had been disbanded after the war and then revived. The division was re-founded in September 1939 and remained on home service until the Dunkirk evacuation in June 1940. Its three brigades were attached to different divisions, 197 Brigade went to the 54th (East Anglian) Division, 198 to the 59th (North Staffordshire) Division and 199 Brigade was disbanded in 1941. The two remaining brigades saw early action in Normandy as part of their divisions but then were disbanded when manpower shortages caused by mounting casualties forced Montgomery to reorganise his forces. 197 Brigade was reduced to a cadre level and used for battlefield recovery and equipment salvage. This was the last hurrah of the division and it is to its credit that it saw action of some form in both world wars. The division was a second line division of the 42nd Division, which still exists as 42 North Western Brigade, based at Fulwood barracks in Preston.

As for the men of the division, they came home and lived their lives as best they could. Colonel Little stayed in the army after General Bethell wanted to give him command of a brigade, which came to nothing. He worked in a collection of huts in Grosvenor Gardens in London, organising and clearing records for the War Office. In September 1920 he was sent to Ireland to command the 2/ East Lancashire Regiment in County Cork against Sinn Fein agitation. In 1922 he went to Malaya but resigned in 1925 as he did not find peacetime soldiering to his taste. After trying a spell on Guernsey growing flowers and potatoes, he was caught up in the depression of 1926. He moved to the Inspectorate of the Labour Branch of the Ministry of Agriculture and Fishery in the Eastern Counties, followed by time as the manager of Richmond Golf Club for the Ministry of works. After a spell with the Rural Industries Bureau and involvement in the quilting industry he moved to Lord Wandsworth College in Hampshire, where he became the first principal of the agricultural college.

In the Second World War Little took a commission in the Royal Air Force and was based in the Middle East from June 1940, when he was in charge of land salvage for the combined forces. In 1944, with the war in the Middle East won, he resigned his commission at the age of fifty-seven. In 1945 he returned as Chief Disposal Officer for three years for the Ministry of Supply until ill health forced his retirement. He retired with a Military Cross, DSO and bar, Croix de Guerre, DSC (USA), mentioned in despatches (five times). In the Second World War he was awarded an OBE and mentioned in despatches twice. He was married to Doris Turner, with whom he had a son and a daughter.

Norman Dunkerley, who served in 42nd Division and was wounded at Gallipoli, was able to recuperate and eventually also ended up in the Royal Air Force. James Jessiman graduated from Aberdeen University with a degree in Medicine in 1923, spending several years in Poplar in London before moving to Malvern, where he found a reputation as a careful, painstaking and knowledgeable doctor. He gained his MD in 1933 and published articles on his specialism of rheumatism. He reluctantly joined the NHS in 1948, although he was strongly opposed to the nationalisation of medicine, and he resigned after two years, though still continuing hospital visits and staying in private practice. He retired to Bromley in Kent in 1968. He married and had a son, also a doctor.

General Lawrence returned to the world of banking in 1919 as managing partner. With Lawrence at its head, the bank acquired Holt and Company, banker to the army, navy and air force, in 1923 and Child and Company in 1924. Lawrence held a string of directorships in industry and was appointed as a member of the Royal Commission on the Coal Industry in 1925, a trustee of the Imperial War Graves Commission in 1926 and a governor of Wellington College. Glyn, Mills & Co. became Britain's largest private bank, with a magnificent new head office in Lombard Street, opened in 1933. In 1934 Lawrence became chairman of Glyn, Mills & Co. By 1939 Lawrence could see that another war was imminent. Fearing the effect of death duties on the bank if the younger partners were killed, he arranged to sell Glyn Mills to the Royal Bank of Scotland. Lawrence remained the bank's chairman and managing partner after the sale. Lawrence was recognised as a senior figure in the City of London and although unassuming he had a reputation for sound financial judgement and wide-ranging business knowledge. He had two sons, who both perished in the war, and a daughter.[7] We might surmise that he worked hard in these posts in order to forget his grief.

Walter Guinness was another officer who went on to great things, and held various ministerial offices, joining the cabinet as Minister of Agriculture for four years from 1925. He was created Lord Moyne in 1932 and wrote two books based on his earlier travels in Asia. He was chairman of the West India Royal Commission in 1938 and 1939. This generation were lucky in the respect that the casualties were so high that employment was easy to gain for some. In the Second World War he was Minister Resident in the Middle East in Cairo until he was assassinated in 1944 by emissaries of the Stern Gang from Israel.

For some of the men, though, life was not so easy. Gilbert Wilkinson, wounded in June 1917, faced six months in hospital in France, where he had his missing cheeks replaced with skin grafts. The photographs of his face were sent to the family to pre-warn them as to his new looks, but even so when they knew he was returning his sister, Maggie, ran out of the house screaming that she did not want to see him. This was the reality of wounded men returning to families and the shock of the reality of severe wounds. He was posted to 193 Hospital in Shrewsbury, where he continued to recover and was granted leave in February 1918. In March 1918, as the division was readying itself for the German offensive, he reported to the 4/ (Reserve) Battalion of the East Lancashire Regiment, serving in the Royal Defence Corps before being discharged in June 1918.

On 11 August 1919 he married his sweetheart, Janey Pilkington, by which time he was working as a bookkeeper in Carter Street in Preston, while Janey was a cotton weaver. Gil later changed his job to being a leather warehouseman and a travelling salesman, so it is obvious that his confidence returned although his health was never good, most nights being disturbed by coughing fits caused by gas in the war. He had three children and died on 20 March 1969 aged seventy-one. The chances are that had he not got his early Blighty wound when he did he would not have survived the March offensive, and he died on the eve of the fifty-first anniversary of the battle in which so many of his friends died.

The removal of General Gough and the criticism of the Fifth Army in the retreat of March 1918 came to a head in March 1937. At a dinner held to honour the Fifth Army by the Old Comrades Association. Lloyd

George, the former Prime minister, was too ill to attend, but sent a letter, which was read out and reported in *The Times*, in which he stated:

> The refusal of the Fifth Army to run away, even when it was broken, was the direct cause of the failure of the great German offensive in 1918. I have the best German authority for that statement. [a Major Otzen of the German army was present]. It was not the fault of the Fifth Army nor of their gallant General [Gough] that, although the attack had been anticipated for weeks, the line was so thinly held at that point. Nor were they responsible for the fact that proper fortifications had not been thrown up on that sector, nor for the further essential fact that the British and French reserves had been so placed that they could not be brought up in time to support the army or the counter-attack.
>
> But the Allied forces were so distributed that at the point of attack we were weaker in numbers, in artillery, and in reserves than at any point of the whole British line. That was not the fault of General Gough.

He was right, Gough had pleaded for more reserves and received few. Haig controlled the overall strategy and should have sent up enough reserves to deal a decisive blow to the Germans. Lloyd George went on that labour and reserves were not increased when they should have been, and laid the blame at Haig's door and of General Headquarters at Montreuil. Gough replied that it was very generous of Lloyd George to admit this so long after the war that he was wrong. Gough added that Lloyd George was misinformed but the blame by inference fell on Haig. That it took so long to make it up to Gough and the Fifth Army was astonishing but it was the death of Haig in 1931 that allowed this rewriting of the Fifth Army's part.

It was not until the eve of the Second World War that General Gough was rehabilitated. In the article in *The Times* it was said of Gough that 'if he considered any slur had been cast upon his ability as an army commander, it never entered the head of anyone serving under him, for each and everyone knew that the army and its gallant commander had put up an epic fight against overwhelming odds, eventually in steadfastness, valour and endurance emulating the tenth Legion of Caesar or the Old Guard of Napoleon'.[8] Gough had lost his command in the March Retreat, but was proven correct that if the British held for eight days then all would be saved.

To play up the part that the East Lancashire Division acted in the March offensive is the reason this book was written. Reading the

Clickety-Click magazine of the annual dinner club, there is a yearly list of those who are ill or some who have died. Whether these were deaths cause by the experiences of war one can only guess but shelling, gas and bullet wounds all affected for years to come the health of those injured or wounded in the war. In the spirit of the Roaring Twenties the officers of the division gathered annually when they could to meet up and to relive their wartime experiences among friends, to pay sober tribute to their comrades who fell in battle, especially the 7,000 casualties of the East Lancashire Division in March 1918 and the men who have not had their story told until now. As for the men who fought and died, their memory will have been rehabilitated in Lancashire with the telling of this story.

NOTES:
[1] L.J. Wyatt served as Lieutenant Colonel of 1st Siege Company (XVIII Corps) at the time of the Somme battle in March 1918.
[2] *Clickety-Click*, The Annual Dinner of the 66th Division, No. 12, 1935, p.1.
[3] Boorman, D. *At the Going Down of the Sun: British First World War Memorials*, York, 1988, p.123f.
[4] Pevsner, N., *Lancashire: Manchester and the South East Yale*, 2004, pp.332–3.
[5] Frost, Barbara, *Memories of the Midland*, Stockport, 2005.
[6] *The Clickety-Click*, Annual Dinner Club of the 66th Division, No.8, 1931, p.28.
[7] Oliver John Lawrence served with the Post Office Rifles (k.1915) and Michael Charles Lawrence with the Coldstream Guards (k.1916).
[8] *The Times*, 22 March 1937.

Appendix I

Principles of Defence on Fifth Army Front

1. Of the Fifth Army front the southern 12 miles are unlikely to be the scene of a serious hostile attack owing to the difficulty of the country. Of the remaining 28 miles either the whole or any part may become the scene of a serious hostile offensive. On these 28 miles of front there would normally be 7 divisions in front line, giving the average of nearly 8000 yards per division. This would leave 4 [infantry] divisions and 3 cavalry divisions in reserve.

2. In the devastated state of the Fifth Army communications are one of the primary difficulties for a determined defence of the Battle and Rear zones.

We have not the means available to render these communications really efficient south of the line Roisel-Péronne.

3. To meet the situation as regards communications, it is for consideration whether our main resistance in the Fifth Army area should not be made behind the line of the Somme.

It would appear that the whole question is one of communications. In other words, are the communications through Péronne of such importance as to render it advisable to cover that place and fight east of the Somme. From the transportation point of view these communications are of great importance. The loss of the crossings at Péronne would seriously affect the supply of troops in the centre and northern portions of the Fifth Army area, and this would indirectly affect the maintenance of the positions on the right of the Third Army.

4. It is considered, therefore, that we should continue at all events to cover Péronne by means of a bridgehead, and that every effort should be made to improve the communications in this vicinity … By falling back to the line of the Somme the situation as regards rear communications

would be improved, but considerable construction work would still be necessary before it could be considered satisfactory. The German communications would be in such a case naturally be very bad.

On the other hand, by falling back to the line of the [Rivers] Somme and Tortille we should have the devastated area of the Somme immediately in rear of our defensive positions.

5. Although it is considered that we should make our preparations to fight east of the Somme, we must, however be prepared to be forced back to the line of the Somme. It is therefore of first importance that an emergency zone should be constructed at once along the line of the Somme and Tortille, and connected by a switch to the existing defensive zones north of Péronne ... this should include and secure the high ground at Mount St Quentin.

6. In view of the importance of Péronne it is considered necessary that a bridgehead should be constructed at sufficient distance from that place to cover the crossings there and to cover the railway communications through Brie. This can best be done by the construction of a switch from about Marquaix via Bouvincourt to the emergency zone at about Pargny.

8. The principles on which the defences of the Fifth Army front should be conducted should, it is considered, be similar to those laid down for the other Armies. That is, we should be prepared to fight for the Battle and Rear Zones. It may, however, at any period of the defensive battle become inadvisable to employ large reserves to re-establish either of these zones, in which case a withdrawal to the line Crozat Canal-Somme-Péronne bridgehead or even to the line Crozat, Somme, Tortille should be carried out. The possibility of having to execute a withdrawal should receive the careful consideration of the Fifth Army, and detailed plans should be worked out. Each Division should be covered by a small rear-guard of all arms. By the skilful handling of these, particularly as regards the employment of machine guns in conjunction with wire obstacles, it should be possible to delay considerably the enemy's advance, cause him to expend considerable force and generally dislocate his arrangements.[1]

J.H. Davidson
February 4, 1918

[1] Reproduced as shown in Gough, *The Fifth Army*, 1968, p.232f.

Appendix II

Prisoners' Statement

66th Division
I G 115 19

Summary of prisoners' statements regarding offensive.

N.C.O. of 28th Foot Artillery Regiment captured west of Bony March 18

Prisoner's battery is in Ossus. Each of four 15 centimetre howitzer has received 1,200 rounds of which 300 are gas shell. German attack expected commence two or three days from March 18. Will be preceded by ten hours intense bombardment, last two hours being gas shell. There will be then two hours to allow air to clear and then infantry and artillery will advance simultaneously.

N.C.O Pilot of 44th Pursuit flight brought down near Ly-Fontaine March 18

Prisoner is certain attack will start March 20 or 21. Large air forces have been brought together opposite this front but have been used sparingly so far and will not be fully disclosed until the day of battle.

Prisoners of 227 Reserve Infantry Regiment 107 Division taken South west of Villers-Guislans March 18/19

They are expecting relief by attacking forces any moment. They have been issued with extra nose pieces for gas masks on March 17 as increased protection. One prisoner mentions March 20 as date of attack but his regiment is to be relieved first.

Two Alsation deserters 414 Trench Mortar Company surrendered south of St Quentin (Pire Aller) March 18/19

Do not know infantry in line. Raid to be carried out March 19/20 and large attack March 20/21 preceded by gas bombardment including trench mortars. Over one hundred trench mortars in position on divisional front.

Addressees all concerned

XIX Corps Intelligence 3 pm.

Appendix III

XIX Corps' Order No.167

19 March 1918

1. Redoubts for all round defence, each for a minimum garrison of one company, are being constructed under Corps arrangements as shown in the following list and attached map [missing].

1.	Yard Redoubt	[D Company 13/ Middlesex with Tunnellers]**
2.	Woodcock Redoubt	[C Company 13/ Middlesex]
3.	Woody Redoubt*	[A Company 13/ Middlesex]
4.	Worm Redoubt*	[B Company 13/ Middlesex]
5.	Viper Redoubt	?7/ Northamptonshire
6.	Vixen Redoubt	?7/ Northamptonshire
7.	Upset redoubt*	?7/ Northamptonshire and men attached to Tunnelling Company
8.	Uplift redoubt	?7 Northamptonshire
9.	Upstart redoubt	[D Company 9/ Sussex]
10.	Trinket redoubt	[C Company 9/ Sussex]
11.	Trinity redoubts	[A Company 9/ Sussex]
12.	Triple redoubt	[platoon?? B Company 9/ Sussex with Tunnellers]

[authors note * redoubts where work had hardly started by 20 March]
[authors note ** reconstructed reserve formations of 73rd Brigade, 24th Division]

2. The role of these redoubts is
    a) to act as centres of resistance to break up an enemy attack and bring his advance to a standstill should he penetrate to a considerable depth

b) To cover the deployment of the troops employed under orders of the Corps for deliberate counter-attack in the battle zone and to support that counter-attack when launched.

Obligatory garrison for these redoubts will be found by the brigade in corps reserve as follows;

1–4 A battalion	headquarters at Vermand
5–8 B Battalion	headquarters at Jeancourt
9–12 C Battalion	headquarters at Hesbécourt

Division concerned will arrange to mark and mark and make available when required, accommodation for battalion headquarters at the above places. The marking should be 'Corps redoubts', 'A battalion headquarters' etc.

Unless orders to the contrary are issued, garrisons of one company each will move to these redoubts on the order to 'Man Battle Stations'.

The Companies of the brigade now in Corps Reserve employed with Tunnellers will occupy the following redoubts:

Yard redoubt
Upset redoubt
Triple redoubt

Should the order to 'Man Battle Stations' be issued before the sites of the redoubts are complete, garrisons will proceed to the site of the work and make use of and develop such defences as exist. A few days will elapse before any defences at all will exist at numbers 3, 4 and 7, and in the event of immediate necessity arising, the companies concerned must take an adequate supply of entrenching tools with them.

From the time of their arrival in position, garrisons will come under orders of the divisions in whose areas they are located, UPSET REDOUBT being included in the 66th Division area.

It is, however, to be clearly understood that these troops are obligatory garrisons, and no movement from the redoubt, either in withdrawal or otherwise, is to take place without authority from the Corps Headquarters.

Should circumstances subsequently permit, the whole or a portion of these garrisons will be relieved by troops of the division concerned, the relieved garrisons being again withdrawn into Corps reserve.

3. 24th Division will arrange for the necessary reconnaissances to be carried out <u>forthwith</u> by all concerned, so as to ensure the movement to redoubts being carried out as smoothly and as rapidly as possible on the order bring issued.

Similar reconnaissance will be carried out whenever the brigade in Corps reserve is relieved.

4. Copies of all orders issued this subject by the 24th Division and the Brigade concerned will be forwarded to Corps headquarters and the 66th Division.

5. A. D. Signals, XIX Corps, will arrange for immediate construction of telephonic communication with all redoubts and battalion headquarters by means of cable in shallow trenches, and will link them up with a deep buried cable system as progress on the work permits.

6. Divisions will arrange to stock the following at each site as soon as possible;

SAA for Rifle and Lewis Gun	30 boxes
Grenades Mills Hand	144
Grenade Mills Rifle	252
Grenades No. 35	252
Flares Red	250
Very Pistol Ammunition	100
S.O.S. Grenades	25
Sandbags	200
Picks	12
Shovels	24

<u>Rations</u>
Beef   300
Biscuits   300

<u>Water</u> (2 gallon petrol tins)   60

Two wardens per redoubt will be detailed by division to take charge of the above and to maintain the defences constructed in good condition.[1]

___

[1] TNA, WO95/3121/6.

Appendix IV

Casualties During Operations 21.3.18 to Date

Key: **K** = Killed
    W = Wounded
    M = Missing

Unit	Officers K	W	M	Total	Other Ranks K	W	M	Total
Divisional Headquarters		1	1	2		1	4	5
330 Bde RFA	1	6	8	15	16	51	65	132
331 Bde RFA	4	6	3	13	35	96	31	162
66th DAC						2		2
X 66th TMB		1	1	2		6	7	13
Y 66th TMB			1	1	1	2	40	43
66th Div Signal Coy						3	2	5
R E HQ						1		1
430 Field Coy RE	1	1		2	2	32	11	45
431 Field Coy RE		1		1	6	13	12	31
432 Field Coy RE		2	1	3	10	22	17	49
197 Inf Bde HQ		2		2		1		1
6/ Lancashire Fusiliers	3	19	15	37	30	218	333	581
2/7 Lancashire Fusiliers	3	13	20	36	30	125	473	628
2/8 Lancashire Fusiliers		10	22	32	30	46	624	700
198 Inf Bde HQ		1*		1*				
4/ East Lancashire R	2	13	21	36	6	29	628	663
2/5 East Lancashire R	5	10	16	31	44	134	516	694
9/ Manchester Regiment	5	16	3	24	20	213	390	623

Unit	Officers				Other Ranks			
	K	W	M	Total	K	W	M	Total
199 Inf Bde HQ								n/a
2/5 Manchester R	2	8	23	33	3	22	670	695
2/6 Manchester R	5	11	14	30	50	171	300	521
2/7 Manchester R	4	11	16	31	80	136	321	537
66th Bn MGC	2	7	7	16	9	58	205	272
5/ Border R (Pioneers)	2	8	13	23	17	102	345	464
66 Div Train					3	6	1	10
2/1 East Lancs Field Amb		1		1			1	1
2/2 East Lancs Field Amb						8	35	43
2/3 East Lancs Field Amb		2		2			22	22
254 Div Empl Coy							2	2
198 LTMB		2	1	3				
199 LTMB		1	1	2		16	28	44
TOTALS	39	152	188	379	392	1516	5081[**]	6989

Compiled 13.4.18

[*] presumed to be at duty
[**] many of these were dead, PoWs or wounded

Appendix V

Poetry

Lines from our tame poet

To Southport, some new recruits joined, not many ages ago,
Training to make themselves fitter, some trade they didn't quite know,
Arrived at the base of our ladder, their feet were on the first rung.
Of the future they had no conception.
The Clickety-Clicks were just young

Crowborough, Haywards Heath, Shoreham, Colchester all in its turn,
Took part in the making of soldiers, helped the Division to learn.
Sometimes they grumbled and grizzled, sometimes they whistled and sang;
They took cares and happiness lightly.
The Cickety-Clicks were but young

Suddenly came the great morning, when off they were sent to the war.
Sound in equipment and training, each fellow true to the core.
Their share of the scrap they did bravely, on many breasts medals were
hung;
But the trials of the war didn't change them,
The Clickety-Clicks were just young.

La Bassee and Nieupoort, then Wipers,
The wonderful Passchendaele fight,
Reorganisation; St Quentin- retiring (by programme) each night.
All took great toll of the units, the rest, with their rifles well slung
Reinforced and reorganised quickly
The Clickety-Clicks thus kept young

Today with the war far behind us, and men settled down – more or less –
Generals Lawrence, Neill Malcolm and Bethell

Join us as each year at our Mess.
Hard are the fights reconstructed and
Tales from some lips are wrung.
But nevertheless its a Hell of a mess
And keeps the Clickety-Clicks young.[1]

Passchendaele
Night 8–9 October 1917

Night, Storm and war
No mercy in the sky;
The earth was foul
And from the hostile East
A wild wind swept
Chill as dark fingered Death
While rain slashed down
Upon a corpse strewn swamp.

Burdened with fighting kit,
Men struggled on;
Dragging their leaden feet
Through waste of slime
Past shell holes waterlogged
Where some were drowned
In the slow yellow mud
Amid contorted dead.

Through crash of shell,
And burst of light,
whence ragged metal leapt
Whipping the air
That moaned with evil sound;
Past bleeding flesh
And newly stricken clay,
Hour after hour
Up tape marked tracks,
With frequent halts
Where weariness was pain.
Throughout that night
Which horror held in sway
With shambling steps-

Yet jesting at grim fate-
The files moved on
To the attack at dawn

Oh! Saviour, Christ!
May they rest light
In Flanders Fields
Who passed that night

[1] Annual Dinner Club of the Clickety-Clicks, 1926, p.33.

Order Of Battle

66th (2nd East Lancashire) Division

197 Brigade
    3/5 Lancashire Fusiliers
    2/6 Lancashire Fusiliers 'Half Crown Battalion'
    2/7 Lancashire Fusiliers
    2/8 Lancashire Fusiliers

198 Brigade
    2/4 East Lancashire Regiment
    2/5 East Lancashire Regiment
    2/9 Manchester Regiment
    2/10 Manchester Regiment

199 Brigade
    2/5 Manchester Regiment 'The Collier Battalion'
    2/6 Manchester Regiment
    2/7 Manchester Regiment
    2/8 Manchester Regiment

Mounted Troops
    66th Division Divisional Cycle Company

Artillery
    2/I East Lancashire Brigade
        2/4 Lancashire
        2/5 Lancashire
        2/6 Lancashire

    2/II East Lancashire Brigade
        2/15 Lancashire

2/16 Lancashire
2/17 Lancashire

2/III East Lancashire Brigade
2/18 Lancashire
2/19 Lancashire
2/20 Lancashire

2/IV East Lancashire (Heavy) Brigade
2/I Cumberland (Heavy) Battery
2/II Cumberland (Heavy Battery

Brigade Ammunition Columns
2/I East Lancashire
2/II East Lancashire
2/III East Lancashire
2/IV East Lancashire (Heavy)

Divisional Ammunition Column
66th East Lancashire

Engineers
2/I East Lancashire
2/2 East Lancashire

Signal Section
66th East Lancashire

Field Ambulance
2/I East Lancashire
2/II East Lancashire
2/III East Lancashire

Divisional Train
66th 2/I East Lancashire

SEPTEMBER 1916

197 Brigade
3/5 Lancashire Fusiliers
2/6 Lancashire Fusiliers
2/7 Lancashire Fusiliers
2/8 Lancashire Fusiliers

198 Brigade
> 2/4 East Lancashire Regiment
> 2/5 East Lancashire Regiment
> 2/9 Manchester Regiment
> 2/10 Manchester Regiment

199 Brigade
> 2/5 Manchester Regiment 'The Collier Battalion'
> 2/6 Manchester Regiment
> 2/7 Manchester Regiment
> 2/8 Manchester Regiment

Mounted Troops
> B Squadron 2/1 Bedfordshire Yeomanry
> 66th Divisional Cyclist Company

Artillery
> 2/I East Lancashire Brigade
> > 2/4 Lancashire
> > 2/5 Lancashire
> > 2/6 Lancashire
>
> 2/II East Lancashire Brigade
> > 2/15 Lancashire
> > 2/16 Lancashire
> > 2/17 Lancashire
>
> 2/III East Lancashire Brigade
> > 2/18 Lancashire
> > 2/19 Lancashire
> > 2/20 Lancashire
>
> 2/IV East Lancashire (Heavy) Brigade
> > 2/I Cumberland (Heavy) Battery
> > 2/II Cumberland (Heavy Battery

Divisional Ammunition Column
> 66th East Lancashire

Engineers
> 2/I East Lancashire
> 2/2 East Lancashire

Signal Section
    66th East Lancashire

Field Ambulance
    2/I East Lancashire
    2/II East Lancashire
    2/III East Lancashire

Mobile Veterinary Section
    I/I East Lancashire

Divisional Train
    66th 2/I East Lancashire

JUNE 1917

197 Brigade (Lancashire Fusilier Brigade)
    3/5 Lancashire Fusiliers
    2/6 Lancashire Fusiliers
    2/7 Lancashire Fusiliers
    2/8 Lancashire Fusiliers
    202 MG Company
    197th TMB

198 Brigade
    2/4 East Lancashire Regiment
    2/5 East Lancashire Regiment
    2/9 Manchester Regiment
    2/10 Manchester Regiment
    203 MG Company
    198th TMB

199 Brigade
    2/5 Manchester Regiment
    2/6 Manchester Regiment
    2/7 Manchester Regiment
    2/8 Manchester Regiment
    204 MG Company
    199th TMB

Mounted Troops
    B Squadron 2/1 Bedfordshire Yeomanry
    66th Divisional Cyclist Company

Artillery
    2/I East Lancashire Brigade
        2/4 Lancashire
        2/5 Lancashire
        2/6 Lancashire

    2/II East Lancashire Brigade
        2/15 Lancashire
        2/16 Lancashire
        2/17 Lancashire

    2/III East Lancashire Brigade
        2/18 Lancashire
        2/19 Lancashire
        2/20 Lancashire

    2/IV East Lancashire (Heavy) Brigade
        2/I Cumberland (Heavy) Battery
        2/II Cumberland (Heavy Battery

Trench Mortar Batteries
    Medium
    X Y Z
    Heavy
    V

Divisional Ammunition Column
    66th East Lancashire

Engineers
    2/I East Lancashire
    2/2 East Lancashire

Signal Section
    66th East Lancashire

Pioneers
    10/ Duke of Cornwall's Light Infantry (Pioneers)

Field Ambulance
    2/I East Lancashire
    2/II East Lancashire

2/III East Lancashire

Mobile Veterinary Section
    I/I East Lancashire

Divisional Employment Company
    254th

Divisional Train
    66th 2/I East Lancashire (Royal Army Service Corps)

MARCH 1918

197 Brigade
    6/ Lancashire Fusiliers
    2/7 Lancashire Fusiliers
    2/8 Lancashire Fusiliers
    197 Trench Mortar Battery

198 Brigade
    4/ East Lancashire
    2/5 East Lancashire
    9/ Manchester Regiment
    198 Trench Mortar battery

199 Brigade
    2/5 Manchester Regiment
    2/6 Manchester Regiment
    2/7 Manchester Regiment
    199 Trench Mortar Battery

Artillery
    CCCXXX
    A, B, C, and D (Heavy)
    CCCXXXI
    A, B, C, and D (Heavy)

Trench Mortar Batteries
    Medium X 66, Y 66

Divisional Ammunition Column
    66 Divisional Ammunition Column

Engineers
    430, 431, 432 Field Company

Signal Section
    66th

Pioneers
    1/5th Border Regiment (Pioneers)

Machine Gun Unit
    No.66 battalion Machine Gun Corps

Field Ambulance
    2/I East Lancashire
    2/II East Lancashire
    2/III East Lancashire

Veterinary Section
    I/I East Lancashire

Divisional Employment Section
    254th

Divisional Train
    66th (Royal Army Service Corps)

SEPTEMBER 1918

198 Brigade
    6/ Lancashire Fusiliers
    5/ Royal Inniskilling Fusiliers
    6/ Royal Dublin Fusiliers
    198 Trench Mortar battery

199 Brigade
    18/ Kings (Lancashire Hussars)
    9/ Manchester
    5/ Connaught Rangers
    199 Trench Mortar Battery

South African Brigade
    1/ South African Infantry

2/ South African Infantry
4/ South African Infantry
South African Trench Mortar Battery

Artillery
CCCXX
A, B, C, D (Heavy)
CCCXXXI
A, B, C, D (Heavy)

Trench Mortar Batteries
Not replaced

Divisional Ammunition Column
66 Divisional Ammunition Column

Engineers
430, 431, 432 Field Company

Signal Section
66th

Pioneers
9th Gloucester Regiment

Machine Gun Unit
No.66 battalion Machine Gun Corps

Field Ambulance
2/I East Lancashire
2/II East Lancashire
2/III East Lancashire

Veterinary Section
I/I East Lancashire

Divisional Employment Section
254th

Divisional Train
66th (Royal Army Service Corps)

General Officer Commanding
6 November 1914	Brigadier General C.E. Beckett
14 November 1915	Major General C.J. Blomfield
10 February 1916	Colonel C.S. Gordon Steward (acting)
1 March 1916	Major General C.J. Blomfield
12 February 1917	Major General Hon. H.A. Lawrence
22 December 1917	Brigadier General N. Malcolm (wd 29/3/18)
29 March 1918	Brigadier General A.J. Hunter
31 March 1918	Major General H.K. Bethell

General Staff Officer 1
11 November 1914	Major E.M. Lang (acting)
12 April 1915	Lieutenant Colonel L.W.G. Butler
2 March 1916	Lieutenant Colonel A.R. Burrowes
29 March 1918	Lieutenant Colonel F.P. Nosworthy

A A and Quarter Master General
6 November 1914	Lieutenant Colonel W.S. France
1 February 1917	Lieutenant Colonel R. Luker
26 November 1917	Lieutenant Colonel G.N. MacReady
24 April 1918	Lieutenant Colonel F.J. Lemon

Brigadier General Royal Artillery
November 1914	Lieutenant Colonel J. Magnus (acting)
1 February 1915	Colonel C.B. Watkins
30 March 1916	Colonel E.H. Armitage
17 February 1917	Brigadier General J.J. MacMahon
3 July 1917	Lieutenant Colonel J. Laird (acting)
13 July 1917	Brigadier General D.B. Stewart (wounded 28/8/17)
28 August 1917	Lieutenant Colonel H.E. O'B. Traill (acting)
12 September 1917	Brigadier General A.C. Lowe (killed 24/11/17)
24 November 1917	Brigadier General A.B. Forman (temporary)
25 November 1917	Lieutenant Colonel J. Laird (acting)
1 December 1917	Brigadier General A. Birtwistle

Commander Royal Engineers
9 November 1914	Lieutenant Colonel H.A. Fielding
20 November 1916	Lieutenant Colonel F.G. Guggisberg
10 May 1917	Major G.S. Knox (acting)
12 June 1917	Lieutenant Colonel G.C. Williams (to 199 Brigade)

15 March 1918	Captain C.A. West (acting)
2 April 1918	Lieutenant Colonel G.J.P. Goodwin
11 August 1918	Major S.H. Morgan
19 August 1918	Lieutenant Colonel G.J.P. Goodwin
1 September 1918	Major S.H. Morgan (acting)
30 September 1918	Lieutenant Colonel O.S. Davies

197 Brigade
(2/1st Lancashire Fusiliers)

5 November 1914	Colonel A.A. Garstin
19 May 1916	Brigadier General F.L. Banon
13 July 1917	Brigadier General O.C. Borrett (wounded 30/3/1918)
30 March 1918	Lieutenant Colonel G.P. Norton (acting)
3 April 1918	Brigadier General L.L. Wheatley

On 20/9/18 197 Brigade left 66th Division for Line of Communication

On 22/9/1918 Brigadier General Wheatley left 197 Brigade and assumed the command of 1 Brigade, 1st Division. Thereafter until the Armistice 197 Brigade was commanded by the following officers:

22 September 1918	Lieutenant Colonel A.W. Blockley (acting)
1 October 1918	Lieutenant Colonel G.V.W. Hill (acting)
6 November 1918	Brigadier General J. Hamilton Hall

198 Brigade
(2nd/1st East Lancashire)

5 November 1914	Colonel C.S. Gordon Steward
10 February 1916	Lieutenant Colonel W. Patterson (acting)
1 March 1916	Colonel C.S. Gordon Steward
8 June 1916	Brigadier General G.E. Matthews (wd. 12/4/1917 d. of w. 13/4/1917)
12 April 1917	Lieutenant Colonel G.T.B. Wilson (acting)
17 April 1917	Brigadier General A.J. Hunter

199 Brigade
(2nd/1st Manchester)

16 November 1914	Colonel B.N. North
20 May 1916	Brigadier General J.O. Travers
16 March 1918	Brigadier General G.C. Williams

South African Brigade

Transferred from 9th Division and joined 66th Division on 23/9/1918
1 April 1918   Brigadier General W.E.C. Tanner

The following units and training cadres also served with 66th Division between 18 May 1918 and 10 September 1918:

18/ Northumberland Fusiliers
23/ Northumberland Fusiliers
25/ Northumberland Fusiliers
14/ Kings
17/ Kings
19/ Kings
2/5 Lincoln
10/ Lincoln
7/ Suffolk
7/ Bedford
6/ York
12/ Lancashire Fusiliers
13/ Gloucestershire
11/ Border
2/6 South Staffordshire
11/ South Lancashire
10/ Black Watch
7/ Sherwood Foresters
17/ Kings Royal Rifle Corps
13/ Manchester
17/ Manchester
2/6 North Staffordshire
14/ Highland Light Infantry
5/ Royal Irish Fusiliers
16/ Rifle Brigade
6/ Leinster
2/20 London
2/24 London

Bibliography

Anonymous, *A History of the East Lancashire Royal Engineers*, Manchester, 1920.

Ashurst G., *My Bit*, Marlborough, 1987.

Boorman, D., *At the Going Down of the Sun*, York, 1988.

Boraston and Bax, *The Eighth Division*, Eastbourne, 1926.

Brown, *IWM Book of 1918*, London, 1998.

Carnock, Lord, *The History of the 15/ King's Hussars*, Gloucester, 1932.

Conan Doyle, A., *The Great Boer War*, quoted online source The Museum of the Lancashire Fusiliers.

Edmunds E., *The Official History of Military Operations France and Belgium* Vol. 1–5 1918, various dates.

_____, *The Official History of Military Operations France and Belgium* Vol 2 1917, various dates.

— Official History; The Union of South Africa and the Great War, reprint Nashville, 1924.

Farndale, M., *History of the Royal Regiment of Artillery*, 1914–1918.

Francis, A.E., *History of the 2/3 Field Ambulance in the Great War*, Salford, 1930.

Frost, B., *Memories of the Midland*, Stockport, 2005.

Gough, H., *The Fifth Army*, Bath, 1931, reprint 1968.

Guinness, W., *Staff Officer*, London, 1987.

Henniker, A., *Transportation on the Western Front*.

Nicholson, C.N., *History of the East Lancashire Regiment in the Great War*, Liverpool, 1936.

Latter, J.C., *The Lancashire Fusiliers 1914–1918*, 1949.

Locicero, M., *A Moonlight Massacre*, Solihull, 2014.

Macdonald, L., *They Called it Passchendaele*, London, 1978.

MacReady, G., *In the Wake of the Great*, London, 1965.

Martin, D., *Londoners on the Western Front*, Barnsley, 2014.

McCarthy, C., *The Third Ypres, Passchendaele The Day to Day Account*, London, 1995.

Michelin, *Bygone Pilgrimage Guide to the Battlefields 1916–1917*, Uckfield.

Moorhouse, G., *Hell's Foundations*, London, 1992.

Murland J., *Retreat and Rearguard – Somme 1918*, Barnsley, 2014.

Pevsner, N., *The Buildings of England, Lancashire: Manchester and the South East*, Yale 2004.

Potter and Withinshaw, *History of the 2/6th Battalion*, 1926, LF.

Sparrow, W. Shaw., *The Fifth Army in March 1918*, Uckfield.
Wyrall, E., *The Fiftieth Division 1914–1919*.

Imperial War Museum, Department of Documents
Papers of John Gore.
Papers of P.R. Hall.
Papers of Tom Hardman.
Papers of Withinshaw.
Papers of N. Dunkerley.
Papers of R.C.A. Frost.
Papers of Roland Bate.
Papers of T.H. Westmacott.
Papers of W.B. Little.

Other Sources
Birmingham University, The Avon Papers, Cadbury Research Library
Clickety-Click, The Annual of the East Lancashire Division Dinner Club, LF
Online Source, The 1/4 Battalion Alexandra Princess of Wales Own Yorkshire
    Regiment
Royal Bank of Scotland, online source
The Cairo Gang, online source
The Godfrey Edition of Maps
The London Gazette
The National Library of Scotland, Trench Maps Archive
The Tank Museum, Bovington. History of 5 or E Battalion, Royal Tank Corps
The Times

Index